DEATH WAS COMING

For many days, the woman Kooyuk had refused her bit of food so that the children might have more. Now she stripped off her rags and, naked, stumbled into the white night to die...

The orphan Pameo, four years old, had no hope of life. She was a woman-child and worthless, the last to be fed. She starved until her huddled little body no longer shivered beneath its tattered robes...

And close to the dying Eskimos, and their already dead dogs, stood the warm, well-stocked camp of their civilized white guardians.

THE
DESPERATE
PEOPLE

Farley Mowat

With Woodcuts by Rosemary Kilbourn

SEAL BOOKS
McClelland and Stewart-Bantam Limited
Toronto

For the People of the Deer—
in the belief that we will make amends

*This edition contains the complete text
of the original hardcover edition.*
NOT ONE WORD HAS BEEN OMITTED.

THE DESPERATE PEOPLE
A Seal Book / published by arrangement with
McClelland and Stewart Limited

PRINTING HISTORY
McClelland and Stewart edition published 1959
Seal edition / November 1980

*The author is grateful to Maclean's for permission to include
material previously published in that magazine under the title
"The Two Ordeals of Kikik"; and to Weekend Magazine for
permission to reprint portions of an article by R. A. J. Phillips
entitled "Slum Dwellers of the Wide-Open Spaces."*

Front Cover Photo Courtesy of Bruce Coleman, Inc.

ISBN 0-7704-2323-X

PRINTED IN THE UNITED STATES OF AMERICA

KR   15 14 13 12 11 10 9 8 7

Contents

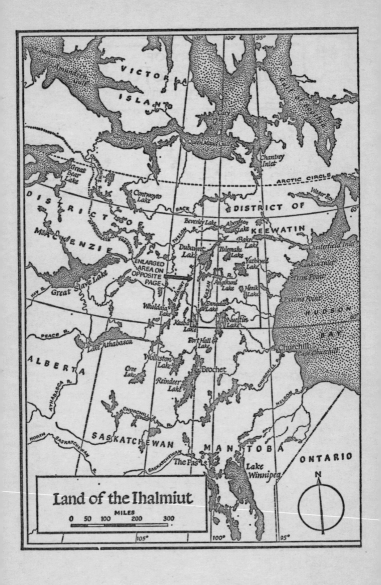

Land of the Ihalmiut

MILES
0   50 100   200   300

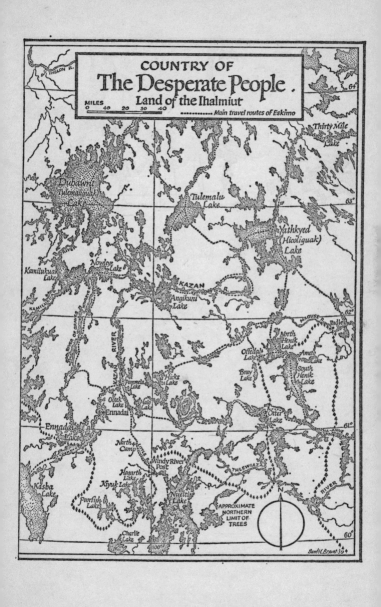

COUNTRY OF
The Desperate People
Land of the Ihalmiut

MILES
0   10   20   30   40

·········· Main travel routes of Eskimo

Thelon R.

64°

Thirty Mile Lake

Dubawnt Tulemaliguak Lake

Tulemalu Lake

63°

Yathkyed (Hicoliguak) Lake

Kamilu River

Nowleye Lake

Kamilukuak Lake

KAZAN

Angikuni Lake

62°

Maguse R.

Padlei

North Henik Lake

RIVER OF GRAVES

KAZAN RIVER

Offedal Lake

Bray Lake

Ameto

South Henik Lake

Hicks Lake

Pommela Lake

Halo Lake

Ootek Lake
Ennadai

Otter Lake

Ennadai Lake

61°

HA-ANNE R.

North Camp

Windy River Post

THLEWIAZA

Hogarth Lake

Kiyuk Lake

Nueltin Lake

Kasba Lake

Poorfish Lake

APPROXIMATE NORTHERN LIMIT OF TREES

RIVER

N

Charlie Lake

100°

60°

Sam'l H. Bryant 59

Foreword

This is the second of two books of mine about the inland Eskimos of Keewatin District in the Northwest Territories. The first, *People of the Deer*, which was published in 1952, concluded with these words:

"In the days of Inoti, the son, the strength of a great people might be made to live once more. In time it would be *our* strength, and the people would be *our* people.

"And then the dark stain which is the color of blood might at last be wiped from the record of the *kablunait* [the white men] in the place of the River of Men."

The present book is a chronicle of how, during the seven years after 1952, that stain did not disappear, but spread beyond the River of Men until it came to encompass the greatest portion of the inland plains we call the Barren-grounds—and to leave them empty of mankind.

It is a chronicle of the virtual extinction of a native people in this, the *present*, hour of Canadian history. It is also, so I believe, an irrefutable argument for the full and immediate emancipation of the surviving Canadian Eskimos from the intellectual, spiritual, economic and social domination which we have imposed upon them.

Most of the people of whom I write are gone, and cannot be recalled. It is for us to say whether the surviving Eskimos of the Canadian north will follow them or whether, as has happened in Greenland and in Siberia, they will become a revived and vigorous element in the variegated complex which is mankind.

There are now belated signs of a lightening on the somber horizon of the Canadian arctic; but this may be no more than the illusion of a false sunrise in a polar winter, unless we resolutely set ourselves to expunge a damning reflection upon our own pretensions to humanity, and unless we commit ourselves unequivocally to make amends.

The preparation of this book has been made easier for me by the degree of help which I received—sometimes from unexpected sources.

To the Hudson's Bay Company for assistance, including arctic transportation and access to certain of its records, I return my gratitude. My thanks are also due to the Royal Canadian Corps of Signals; the Territorial Court of the Northwest Territories; a number of scientists and scientific organizations; and to a great many individuals of experience in the arctic who provided me with invaluable material, including personal journals and diaries. In some cases the transmission of this material involved a considerable degree of potential risk—a fact which I am not free to dwell upon but which I feel bound to acknowledge publicly.

Finally I wish to acknowledge my debt to the several members of the Department of Northern Affairs of the federal government who gave me the most unstinted cooperation even when it was clear that the results would not redound to the credit of the Department.

All the major events in this book, and most of the minor ones, have been documented from official sources. Other sources which were used included published works, signed statements and private correspondence, together with many hours of tape-recorded conversations with survivors of the Ihalmiut, other Eskimos, and white men who were involved in the recorded events. To obviate the possibility of error, all Eskimo conversations were independently translated by at least two Eskimo linguists.

At the time *People of the Deer* was written it was impossible to obtain documentary corroboration of much of the material. Consequently I was obliged to use pseudonyms for some of the Eskimos and many of the whites as well as to deliberately misidentify some individuals. I was also obliged to refrain from identification of certain events in terms of time and place. In the present book these problems no longer exist and all names given are the correct ones, while all the events are presented in their actual spatial and temporal contexts. Where apparent discrepancies occur between this book and my earlier one, the version given here is the factually correct one.

In the Appendix I have given a detailed list of all the Ihalmiut who were alive in 1946 or who were born thereafter, together with their relationships, ages, and brief notes as to their eventual fates.

F. M.

Palgrave, Ontario
May, 1959

Foreword to the New Edition

In the original Foreword I wrote: "There are now belated signs of a lightening on the somber horizon of the Canadian arctic; but this may be no more than the illusion of a false sunrise in a polar winter ..."

It is now fifteen years since those words were written and the sunrise has proved to be an illusion in all truth. The physical disruptions which our society inflicted on the Eskimos during the first half of this century have been ameliorated to the extent that few Eskimos now die of physical neglect. Since about 1960 we have made considerable efforts to ensure that they will survive in the flesh; but at the same time we have pursued a policy which is very efficiently destroying them psychically. We have made a ruthless and concerted effort to dispossess them from their own age-old way of life and thought and to force them into the mold of our modern technological society. Assimilation has been our goal ... and it has failed disastrously. In 1974 almost all Canadian Eskimos have been broken away from the support of their land (which is theirs no longer) and live clustered in modern slums—many of them hardly better than ghettos—in not many more than a score of artificial settlements along the rim of the Canadian north. Here they exist for the most part on welfare payments of one kind or another—no longer taking sustenance from the land and the sea. Effectively they live in unguarded concentration camps, provided with the basic requirements for mere physical survival, but deprived of the freedom to shape and control their own lives. We have salved our national conscience by ensuring that they do not die anymore of outright starvation, but we have resolutely denied them the right to live according to their own inherent needs— the right to *function* as viable human beings according to their own desires and capabilities.

Genocide can be practiced in a wide variety of ways.

The Desperate People, of whom I wrote in 1959, are desperate still. But *now* they include *all* the native peoples of Canada—Indian, Eskimo and mixed bloods. They are making what may be their last convulsive effort to achieve survival apart from, and despite, a society which will accept them only if they transform themselves into second-class simulacrums of Western man. They are fighting what may well be their ultimate battle to exist in the world according to their own concept of what their lives should be. They are making what is probably their final effort to achieve the freedom to be themselves.

We have long prided ourselves on being a democratic nation, dedicated to the altar of freedom. Freedom for whom? If it is only freedom for ourselves to do as we please at the expense of others, then our pious stance is even more abhorrent than that of any overt tyrant—for ours is based upon a vile hypocrisy.

To have freedom one must give freedom. Let us put our vaunted belief in freedom to the test. Let us give back the freedom that we have taken from the native peoples of this land. If we cannot do this, then not only are they doomed, but we will have doomed ourselves as well.

Because the time is short, and the time is now, and that time will not come again, I am re-issuing this book in the hope that it may help us to understand and to acknowledge the crimes against humanity we have perpetrated here, *in our country*, under the aegis of a free democracy ... crimes which we are perpetrating still in a more subtle guise.

F. M.

Port Hope, Ontario
March, 1974

1

People of the Deer

Across the northern reaches of this continent there lies a mighty wedge of treeless plain, scarred by the primordial ice, inundated beneath a myriad of lakes, cross-checked by innumerable rivers, and riven by the rock bones of an elder earth. They are cold bones into which an eternal frost strikes downward five hundred feet beneath the thin skin of tundra bog and lichens which alone feel warmth under the long summer suns; and for eight months of the year this skin itself is wrinkled by the frosts and becomes a part of the cold stone below.

It is a naked land, bearing the deep excoriations which are the legacy of a glacial incubus of ice a mile in thickness which once exerted its colossal pressures on the yielding rock. Implacable and irresistible the ice flowed outward, crushing mountains, filling lakes with the mountains' broken bones, and lacerating the tilted planes of the land's face with great gouges, some of which are fifty miles in length. The scars made by the ice are open still; the wounds have never healed.

It is a land uncircumscribed, for it has no limits that the eye can find. It seems to reach beyond the finite boundaries of this earth. Brooding, immutable, given over to its own essential mood of desolation, it showed so bleak a face to the first white men who came upon its verges that they named it, in awe and fear, the Barrengrounds.

Yet of all the things that it may be, it is not barren.

During the brief arctic summer it is a place where curlews circle in a white sky above the calling waterfowl on icily transparent lakes. It is a place where gaudy ground squirrels whistle from the sandy casts of vanished glacial rivers; where the dun-colored summer foxes den, and lemmings dawdle fatly in the thin sedges of the bogs. It is a place where minute flowers blaze in microcosmic revelry, and where the thrumming of insect wings assails the greater beasts, and sets them fleeing to the bald ridge tops in search of a wind to drive the unseen enemy away. It is a place where the black muskoxen still stand foursquare to the cautious feints of the white wolves, and where the shambling giant of the land, the massive Barrens grizzly, moves solitary and untouchable. And, not long since, it was a place where the caribou in their unnumbered hordes could inundate the land in one hot flow of life that rose below one far horizon, and reached unbroken past the opposite one.

In all its harsh hostility it is not barren; nor has it been since the first crawling lichens spread like a multicolored stain over the scoured rocks. And through the cold millennia since the lichens came, life in ten thousand forms has prospered on the plains where the caribou became a living pulse, fleshed by the other beasts, and waiting for the day when man would come bringing sentience into a new world.

And man came early.

Three or four thousand years ago, caribou were already dying with stone points embedded in their flesh. Along the ancient gravel beaches that now cling crazily to hillsides three hundred feet above the shrunken levels of the present lakes, the quartz flakes lie profusely and the broken points made by clumsy or unlucky workmen keep them company. They are as fresh now as when men's hands gave them their present form, for no leaves have fallen in that treeless land to bury them in detritus, and the long winter winds have covered them with no more permanence than that of snow.

For all their freshness, the flaked stones have not yet

2

been made to speak, and almost nothing is known with certainty of those first comers, nor of the manner of their passing. There is only conjecture to suggest that the first men upon the plains may have been the ancestors of the dispersed family of Athapascan Indians whose descendants include the Chipewyans of the thin forests on the Barrens' southern boundaries. There is no way of telling if these first men still held the plains when out of Asia there came a wave of new and different men.

The early history of these newcomers is not recorded either—not even upon the land which they made theirs. Skin tents, bone implements and the greater part of the tools and weapons which they possessed could not resist the years when they lay naked on the wind-swept rocks. Yet something of their early tale still lingers in the memories of surviving men whose memories are contiguous with the memory of their race. And the story says that in the opaque time which has no name, a people came out of Asia, driven from the inland plains of Siberia by encroaching hordes who were well skilled in war. The plains dwellers themselves knew almost nothing of warrior skills. They were reindeer hunters, peaceful people, and they could not fight back. So they moved west and entered a new continent along a narrow defile of tundra plain that lies between the Brooks Range of Alaska and the arctic sea.

The unfamiliar sea was close upon their left flank, and they were afraid of it, so that as they came eastward and the boundary of the tundra plains receded into the southeast, they also swung southward away from the seacoast. For a time, so the old memories insist, they lingered near two mighty inland lakes which may be those that we now call Great Slave and Great Bear Lakes. But the plains drew them on, and to the east the plains grew ever broader, and so they continued to the east. Eventually, at least as early as ten centuries ago, they reached the land which was to be their home.

They came to the heart of the Barrengrounds, which encompasses the great plateau about Dubawnt, Yathkyed and Angikuni Lakes, in the present district of Keewatin; and here they stayed. They were men belonging to the race we now call Eskimos, but who have always called themselves *Innuit,* which is to say, The People.

They were The People in truth, for if the greatest Eskimo ethnologist, Knud Rasmussen, is to be believed, it was from this reservoir of inland-dwelling Innuit that many of the coastal and sea-culture Eskimos subsequently originated. Rasmussen called the inland dwellers the proto-Eskimos, and there is little reason to doubt that he was right, for the surviving Eskimos of the great plains have no memory of life by the sea, and no knowledge of such a way of life, or of its manifest tabus and mysteries; yet they have a long memory for the past—perhaps a longer memory than that possessed by any other group of Eskimos.

People who remain in one place for a great stretch of time often have such memories; but those who drift and move before the years have shorter ones. Pommela, who was a shaman and a wise man, could, as late as 1948, recall eleven generations of his people who had lived beside the lake called Angikuni, and when he had recited to me the names of the men of each of these generations in direct descent down to himself, he concluded with the remark that the earliest of these had been no newcomer to the land.

In any event it is certainly established that when the first Europeans came to Hudson Bay in the beginning of the seventeenth century, the people who had come out of Asia millennia before had long been settled in the heartland of the Barrens. When the first whites arrived, the whole of the inland plains westward from Hudson Bay to the headwaters of the Back River and to the Great Bend in the Thelon River, and north from near timberline to the fringes of the arctic coast, were in the hands of a great multitude of inland Eskimos who depended for their whole livelihood upon the caribou, and who were in truth the People of the Deer.

They were a singularly fortunate people. Through the next two centuries, while the white men changed and mutilated the faces of the nations of coast Eskimos, and of the Indians, the People of the Deer remained remote, their presence unsuspected behind the grim ramparts of the Barrengrounds which presented such a frightening aspect to the Europeans that it was not until late in the eighteenth century that any white man dared to venture into them.

Yet, indirectly, the coming of the white men wrought a catastrophic change in the lives of the inland Eskimos.

Through countless centuries the inland people had been bounded on their southern flank by the Athapascan Indians, of whom the most important were the Idthen Eldeli—the Eaters of the Deer—who formed a major segment of the Chipewyan group. Yet, though there had always been a bitter enmity between the Eskimos and the Chipewyans, there had not been much bloodshed, for neither group knew much of war. By tacit agreement they left a broad band of unoccupied country between them, and though there were isolated massacres when a band of one race was able to surprise a smaller group of the enemy, for the most part there was a state of armed but impotent hostility.

In the middle of the seventeenth century this state of things began to change. Far to the south of the Idthen Eldeli lands, which may then have stretched as far as Churchill River, the Indians of the open prairies began to acquire firearms. With these magnificent new weapons, the Plains Crees began to strike northward against the Woodland Crees who, in their turn, edged northward into Chipewyan country. The Chipewyans had always been inferior fighters, so they gave way before the pressure; and their retreat was hastened when the Woodland Crees began to obtain guns from the outposts of the Hudson's Bay Company. The Idthen Eldeli were rapidly driven north to the edge of the forests until they were impinging on the southern fringes of the Eskimo lands. Here they halted for a time; but before long they too began to barter for guns, mainly at Fort Prince of Wales, the present site of Churchill. Before the middle of the eighteenth century the Idthen Eldeli, made warlike by the new weapons in their hands, had begun to strike far out into the Barrens.

The inland Eskimos could not resist the invasion, and so they in their turn drew back toward the north, abandoning the land which had been theirs for many centuries.

As yet they had had no contact with the whites, and very little even with the coast Eskimos with whom the Hudson's Bay Company was now trading at Eskimo Point and Marble Island. Since they could obtain no guns, the only defense open to them was to continue to withdraw until sheer distance eased the pressure, and they were at last able to draw breath and pitch their camps in the twin valleys of the Thelon and Back Rivers.

During the years between 1770 and 1772, when Samuel Hearne became the first (and last) white man ever to traverse the Barrengrounds on foot, he found the heartland to be in the possession of the Idthen Eldeli bands. Hearne walked north to within a hundred miles of the lower Thelon River and saw no Eskimos, yet though the Eskimos were gone, the Indians held only a precarious tenure on the land, for they could not live upon it in the winter and were forced to withdraw south of timberline each autumn. Nor was even this partial possession destined to endure for long. During the final decade of the eighteenth century, smallpox came burning up from the south of the continent and it swept north in as destructive an epidemic as any known to human history. Entire Indian tribes were decimated until the dead must have numbered in the tens of thousands. The plague came at last to the Idthen Eldeli, by way of the traders at Great Slave Lake, and when it had burned its way through their scattered camps they had melted, in the space of a single winter, from several thousand people to a few hundred who clustered in fear and desperation close to the trading posts at Churchill and Great Slave. It was to take them generations to rebuild a fraction of their former strength and, before they could recoup their losses, they were again on the decline as the lesser ravagers, tuberculosis, influenza, and diphtheria, followed quick upon each other's heels. By 1800 the great plains which had been so briefly theirs were lost to them forever. For a time, small and timid parties were sometimes driven by starvation to follow the migrating deer northward into the tundra during the summer months, but even these desperate sallies eventually ceased, for the land was no longer empty.

The Innuit had returned to claim their own.

The People had been spared the plague, for they had no contact with white men. Thus, when the Indians failed to reappear in the summers immediately after the smallpox scourge, the Eskimos began to edge southward. They came cautiously up the Dubawnt River to the great inland sea which they called Tulemaliguak. They were a numerous people, and they were anxious to regain their old lands, for they had been able to obtain too little meat in the narrow confines of the Thelon and Back River valleys, and they knew, as had the Indians, that the best hunting grounds lay in the Dubawnt-Yathkyed-Angikuni country.

Before the end of the first decade of the nineteenth century the repossession was complete, and the inland people again held the whole of the central plains. To the north the Hanningaiormiut lived along the shores of Black River. South of them, on the Thelon Lakes, were the Akilingmiut. Southward again were the Tulemaliguamiut, and east of them were the Kingnetuamiut, so named after the high hill which guards the entrance to Angikuni Lake. From Angikuni the People had spread up and down the Kazan River, northward past Yathkyed as far as Thirty Mile Lake where their expansion was contained by the Harvaktormiut who held the mouth of the river. Those who lived near Yathkyed called themselves Padliermiut, and some of them spread even farther to the east, coming eventually to the lakes which we call North and

6

South Henik, and thence down the coastal rivers to the shores of Hudson Bay.

Southward from Angikuni, along the Kazan (which they called the River of Men), the People came to Kekertarahatok, which we now call Ennadai Lake, but they did not halt until they reached the northern edge of the forests. These, the most southerly of all People, became the Kekertarahatormiut.

The inland Eskimos were a great people in those days, numbering perhaps two thousand in their many camps; and though each group of camps had its own local identity, they were all united under a common name, Ihalmiut. It is a name with a proud ring, for it means The Other People, in the sense of those who are set apart from, and who are superior to, all others. And the Ihalmiut were indeed set apart, for it was not until the year 1867 that the first of the strangers who had already usurped a continent came into their land.

It was in 1867 that Father Gasté, an Oblate priest, set out from his mission at Reindeer Lake to proselytize the pagan inland Eskimos to the north, of whom he had heard from his own Idthen Eldeli Indians. Gasté underwent terrible hardships but, if report speaks truth, he eventually met the Kekertarahatormiut somewhere northwest of Nueltin Lake. He remained with them for most of that summer, and he may even have penetrated as far north as Angikuni Lake where the Kingnetuamiut camps were massed in such propinquity that the shores of the eastern bay were like a city of skin tents. Gasté was repulsed in his efforts to convert the Innuit, and in the autumn he fled south, barely regaining his mission post alive. It took him years to recover from the spiritual and physical ordeals he had suffered, and he never again ventured north into the tundra plains. Nevertheless, and as a direct result of his visit, a trade link was established for the first time between the inland dwellers and the whites. From 1868 onwards a small and courageous handful of the best hunters and bravest men amongst the Kekertarahatormiut each year dared the long journey south, penetrating two hundred miles into the forests, and into the lands of their old enemies the Chipewyans, in order to trade with the priest, and with the Hudson's Bay Company post at Reindeer Lake. Those were hard journeys and sometimes there was bloodshed between Indians and Eskimos. Nevertheless, having once discovered guns, steel hatchets, knives and metal cooking pots, the Ihalmiut desired more and more of these rare things.

7

So it happened that individuals amongst them began to engage in a series of quite fantastic trading journeys. From Angikuni and Yathkyed the Padliermiut began to drive their sleds southeastward as far as Churchill, taking a full winter season to complete the round trip; and the following winter these trading Eskimos turned north carrying trade goods clear to the arctic coast at Chantrey Inlet. The Ennadai and upper Kazan Eskimo travelers journeyed to Brochet at Reindeer Lake each winter, and in the summer they went north by kayak or with pack dogs to Beverly Lake where they and the Akilingmiut traded with the dreaded Kidliermiut—the men who kill all strangers—who came to meet them at Beverly Lake from the south shores of Coronation Gulf and from as far to the northeast as the mouth of the Coppermine River.

Yet despite these contacts with the whites, the land of the Ihalmiut still remained inviolate, and the Peoples' lives were little changed. Not more than a handful of the men were engaged in the trading journeys, and the vast bulk of the People had no contact with the world beyond the Barrens. They wished it so. They went into the strangers' lands and procured those things for which they had need; but the strangers did not come into *their* lands and force new appetites and new ideas on them.

But just before the turn of the century a stranger did come amongst them. He was J. B. Tyrrell, a geologist and government explorer, who in 1893 and 1894 made two masterful journeys through the Barrens from timberline north as far as the Thelon, thus becoming the first white man ever really to penetrate the interior plains since the time of Hearne. In 1893 Tyrrell explored the Dubawnt River system from its headwaters to Baker Lake, and so home along the shores of Hudson Bay to Churchill. Not content with this spectacular journey he paralleled it the next year by traveling from the headwaters of the Kazan to a point north of Yathkyed, and then swinging east to reach the Bay at the mouth of the Ferguson River.

Between Ennadai and Yathkyed he found the country heavily populated and, being a scientist and a methodical man, he mapped and located the camps he passed and tabulated the number of people whom he saw. In his official report to the government, Tyrrell estimated that he *encountered* between five and six hundred Eskimos along his route of 1894; but when I talked to him in 1949 he told me that he had actually seen only a portion of the people, and that he believed they may have numbered well above a thousand on the Kazan alone.

His estimate is confirmed by the observations of the Oblate priest, Father Turquetil. Like Gasté, Turquetil was stationed at Reindeer Lake, and he too burned to establish a mission amongst the inland Eskimos. From 1901 to 1906 he made five attempts to reach the inland people, and in 1906, with the assistance of a group of Eskimo traders from Ennadai, he at last succeeded in reaching that lake. He stayed for seven months in the land of the Kekertarahatormiut, and on his eventual return south he estimated the Eskimo population of Ennadai, the upper Kazan, and Angikuni Lake as totaling 858 souls—and this estimate *did not include* the Padliermiut of Yathkyed. Including the people north of Dubawnt Lake (which would presumably embrace the Thelon and Garry Lake Eskimos) Turquetil's estimate of the total numbers of the Ihalmiut was close to two thousand.

In those days immediately after the turn of the century the Ihalmiut must have been the most numerous cohesive group of Eskimos extant. They must also have been amongst the most secure, and the most vital. Unlike the majority of the coastal and sea-culture Eskimos, they were not nomads, for they had no need to pursue different kinds of game at different seasons. They were a settled people of long-established residence in their camps along the rivers and beside the lakes. The caribou, on which their entire way of life was based, came to them twice, and often four times a year, in mighty herds that stretched as far as a man's eye could encompass. They were a people of great strength and certainty, and this they clearly demonstrated by the manner in which they rejected the attempts of Father Turquetil to Christianize them. The old men of the Ihalmiut still recount how the Black-robed One set himself against the *angeokoks*—the shamans and the wise men—whose magic defeated him so severely that he believed his life was in jeopardy, and fled the inland plains. It must indeed have been a salutary experience, for no other missionary again attempted to penetrate the heartland of the People until almost half a century had passed.

The People proved their certainty and pride by their steadfast refusal to follow the coastal Eskimos into virtual servitude to trading post and mission. They chose to remain remote, untouchable, and their own masters, and only a selected few continued to trade with the whites on the borders

9

of the land. Kakumee, Ooliebuk, Igluguarduak, Pommela and no more than a dozen others did the trading for more than a thousand people, who refused to pursue the white fox, and their own future, into decay and ultimate extinction.

They were a people with a niche in time, for, unlike the coast Eskimos, they had a genuine sense of their own antiquity. Their legends spoke clearly of their primacy amongst the nations of the Innuit.

They were a rich people, as richness is measured in their world, for they seldom knew hunger; they had an abundance of the warmest clothing a man could want—caribou skins; their dogs were numerous and strong; the children in the tents were also numerous, and there was little or no need to face the horror of putting babies that could not be fed under the snow to die. They had no effective enemies amongst men. The deer were incredibly numerous, and the muskoxen were still abundant. The Ihalmiut had no need to suffer through bitter winter days upon the ice floes seeking seals; nor on the frozen lakes jigging stubbornly for the fish which are, at best, a starvation diet in the north. Instead of being a time of hardship and of dread, the Ihalmiut winter was a time for feasting, for visiting, for songs and stories. Almost alone amongst the Eskimo peoples the Ihalmiut possessed the rarest of all riches—time. They had time to remember what was past and to speculate upon what was still to come. They had time to dream, and time to work with words and thoughts— while their cousins on the hard seacoasts had little time for anything save the eternal struggle to survive.

Such was the hidden world of the Ihalmiut as the second decade of the present century began. Such were the people who had as much of contentment as they could desire. Such were the People of the Deer.

2

Of Many Graves

It was in the year 1912 that the defenses which the land had built about its people were suddenly and ruthlessly pierced by an enemy which could not be denied. The assailant was brought into the land hidden within a man of the people, the shaman Pommela, who was returning from a trading trip to Reindeer Lake. When it reached the heart of the plains, it burst out of him and ran an untrammeled course along the river routes. It leapt from camp to camp with an appalling swiftness and, as it passed, the camps stood desolate and still. It had no name, this unseen nemesis, for it was a stranger. Perhaps it was influenza, but whatever we might call it, it became known to the Ihalmiut as the Great Pain.

Those who survived its passage remembered its effects with dreadful clarity. Pommela remembered it, and he spoke of how men, women and children, driven mad by the flaming fever within their bodies, flung off their clothes and plunged themselves into the last spring snowdrifts—and did not rise again. Of the countless families whom Pommela knew, half vanished within the space of a spring and summer, and those families which remained were shattered so that here a father might have survived alone of all his children and his wives, and here a young child might have survived its parents, its brothers and its sisters.

Word of the disaster was slow to reach the outer world, but some years later Father Turquetil, at his new mission post on the coast at Chesterfield, heard that between five and six hundred of the inland people had perished in that one stroke of death. No one will ever know with any certainty how many died, for no one kept count. The greatest dying probably took place at Angikuni Lake, for this was the center of the Ihalmiut country and it was here that the people were most heavily concentrated. The evidence of the plague remains there still, for the shores of the western bay are so thickly strewn with hurriedly built graves that in places it is difficult to walk between them.

When the disease had run its course, the scattered survivors of the people of the plains slowly drew together again to form new camps of widows, orphans, and widowers. The Angikuni area itself was almost abandoned, and most of the surviving Kingnetuamiut withdrew north and south along the Kazan. Thus a major break appeared in what had been a continuous population stretching from Ennadai northward to Thirty Mile Lake. The heartland came to be almost empty of the People, who were now concentrated largely in the vicinity of Yathkyed, and about Ennadai Lake, and who were therefore perilously near the north and south frontiers of their own land, and thus more easily accessible to new invasions of another kind.

These were not long in coming. Now, from the north, the east and the south, the traders began to move in upon the Ihalmiut.

In 1913 a trading post had been established at Baker Lake and the next year an outpost from it was pushed up the Kazan to a point on the edge of the Padliermiut country. For the first time the Padliermiut were in direct contact with the whites, and within a few years they became slaves to new appetites, for trinkets, flour, cloth, and much other sorcery that could wean a hunter away from his allegiance to the deer and turn him into a trapper of white foxes. They paid an early price. According to Rasmussen, about a hundred of them died in 1919 of starvation and disease.

The more southerly Padliermiut were invaded from the eastern flank. In the early 1920's traders pushed in from Eskimo Point to Yathkyed itself, with the intention of establishing a permanent outpost there. When it proved impossible to maintain such a post, due to the difficulties of supply along the wild rivers running eastward to the sea, the post (called Padlei) was built instead near the headwaters of the Maguse River, and from here it exerted its steady pull, drawing to it many of the Padliermiut and the last remnants of the Kingnetuamiut. These came to take up residence in a new country which was not generous of meat, and they, too, rapidly became slaves of the demand for foxes.

The invasion of the Kekertarahatormiut from the south moved at a slower pace, for the distances were greater there, and the defenses of the land were stronger. Nevertheless, outposts from Reindeer Lake were established at Fort Hall Lake by 1914 and then, as competing traders entered the country, the outposts began to leapfrog each other north until by 1924 they had reached the edge of the true Barrens west of Nueltin Lake, and were in direct contact with the outlying camps of the inland Eskimos of Ennadai and the upper Kazan.

The effects of the new invasion were manifold.

In the first place the People, still disorganized by the blow which had crippled them in 1912, no longer were secure, no longer felt the certainty they had once known, and they could not so easily resist the temptations which the traders offered. The old framework of their life, already cracked, began to crumble and they began to build a new structure, a slipshod, jerry-built affair whose foundation rested uneasily upon a wildly fluctuating factor—the value and abundance of the white fox. They began to spend much of their time in the hunt for foxes. The locations of good trapping areas and proximity to the nearest trading posts came more and more to determine the places where they chose to live. They obtained rifles and almost limitless supplies of ammunition in exchange for foxes, and for a time this mighty increase in their ability to kill the deer—even at poor hunting places—compensated for their abandonment of the old camp sites at the main deer crossings, and of their old ways which had been determined by the ways of the deer. But the very efficacy of the rifle was also its most evil attribute.

To a people who had known no other restrictions on their hunting than those imposed by the nature of their crude weapons, the thought that it might be possible to kill *too many* deer did not occur. Nor did any of the white strangers to the land attempt to introduce this idea into the People's minds. In truth, the white men themselves were the most pitiless butchers of the deer the land had ever seen, and by their example they greatly encouraged the People to the excessive slaughter which the rifle now made possible.

The herds of deer, mighty as they were, were delicately balanced between the toll taken by their natural enemies and their ability to reproduce. As the toll suddenly grew heavier, there was no corresponding increase in the annual fawn crop. Slowly death gained the upper hand. What had been a river of life flowing through the Barrens began to shrink; the tributaries began to dry up altogether. Where once there had been a myriad roads belonging to the deer, now there were fewer with each passing year. And in 1926 the consequence of the slaughter fell full upon the People.

Harried and decimated, the deer changed their ancestral routes in the autumn of 1926, and during the winter which followed nemesis came again to the Ihalmiut camps. That winter there was starvation on a massive scale throughout the inland plains. At Ennadai one trader heard of fifty deaths, while from the vicinity of Hicoliguak a report of the deaths of more than two hundred people filtered through to Baker Lake.

The Ihalmiut were not only wasting in the flesh; they were also stricken in the spirit. The nature of the epidemic of the earlier decade had been completely inexplicable, and less terrible for that, since it did not strike at the familiar certainties upon which men depended. But this new catastrophe struck at the very roots of the Ihalmiut existence since, for the first time in memory, the sustainer, the foundation of life itself—*tuktu*, the deer—had failed the People.

This disaster resulted in the virtual obliteration of the Padliermiut as a people of the deer. Wracked by the terrible uncertainty which resulted from the failure of the herds, the majority of the survivors sought for a new certainty in an increasing reliance on the fox. They abandoned Yathkyed and the Kazan from Angikuni north to Thirty Mile Lake, and fled to Padlei.

There they became completely dependent on the fur trade, and although they still hunted deer, ate deermeat when they could get it, and dressed partly in deerskins, they were no longer *of* the deer. The old ways were no longer valid and, when missionaries came inland from Eskimo Point a short time later, the final dissolution was assured. The Padliermiut became mere fragments of a people whose identity and strength were gone.

But not all of the Padliermiut fled to Padlei.

There were some whose faith was strong enough so that even the inconceivable failure of the deer in the autumn of 1926 could not destroy it. Of these, about fifteen families remained in the ancestral lands, and there most of them perished before 1932 as starvation came again and again into their camps. Some, the strongest and most obdurate of all, traveled up the Kazan through the deserted land, seeking their kinsmen at Ennadai. Amongst them was the towering figure of Igluguarduak who brought his four surviving children into the camps of the Kekertarahatormiut, together with some score of relatives and followers. They were not the only strangers at Ennadai, for others of the broken people had preceded them, and still others followed. Some came from Padlei itself, and these were men who could not bear the servitude to the trap and to the Black-robes. Some came out of the lonely country to the northeast, between Tulemaliguak and Angikuni. A few even came from the Thelon country where the Akilingmiut had also become a people of the trap—the steel trap for the fox, which had become a greater trap for the people. Throughout the lands of the Ihalmiut those who could not, and would not, discard the old for the new, drifted toward Ennadai, so that before 1930 it had become the last stronghold of the People in the southern half of the Keewatin plains. There was one other stronghold, a small one, far to the north in the vicinity of Garry Lake, but it was now cut off from intercourse with the rest of the inland people, and was to remain so until its ultimate collapse and disappearance.

The remnants of the Ihalmiut who were now concentrated near Ennadai could not have numbered more than three or four hundred. Yet, though their numbers had been so greatly reduced, they were still able to feel themselves a people, and there was strength in them. Here, through the decade ahead, they were to remain and wage their struggle for survival.

In the last years of the 1920's they consisted of four groups. One of these, under the leadership of a man called Ilupalee, occupied the pocket of tundra which thrusts south into the forests just west of Nueltin Lake, and their camps stood beside the shores of Kiyuk, Poorfish and Hogarth

Lakes. A second group lived along the Nowleye River, while a third occupied the Kazan itself for a distance of some forty miles north of Ennadai. But the largest and most important group of all were those who called themselves the People of the Little Hills, and who held the northeastern shores of Ennadai and the land about the lakes which are now called Hicks, Stern, Calhoun and McCourt.

This latter band consisted of more than a hundred people, and the two greatest men amongst them were the brothers Kakut and Pommela, whose uncle was Kakumee, the most famous of all the inland Eskimos. These people occupied the central keep, while the three smaller bands held the outer bastions of the shrunken lands of the Ihalmiut.

In the early years of the 1920's there had been probing attacks upon this fortress by the traders from the south, but by 1927 a new and far more formidable invasion had begun. Out of the forests swarmed a strange breed of white men who were to become known as the Barrenland trappers. They were the last wave of the savage flood of anarchy which, a century earlier, had flowed westward to overwhelm an entire continent and to debauch the native peoples in its path. The Barrens trappers were the backwash of that flood, diverted into the bleak lands of the north, and doomed to break and disappear upon the edges of the last frontier. They were men who had cast off the ways of their fellows, or who had been cast off. Restless, unfulfilled, driven either by some consuming hunger within themselves or else by the antipathies of the herd behind them, they came thrusting north seeking to live by the white fox.

For a decade and more the land about Nueltin, Ennadai, and south of Dubawnt Lake was theirs. Most of these men had no law, nor knew of any. The majority hunted foxes not with traps, but with strychnine. They slaughtered the deer with an annihilating savagery in order to leave hundreds of carcasses strewn along the perimeters of their vast hunting areas as bait for foxes. The land was theirs, and they took what they wanted from it, and did what they wanted with it. And the People of the land had no recourse against them. Only twice in twenty years was any shadow of authority seen near the inland country and on these two occasions police patrols approached the verges of the land and then withdrew in haste, having accomplished nothing. In 1932 a Royal Canadian Mounted Police constable stationed at Eskimo Point heard rumors of what was happening in the interior, and reported to his superiors—but no action was taken.

16

There was no law in the interior plains where the last of the Ihalmiut fought their losing battle.

There were some amongst the Ihalmiut who attempted to defend themselves. When one of the trappers entered Igluguarduak's camp and, at gun point, stole a team of dogs, a sled and a woman, he did so in the firm belief that the "Huskies" would not resist. And they did not resist. But some hours later Igluguarduak hitched up his own team of dogs, and in the dark of a winter's evening he caught up to the white man. Igluguarduak returned to his camp with the woman and the stolen team—and when the spring came and the ice melted, the body of the white man floated on the surface of the bright waters.

Yet the Ihalmiut were not fighting men. Even Igluguarduak did not have the courage to remain in that place after the deed was done. Before the spring came he had vanished, accompanied only by his wife and one child. He returned to his old land north of Hicoliguak where he remained, almost alone, eschewing any contact with the whites of Baker Lake, until he died in 1948—the last survivor of the Padliermiut to live in the ancestral land.

By 1930 the southern bastion of the Ennadai fortress had been reduced to dust, for Ilupalee's band was scattered and the traders had reached north as far as Ennadai itself. The Barrens trappers roamed at will over the entire area, and with their poison baits they took most of the fur that was available, so that those of the Ihalmiut who had learned to live by the trap could not live. To make matters worse, the Idthen Eldeli had again begun to push northward, drawn by the trading posts, and assured of safety by the presence of the whites.

The slaughter of the caribou became a bloodletting on an almost unprecedented scale, not only on the open plains, but also in the thin forests where the majority of the deer herds wintered. Here, too, the trappers, both white and Indian, needed immense numbers of deer to provide bait and dog feed so that they could operate their long trap lines. Where once the deer had died so that men might be fed and clothed, now these were the least of the reasons for their slaughter.

Starvation became an annual occurrence in the Ihalmiut camps. In 1929 the whole of the Nowleye River band perished of famine, and that river received a new name, becoming the River of Graves. One more bastion was gone. By 1932 the surviving Ihalmiut numbered no more than two hundred

17

people and, in order to survive at all, these had also become slaves to the fox. They were not yet totally enslaved, for they still hunted the deer and, when they were lucky, they were still able to make good hunts. But what had been a certainty to them once had now become entirely a matter of luck, and each year saw their luck grow worse. Only a very few of the best and most determined hunters now dared depend upon the deer. For the rest, their dependence on the fox, and on the food the fox could buy, became greater with each year that passed. It was a poor support at best, for the white trappers took most of the fur, and the traders gave very little in exchange for what fur the Eskimos could catch.

Then, in 1932, the value of white fox pelts, which had declined steeply over the previous two years, suddenly and catastrophically collapsed. Within a year more than three-quarters of the white trappers and traders in the southern Keewatin plains had withdrawn from the land, never to return.

The Ihalmiut were once again in possession of their own country—but the nature of that country had altered drastically. The great and assured herds of deer had vanished, and the people who had once been the People of the Deer could no longer predicate their lives upon the caribou. Thus they were forced to turn more and more to the white fox, even as the value of the fox declined.

Never before in the history of the Barrens had the lives of man and fox been interrelated. Man had depended on the deer, and the fox had depended on the lemming. But the lemming—that mouselike creature of the high arctic—is a cyclic animal. Through four or five years its numbers mount until, usually in the fifth year, there are too many lemmings for the land to support. Then nature takes a hand and disease goes raging through the myriad runways. In the next year there are so few lemmings that many of the predators who depend on their flesh must starve. The white owls flee to the distant south. The foxes grow thin, and disease comes to them also, and in the following year a man may trap all winter and take no more than a dozen white fox pelts.

In the late 1920's when a fox pelt was worth as much as fifty dollars, the low point in the cycle of abundance could be borne by those who depended on the fox, but in 1933, when a prime white fox pelt was often worth less than three dollars, a man who depended on the fox in the years of its scarcity would starve.

It was because of this that the Ihalmiut lands were

emptied so abruptly of the white interlopers—but the Ihalmiut could not flee. This was their home, their only and their final home.

So they remained, but they were no longer the People of the Deer. Now they were the People of the Lemming.

And there were fewer of them with each new year. By 1940 when the last official trader, an outpost manager for the Hudson's Bay Company, withdrew from the land, there were 138 Ihalmiut left. After 1940 their sole hope for a futurity lay in an immigrant German, an ex-manager of the company post, who had chosen to remain on in the land. He was the last of the many whites who had come to the Ihalmiut country, had taken what they could get, and who had departed when there was no more to take. He remained not because of any sense of obligation to the People but because he was married to a Cree wife, and had five children who would have found little to their taste in the color-conscious settlements far to the south. Although he continued to hold a trader's licence, he actually did very little trading. The tremendous difficulties of freighting supplies by canoe along the three-hundred-mile waterway from Reindeer Lake ensured that he could make no significant contribution to the growing needs of the Ihalmiut for white men's goods. Though he was a trader in name, he supported his family largely through the efforts of his elder children as trappers on their own account. The furs they caught were the mainstay of the family's precarious existence on the border of the Ihalmiut country.

In effect, therefore, the Ihalmiut were almost totally abandoned, and they could neither return to the old ways nor find a sufficient source of sustenance in the new ways that the whites had taught them.

In the fall of 1942 the people who lived near the head of Ennadai Lake missed the caribou entirely. No one knows which route the shrunken herds followed during the autumn's migration, but they did not come to the old crossing places. And that winter forty-four people, a third of the total surviving population, died of hunger. The trapper-trader at the mouth of Windy River on Nueltin Lake could not help them, for his family also failed to kill sufficient deer to last the winter through, and he had nothing to spare for the Ihalmiut.

By 1946 the land had become a land of graves. In all the many places where the tents of men had stood, from Ennadai to Hicoliguak and even farther north, from Angikuni west to the great sweep of Tulemaliguak, the tents had vanished.

Only the circles formed by the anchor stones marked where they had stood, and only the mounded rocks upon the ridges marked where their owners lay.

The Ihalmiut of South Keewatin, who had been a great and numerous people less than forty years earlier, had vanished—save for one tiny pocket of humanity which still gave a semblance of life to a land almost dead. These were the three score People of the Little Hills who still clung stubbornly to the cluster of small lakes northeast of Ennadai, and to a way of life which had become a way of death.

3

A Spring to Remember

Along the borders of the Barrens, where the trees grow thin and stunted, stood a score of rough log shanties, many of them no more than hovels, which had been the transient homes of the now vanished white men. In the summer of 1946 all of these were empty; even the squat cabin which crouched below a protecting northern ridge near the mouth of Windy River on Nueltin Lake, and which was the home of the German trapper-trader, held no life. In the spring, when the ice passed from the lakes, the trader and his family had taken their canoe and had made their way southward.

The last white man had gone, but the Ihalmiut had no knowledge of his departure and so it was that in the early summer days two men whose names were Hekwaw and Ohoto set out from their camps near Ennadai to find the

21

white man. They had urgent need of him—they and all the people; for in the hot days of July death had come in a new guise to the camps. Men, women and children lay moaning on the worn deerskin robes. Their throats were choked with swollen membranes and with mucus, and they fought desperately for breath—and none could help them fight. Pommela, the chief shaman of the band, who had many spirits at his command, could do nothing to ward off the new evil which had entered into so many of the People. Ootek, a young man, but a shaman too, had sung his magic songs and had sought out the spirits in a score of trances, but he had failed as well. The two men differed only in the fact that Pommela, recognizing the impotence of his magic, finally took his family and moved away from the tents of the stricken people so that he and his own might not be endangered—while Ootek remained and exhausted himself in the useless struggle until he too fell sick, as did his only child. One shaman had fled, and the other lay stricken in his tent, when Ohoto and Hekwaw took counsel and decided that they must seek the white man's aid.

They walked the sixty miles from their camps to Windy River in two days—and when they came to the cabin where their hopes dwelt, they found the door barred against an emptiness within. So they returned again to their own place, and they came back in time to help heap rocks over the bodies of eighteen people.

Three times during the summer men came out of the north seeking help at the cabin, and found none. But on the fourth visit, in mid-August, the door of the cabin stood unbarred at last.

The trader himself had not returned, nor was he ever to return again, but he had sent his three sons back to the land and to the river beside whose shores their Indian mother had been buried. There was Charles, who had just turned nineteen, and his brothers Fred and Mike, who were, respectively, sixteen and seven years of age. The three had come back to earn their living as trappers. They had not come unwillingly, for this was the only land that they had ever known, and they had suffered intolerable rebuffs amongst the whites during their brief excursion south, because their skin was dark and their blood mixed.

Their canoe, a nineteen-foot freighter, could carry less than a thousand pounds of ammunition, food, clothing and other essential supplies, in addition to the drums of gasoline

22

and its human cargo. This was not enough to see the three boys through the eight months of winter which lay ahead, and it was clear to Charles that he would either have to journey south by dog team and obtain further supplies once the snows had come, or else he and his brothers would have to abandon their trap lines and retreat out of the land long before the winter ended. It is not to be wondered at that there was little space in the canoe for goods to give more than token meaning to the trader's licence which Charles carried folded between the pages of his diary.

Windy River Cabin was thus occupied when, on August 16, Pommela and three other men of the Ihalmiut came to it—but there was little enough for them at the end of their journey.

They told Charles and Fred of the events of the summer, and the two youths listened silently. There was no display of emotion on the part of the tellers, nor of the listeners, for they were equally helpless to change what was past. Charles heard that eighteen people had died of the disease, and though he knew most of them, he could do no more than echo Pommela's fatalistic conclusion to the grim tale, *ayoranamut*—it could not be helped.

Moreover, it was not on behalf of the dead that Pommela and the others had come south. The disease was gone, and the dead were dead. Now the summer was coming to its end, and in a few weeks the deer would begin to mass for the trek to the forest country. The people needed rifle ammunition in order to ensure a good hunt during those critical weeks so that the living would remain alive until spring. It was on account of the living that Pommela and the others had come for the fourth time to the cabin of the traders. There was no ammunition in the camps, nor had there been since late in the preceding winter. Throughout the summer, fear of the diphtheria epidemic had been second only to the fear that, if the traders had indeed left the land for good, there would be no more shells for the ancient rifles, and therefore no deer stored in the meat caches against the winter months.

When Pommela and his companions breasted the ridge by Windy River they carried with them a great apprehension; but the sight of smoke rising from the tin-can chimney, and of the canoe drawn up upon the shore, had seemed to mean release from fear. They had been smiling as they hurried down the slope toward the shack.

Charles knew these people, and he knew what was in

their hearts. It was not easy for him, yet he had no choice but to explain that he had very little ammunition—not enough in fact for his own needs.

In the end he gave Pommela and the other men more shells than he could safely spare—but he knew that it was not enough. The Ihalmiut hunters also knew that it was not enough; yet there was nothing to be done. They took what they had been given and turned north, and Charles stood on the ridge above the cabin and watched them diminish into the illimitable distances of the great plains; and the youth was troubled for them.

He had no time to dwell upon it. He was young, and the responsibility he bore was overwhelming. Three people's lives were in his hands, and there was much to do. The deer were coming, and he and Fred must meet them, not only at the cabin, but along as much as possible of their joint trap line which extended northwest a distance of more than two hundred miles to the south shores of Nowleye Lake. Deer carcasses were the essential bait for foxes, and meat caches were the equally necessary fuel depots for the dogs which must drag the heavy winter sleds into the faceless land from which all but a few isolated deer would vanish when the snows had come.

In late August the caribou which were scattered over that measureless expanse of plain had already begun to coalesce and to drain life from the intervening spaces. As the month ended, the growing herds began to drift toward the south, drawing to themselves other small herds in the abortive migration of late summer which reaches to the edge of timber, but no farther. There, milling in indecision on the borders of the Barrens, the herds await a signal known only to themselves which sends them surging north again, driven by the frantic madness of the rut.

As the deer drifted south in this August of 1946, the people who awaited them beside the Little Hills took toll of them, for it is at this season that the hides are best for winter clothing. The toll was small, for the herds also were small, dispersed, and therefore wary. And the hunters had few shells.

In early September the herds suddenly heard the call, and swung northward, and they were followed by Charles and Fred, who hunted while they traveled. Some of the animals which they shot were left to lie where they had fallen, to serve eventually as bait for foxes, though in the meantime they became prey for the many scavengers—the ravens, gulls,

24

foxes and wolves. Other carcasses were cached beneath rock piles, to be used later on for dog feed. It was too early to put down meat for human use, for the weather was not yet set upon the cold of winter.

Fifty miles north of Windy, Fred turned back, while Charles continued at the heels of the herds until he came to the broad Kazan. Here he found the remnants of the People camped near to crossing places where, in the years gone by, men in kayaks armed with spears had caught the deer between the steep banks of the river, and had killed until there was no more need of killing. In those days the carcasses of the deer had been innumerable, but in this September of another time there were but few dead deer rocked down along the shore. The herds were now too small and too dispersed to give the kayak hunters what they needed, and so most of the hunters had gone out into the plains with rifles, to kill by ones and twos, where once they had killed in tens and twenties at the river crossings.

When Charles came to the camps he found that many of the men were already out of ammunition. He did not investigate the reason for this very closely, but he suspected the truth—that Pommela, into whose hands he had given most of the ammunition intended for all of the Ihalmiut, had retained the bulk of it himself.

Charles did not linger at the camps, for he did not wish to see that which he could not have avoided seeing had he remained—the stone meat caches on the high ridges standing as empty as rifled graves. He was ill at ease in that place of women and children, for he could not escape the knowledge that the children who played by the river edge, and the women who brewed tea for him in the tents, were facing a black future in the months ahead. It made things no easier that no one reproached him for having ammunition which he kept for his own use. He did not like his role, and so he took his dogs, which Pommela and Ohoto had kept for him during the summer, and quickly left the camps.

The first snows had already fallen but there was not yet enough for sled travel, so Charles walked on the frozen plains with the dogs strung out ahead and behind him, half-delirious with their freedom, and driven wild by the heavy scent of caribou which lingered on the long white plains. For the rut was over and the deer too had begun their exodus, so that now the herds were in full flight toward the distant shelter of the forests. Though their paths still seemed innumerable, Charles could remember the time when those faint paths had each been a mighty highway beaten to the rocks beneath. He could remember, as a child, watching the herds come swelling past Windy Cabin in an unbroken river that flowed for days and nights and in his own brief time he had watched that flow shrink and contract until now the remnants of the flood could pass Windy in a single day.

These thoughts were with him when he reached his home. He knew that the best efforts of himself and Fred had not resulted in the slaughter of sufficient deer for their own needs. He guessed, with accuracy, how things would be in the distant camps where the People lived.

When the snows came, and the herds vanished from the plains, most of the People abandoned the camps by the Kazan and retreated to a circlet of little lakes to the eastward where, in times past, occasional small groups of wintering deer had sometimes lingered. Only two families, those of Hekwaw and Katelo, remained beside the river where, in days gone by, they had always known an abundance of deermeat. They remained, partly because of an ephemeral hope that the dead days might again vouchsafe some semblance of their former generosity, and partly because Hekwaw and Katelo, being past the prime of life, could no longer undertake the lean and savage winter hunting expeditions on the wind-swept plains. There were other reasons too. Hekwaw had, in his time, been a great hunter and a famous man, and not the least of his fame was based upon his generosity. Through the long decades he had often taken into his tent unwanted women and orphaned children who might otherwise have perished. In the autumn of 1946 there were many such who had turned to Hekwaw in their extremity. In his skin tent, therefore, there was himself, his two elderly wives, and his two grown sons, together with the widows of two men who had died of disease that summer, and five children who had lost both parents. One of these was an adopted daughter of Pommela's who, in this time of extremity, he had cast off as being only a useless mouth to feed. Thus, even had he wished to follow the rest of the People of the Little Lakes, Hekwaw could not easily have done so.

Hekwaw was sometimes affectionately called *Akla*—the bear—in recognition of his vast bulk, his shambling gait and his broad and placid face. Until the mid-1930's he had resolutely refused to yield his old allegiance to the deer in exchange for the new allegiance to the fox. For years after most of his contemporaries had died, or had moved closer to the trading posts, Hekwaw and his family remained on the Kazan not far south of Angikuni, in the place where he was born. In those days he was like the gray rocks of the Barrens and neither starvation nor disease could break him. Yet it was a lonely life he and his family led, and the Eskimos are a gregarious people. One spring Hekwaw finally succumbed to the nagging of his younger wife and reluctantly joined the remainder of the People near the Little Lakes.

Then his rocklike strength, and his great skill as hunter and provider, proved of no further avail against the fates. From this time onward he shared the torment of the People fully and in his own flesh, for he saw six of his children perish in the country of the Little Lakes, and at the age of fifty he had become an old man.

The tents of the ten families who had moved east from the Kazan were established in two different camps, for though the Ihalmiut were now so few in numbers, they were nevertheless divided against each other. The smallest of the camps was under the hegemony of Pommela and was established by a little lake which bore his name. It consisted of his own two tents and the single tents which housed the families of his followers Alekahaw and Onekwaw.

The members of the other group, who looked to Owliktuk for leadership, had pitched their tents by Halo Lake, five miles from those of the old shaman. The families here were those of Owliktuk, Halo, Yaha, Miki, Elaitutna, Ohoto and Ootek.

Since the days of his youth Pommela had always been full of unpredictable actions and of dangerous passions. He was the antithesis of a true Innuit, for he lived almost entirely for himself, and within himself, and he had early discarded his adherence to the ancient and primary law which binds all Eskimos together in a co-operative way of life. He had been one of those who traded to Brochet and even to Churchill in the early years of the century, and the unique position he had gained as an intermediary between the Ihalmiut and the whites had early given him a taste for personal power. The taste had developed to a consuming hunger as the years advanced, and he had fed it freely. Though he despised all white men, he was astute enough to realize that the source of their power lay in material possessions, and so he had set himself to become something which no Eskimo could ever have envisaged in the past—a wealthy man.

He had succeeded. Now he had two tents, and one of these was filled with an incredible miscellany of useless things purchased over the years from the traders, or taken by stealth or force from his own people. He had not even hesitated at robbing the graves of his dead friends in order to possess himself of their belongings. His second tent was filled with such things as ancient gramophones, rusted and useless rifles, a cast-iron stove for which there was no fuel in this treeless land, and three brassbound trunks filled with an array of junk of indescribable origin and nature. This rusting wealth was not only of no practical value—it was an actual encumbrance, for it made moving camp a considerable problem. Yet these possessions were more than symbols, for Pommela believed they were an actual source of power, and in the tortuous recesses of his mind, the pursuit of power had come to be the motivation of his life. He was possessed of a ruthless and unquenchable vigor which still showed clearly through the darkly wrinkled face of a man of sixty years. He was feared and hated by all the People, even by the two syco-phants, Onekwaw and Alekahaw, who chose to live under his protection.

Pommela had also been cursed with the most terrible physical affliction that an Eskimo man can know, for he was sterile. The fact of his sterility was something that he had never admitted, and during his adult life he had taken seven wives, and had slept with countless other women, in his terrible desire to prove his manhood. As he grew older he had treated the women who failed him with a callousness that had often been their death. In 1946 he was still possessed of two wives, but though there were four children in his tent, none of these were his, for they were the children of his wives by other men, now dead. These children were a symbol of his failure, and he hated them for that.

Pommela was one of the two *angekoks*—shamans—in the band. Amongst the Eskimos an *angeokok* is both priest and doctor, and, like priests and doctors amongst all races of mankind, some of the *angeokoks* are devoted to the welfare of their people, while others are devoted only to their own welfare. Long ago Pommela had turned the special power of an *angeokok* to his own ends. He controlled many spirits, possessed of a great potential for evil, so that it was a foolhardy man who would openly dare the old man's wrath.

Yet, if none could openly resist the will of Pommela, there were those who could do so covertly, and chief of these was Owliktuk.

A darkly saturnine man of middle years, Owliktuk's brown eyes and facial cast betrayed the white blood of some vanished trapper. Within himself he had a strength to equal Pommela's, and as great a certainty. He was by far the most effective hunter and the most thoughtful man amongst the people, and he was devoted to the old ways of his mother's race. He had the gift of unobtrusive leadership, and those who chose of their own will to follow him had been spared the worst of the troubles which had afflicted the People through the past two decades. He was a lusty man whose wife had borne and raised five children. But Owliktuk was not an *angeokok,* and herein lay his weakness, for he could not openly contend against Pommela, who possessed so many allies in the world of spirits. Owliktuk could only disassociate himself and his followers as much as possible from the old man who was so hated and so deeply feared.

There was, however, an *angeokok* amongst Owliktuk's group. This was Ootek, a young man, and a dreamer of dreams. Ootek was a true priest, for he revered the forces that are not of our world, and he was humble before them. All his talents and his energies were pressed into the search for understanding of the omnipotent forces which control human destiny. He was a seeker after truth. And he was no match for Pommela.

When Charles drove his dog team north in mid-November to prepare his trap line he paid a visit to Pommela's camp. The old shaman greeted him with an unction that lasted only until he discovered that Charles could not, or would not, give him a sack of flour. Though he invited the youth into his main tent, he did so with a brusqueness which was nicely calculated to sustain the faint unease Charles always felt in the old man's presence. Charles did not like Pommela, nor did he trust him, yet he had never quite dared to cross him. And Pommela, who knew much of men, was aware that the young trapper harbored the seeds of fear within himself.

Ikok, Pommela's younger wife, served the two men boiled deer tongues on a wooden platter and, while they ate, and drank the broth in which the tongues had been cooked, Pommela dominated the conversation. He told Charles that, due to the lack of ammunition, the people had killed less than half the deer which were required to sustain them until spring. He spoke of hunger that had already come to the camps and, with a bland disregard for visual evidence, he went so far as to claim that even he and his family were on the verge of starvation. "Give me more shells," he demanded.

"I will share them with the other hunters, and then we will all have meat."

It was a demand that expressed his open contempt for the younger man since Pommela knew that Charles would not credit his own protestations of hunger, and he was also fully aware that Charles suspected him of having kept for his own use most of the ammunition which he had obtained at Windy Cabin.

Charles showed no resentment. His belief in his superiority over this sparse-bearded native was not proof against Pommela's powerful presence, and he was afraid to make an open enemy of the old man. He resolved to avoid all the Eskimos as much as possible, particularly Pommela, in the months which stretched ahead. He had done what he could for them, and he could do no more.

Rousing his dogs, the young trapper drove hurriedly away into the northwest. He spent that night in his outpost cabin on the banks of the Kazan and in the morning drove on across the frozen muskegs to the River of Graves. Turning north on its slick and almost snow-free surface, he slipped and slithered along behind his dogs as they struggled for a foothold on the patches of glare ice. Two days later he reached Nowleye Lake and, after a brief night's rest, turned south again, locating and unearthing his caches of traps, and making his "sets" along the route.

Charles had expected to find some wintering deer, for although the main herds abandon the land when the snows come, there are usually a few who lag behind. In this hope he was completely disappointed, for he saw neither deer nor tracks of deer. The fact that he was thus unable to replenish the rapidly dwindling supplies of meat he had brought with him on his sled was cause enough for apprehension. But when he reached the cabin at Kazan he found new reasons for disquietude. Two of the caribou carcasses which he had cached there in the fall were missing, and it was clear from the tracks in the snow that they had been taken by Eskimos. The implications of this theft were obvious to Charles. He knew that none of the Ihalmiut, with the exception of Pommela, would ever rob a cache unless driven to it by absolute necessity. The theft of these two deer, therefore, suggested that the situation in the Innuit camps must already be very serious; yet Charles did not deviate from his route to seek confirmation. He drove on south as fast as his dogs could go until he reached the sanctuary of Windy Cabin.

A growing foreboding as to what he might encounter in the north kept him at Windy Cabin until the end of December. A dozen times he told himself that he must visit his trap line on the Nowleye River, and a dozen times he found a reason for delay. By the end of December he could no longer postpone the trip and so he reluctantly loaded his sled with dog feed for ten days, said good-by to Mike and Fred, and turned into the threatening distances of the north. He made the journey at breakneck speed, driving his dogs unmercifully. Deliberately he avoided the Eskimo camps on the Little Lakes, nor did he linger at the Kazan cabin. The weather was kind to him and there were no storms, so that by January 2 he had reached his farthest north at Nowleye Lake and was ready to turn about. Once more he had failed to find any sign of winter deer, and their continued absence gave rise to an oppressive sense of impending disaster which acted as a goad and sent him south at the best pace his tired dogs could muster. The days were short, and the nights long and very dark. It was a time for the uncouth spirits of the rocks to walk abroad, and Charles's European blood was not wholly proof against their threats.

So it was with a relief bordering on the irrational that he came again to the Kazan cabin and recognized Fred's dogs tied up outside the tiny shack. His relief was short-lived. Fred was indeed there (for this place was the northern terminus of the younger boy's trap line) but he was not alone. With him were Halo and Ootek who had walked the twenty-five miles from Owliktuk's camp, impelled by the faint hope that they might encounter Charles or Fred and obtain assistance from them.

They told their story simply, and it was a bleak account. The meat supplies with which they had begun the winter had proven hopelessly inadequate, for Pommela had refused them any of the ammunition he had obtained from Charles and they had only possessed a beggarly handful of shells which Owliktuk had managed to save over from the preceding spring. Though they had hunted hard at the river during the autumn crossings, using kayaks and spears, the herds had been few and evasive, and the water kill had provided only enough meat for a month or two at most.

With the advent of the first snows, and the departure of the herds, the land had been completely emptied of the deer. Though the best hunters had roamed the plains for days armed with crude bows which they had hurriedly built after

31

the ancestral patterns, they had not found a single winter deer upon which to try their dubious skill with these ancient weapons. Then, in late November, even these desperate journeys had been brutally curtailed. In this of all years the fatal dog disease which comes from the foxes and the wolves (and which is probably a form of distemper) had struck their teams. The dogs, already much weakened by starvation, had so little resistance left that within two weeks only four out of nearly fifty still survived. Nor had these four long outlived their fellows, for there had been no more food to spare for them, and before the end of the month they too were dead.

The people of Owliktuk's camp were already displaying overt signs of famine. Halo and Ootek showed the onset of starvation in the tautness of the skin across the bones of their faces and in the unnatural brilliance of their eyes. They showed it too in the way they ate the meat which Fred had given them, cramming themselves with frozen slivers of deer flesh until their bellies were distended.

By the time Charles arrived at the Kazan cabin, the immediate hunger of the two men had been assuaged, but their fears for the future had been increased. They had hoped against hope that Charles might have received more supplies from the south—perhaps by airplane, as had happened once or twice in the days when the Hudson's Bay Company still operated Windy Post. These hopes dissolved when Fred told them that, far from having supplies to trade, the boys were almost out of food and would soon have to travel south for more if they were to survive.

It was a mirthless irony that this winter found the white foxes at the peak of their cycle and abundance. They had come drifting out of the north that autumn in their hundreds, like small ghosts, and their neat tracks were everywhere. Charles and Fred had already taken more than fifty pelts apiece despite the desultory manner of their trapping. But the Ihalmiut who over the years had been turned into hunters of the fox, and taught to live by the fox, had been unable to take more than a score of pelts amongst them. They had no dogs to enable them to visit distant trap lines. They had no meat for bait, nor enough even to give them strength to maintain short trap lines which could be visited on foot. And now they knew that any foxes which they might manage to procure would be worthless anyway, for there was no way that the pelts could be metamorphosed into food.

To Charles and Fred the news of the outbreak of distemper amongst the Eskimo dogs was of such frightening import that it preoccupied their thoughts to the point where the plight of the Eskimos themselves was virtually forgotten. They knew that if the disease took many of their own dogs they would not only have to abandon their trap lines, but they might be isolated at Windy Cabin without supplies, and unable to make a dash south to the trading posts at Brochet or Duck Lake in order to replenish them. They felt sorry for Halo and Ootek and the rest, but their own plight engrossed their whole attention.

The two Eskimos left the cabin that same day. They took with them a few pounds of frozen meat—but they also took the knowledge that no assistance could be hoped for from the post at Windy River.

Charles and Fred set off for Windy before dawn the following morning. They were consumed by anxiety about their dogs, and even more determined to give the Eskimos as wide a berth as possible; but they reckoned without Pommela. The old shaman, driving the remnants of a team, intercepted the youths as they halted to brew tea at midday. He came up to the little fire as if it had been his own, and truculently announced that all the members of his band were coming south to Windy in a few days' time, and that he expected them to be supplied with food. Charles's residual fear of the shaman was heightened by Pommela's bold demeanor, and he was unable to make any effective protest.

However, Pommela did not make good his threat at once, and during the next week Charles and Fred took stock of their position. It was by no means good. They had only enough "store food" on hand to last, with careful rationing, until the end of January. Their supply of deermeat had been reduced to about forty carcasses, widely dispersed in several caches between Windy and the Kazan, and there was only enough frozen fish on hand to feed the dogs for one long trip. If the Eskimos did not come to Windy Cabin, Charles thought that he and his brothers might be able to hold out until sometime in February; but on January 18, the Eskimos began arriving. The first to come were Onekwaw and Alekahaw and their families—eight hungry people with three starving dogs. Two days later Pommela arrived with one wife and two of his adopted children. Pommela immediately demanded meat for his dogs and for his family, and without waiting for permission he went to a cache behind the cabin and helped himself. Onekwaw and Alekahaw were not slow to follow his example, and Charles made no attempt to stop them.

On the 27th, Pommela announced that he was returning north to get the rest of his family, and Charles decided to accompany him in order to bring back some meat he had cached at North Camp, which was some forty miles from Windy. When the two men reached North Camp, Charles found that the cache had ben completely emptied. It was indicative of Pommela's sense of his own power that he frankly admitted to having been the thief.

Charles's anger was intense, yet he mastered it. The knowledge that Pommela had allowed him to make this trip, knowing full well he would find an empty cache at the end of it, was bitter; but neither bitterness nor rage could free him from the trepidation which the old man inspired in him. Without a word Charles turned his team and headed south.

Immediately upon his arrival at the home cabin he warned Fred that their position had now become dangerous, for they could no longer count on salvaging any of their caches on the land. It was decided therefore that Fred and Mike should take one team and head south at once in a bid to reach Duck Lake trading post and there obtain fresh supplies. Fred took with him the last of the fish that had been set aside for dog feed, and departed on that same day, traveling light and fast.

By the end of January all of Pommela's people were clustered close about Windy Cabin. They very soon consumed the remaining deermeat which Charles had held in reserve, and they were still starving—all of them, that is, except Pommela and his favorite wife who remained well fed and energetic even while Pommela's adopted children grew steadily weaker and more subdued.

Charles soon began to find the atmosphere intolerable. He was aware that Pommela probably possessed more food than he did himself, and he grew increasingly uneasy as the old man's assumption of dominance became more and more blatant. Moreover, while he could shut his mind to some extent to the agonies of famine if the evidence was not before his eyes, he could not now avoid seeing that the children and many of the adults at Windy Cabin were approaching the ultimate stages of starvation.

Five days of this was as much as he could stand. On the sixth day Charles hitched up his team and, though he was very short of dog feed, he too headed down the ice of Nueltin Lake, intending to intercept Fred at the south end, on his return from Duck Lake Post. Charles had made up his mind that, if he could get enough supplies from Fred, he would carry on to Brochet where he could divest himself of some of the unwanted but steadily increasing feeling of responsibility toward the hungry Eskimos, by reporting their plight to someone in authority.

The two boys met near Johnstons Island in south Nueltin on February 3. Fred had a full load of flour, lard, tea and sugar, but he had been able to obtain only a little ammunition, and no dog feed. Reluctantly Charles had to abandon his plan for proceeding south. This decision was made somewhat easier for him when Fred related how he had persuaded the manager of the isolated Duck Lake Post to send out a message on his primitive wireless set, giving at least an indication of the scope and nature of the tragedy which threatened the inland Eskimos.

This message, which appears to have been the first ever to be dispatched to the outside world on behalf of the Ihalmiut, suffered an unknown fate. Almost certainly it reached the federal government department which was responsible for Eskimo affairs. Most probably it then sank into dusty obscurity in some weighty file and was forgotten. In any event, it elicited no response.

The food Fred had brought from Duck Lake was sufficient to hold the hounds of hunger at bay for a week or two, but it was quite insufficient to be of help to the remaining Ihalmiut who were still in their camps to the north of Windy. The condition of these people was now something which Charles could no longer keep out of his conscious mind. A day after he and his brothers returned to the cabin, one of Hekwaw's sons, Belikari, also arrived there, from the Kazan. Belikari was in frightful condition, barely able to walk, and clad in rags of skins. It was some time before he recovered sufficiently to tell his harrowing story. His father's tent, crowded with women and unwanted children, had seen no food for weeks, except scraps of skin clothing, and bones dug from under the snows. No winter deer had come to the Kazan, and attempts to fish through the river ice had yielded almost no results. Death for all the inhabitants of the place was no more than an arm's length away.

This account, coupled with what Charles could see with his own eyes of the apathetic lethargy of starving children at the cabin door, finally resolved the conflict in his mind. He knew he could no longer stand apart. Now he must take sides, and though he must have deeply resented his involvement in something which was, after all, none of his affair, and which would mean that he would have to abandon his own attempts to gain a livelihood from this hard land, he nevertheless consciously now chose the harder course. In doing so he became the first outlander in all time to concern himself with the plight of the inland Eskimos.

On February 8, Charles hitched up his team (from which distemper had already stolen his two best dogs) and, taking with him thirty pounds of rolled oats as food for himself and his remaining dogs, he set out on the three-hundred-mile route south to Brochet.

That was an epic journey. He accomplished it in eleven days, but during the last three days there was not a scrap of food for man or dogs. Both he and his team were so utterly exhausted before they reached the Hudson's Bay post at the north end of Reindeer Lake that they had to be helped up the slope from the lake ice to the settlement. And the hazards of that long trek had been greatly intensified by the fact that at the few isolated camps of the Idthen Eldeli which lay upon the route death stood waiting to receive the traveler. An epidemic of influenza was raging through the thin forests between Nuelti and Reindeer with such ferocity that, before spring came, it was to take the lives of 76 Indians from a total Chipewyan population of 265. Charles encountered the disease at an Idthen Eldeli camp near Kasmere Lake. He had hoped to obtain food at this place, but when no one came out to welcome him he entered the squalid cabin and beheld the naked corpses of three people who had flung off their clothing during the paroxysms of fever, and whose contorted bodies gave a terrible warning to the chance visitor.

Charles remained at Brochet, which was itself in the grip of the epidemic, only long enough to rest and feed his dogs for the return trip. He reported to the Hudson's Bay post manager on conditions amongst the Ihalmiut, and his account was relayed by radio to the Indian Affairs Department doctor at The Pas.

On February 24 he started north again. The snows lay deep and soft in the forests, and no other travelers were moving, so that there were no packed trails to follow. Charles's team could draw the long Eskimo sled only with great difficulty. They could haul no more than five hundred pounds of freight, of which a hundred pounds was frozen fish for dog feed. Even though this was a comparatively light load, Charles was still forced to cache half of it at the south end of Nueltin Lake, and when he arrived back at Windy Cabin on March 7, exhausted and with exhausted dogs, he had with him only sufficient food to last the three boys for a few more weeks.

But fortune, which had forsaken the Ihalmiut, had been kinder to the three outlanders. On March 5, Fred, hunting far afield, had encountered a herd of twenty deer at the edge of timberline and had succeeded in killing eight of them. Together he and Charles hauled the carcasses back to Windy Cabin.

Meanwhile some of the People who had come to the cabin seeking help had given up all hope of it and had gone plodding north again. Alekahaw and his family were amongst these desperate ones, but they were lucky, for they stumbled upon the frozen remains of a deer that had probably died of gunshot wounds the preceding autumn. Alekahaw, with his wife and daughter, camped by the carcass until nothing remained of it but tufts of hair and fragments of cracked bones.

Belikari had traveled with them, but he did not stay to share their good luck. He walked on into the white and hungry land toward the distant tent of his father by the banks of the Kazan, where the people who awaited his coming sustained themselves on hope alone.

At Windy Cabin the eight deer vanished with such incredible rapidity that by March 14 Charles concluded that he and his brothers would have to abandon the post and flee southward while they still could. They had already begun their preparations for the trip when they became aware of a strange sound pulsing in the hard gray sky. They ran out of the cabin in time to see the stubby silhouette of a Norseman ski-plane slip over the Ghost Hills to the south and level off for an approach to the ice of Windy Bay.

The remaining Eskimos had also heard the sound and they had come crawling from their tents to stare incredulously at this salvation coming to them from the skies. Onekwaw's wide and foolish face was contorted in an expression of almost insane relief, while his young wife swayed beside him shrieking with hysterical laughter.

She did not laugh for long.

There was no laughter at that place when the plane came to a halt and Charles, wrenching open the door, discovered that it contained no food of any kind.

The chartered Norseman belonging to Lamb Airways of The Pas, with the Indian affairs doctor as a passenger, had carried food when it set out from The Pas—in fact it had been laden with 1300 pounds of food. At Brochet it had stopped to pick up Charles's father as a guide, but then, for some inexplicable reason, it had flown to the *south* end of Nueltin Lake, where it had landed, and the supplies had been unloaded on the ice, before the flight to Windy was completed.

There was no time for Charles to obtain an explanation. The Norsemen remained only long enough for Tom Lamb, the pilot, to call out that he would return the following day bringing a second load of relief rations direct to Windy, before the plane swung into the wind and in a few more minutes had vanished over the southern hills.

The plane did not return the next day, nor the next. On the morning of the sixth day of waiting Charles hitched up his remaining dogs—four had now died of the disease—and he had already started for south Nueltin when he heard the roar of the plane approaching.

He hurried back and was in time to help unload the relief supplies. These totaled eight hundred pounds, one hundred pounds of which consisted of dried white beans that were of as little use to the starving people of the plains as lead pellets might have been. In a land where half a day's hard searching may sometimes yield only enough willow twigs to melt sufficient snow to make a pint of water, these beans were worthless. They were still lying, untouched, in Windy Cabin a full year later.

This "mercy flight"—it was later publicized as such—represented the total assistance which the authorities considered was required to meet the needs of the Ihalmiut. The doctor departed, having visited none of the camps and having seen no Eskimos at all except the watching figures of Pommela's and Onekwaw's families on the distant shore of Windy Bay.

It was a gesture which presumably served a purpose as far as Ottawa was concerned, but it had no meaning for the people of the land. It had no effect upon Owliktuk's camp, for instance, where thirty people clung upon the brink of dissolution. As early as the first week in February all the food in this camp had been exhausted and the people had been forced to scrabble beneath the hard-packed snow for the refuse discarded in the fall. Huddled in their deerskin tents, which had been banked with blocks of snow, these people endured the searing cold of winter with empty stomachs, and with only remnants of fur clothing upon their bodies. They had no fires, for no one had the strength to spare for the arduous search for willow twigs beneath the drifts. They lived on scraps of skin, on frozen carrion, and some of them even searched out and ate human excrement; for there are no niceties of taste when death lies hard and cold within the belly.

Near the end of March, and at about the time that the authorities concluded their rescue mission, the situation in Owliktuk's camp reached a climax. Owliktuk was aware that if his people remained where they were for even a few more days, they would be incapable of ever moving again. They had held on at the old camp site in the desperate hope that some winter deer would come within their reach, but Owliktuk now recognized that this was a forlorn hope. He knew it would be fatal to remain, but that it might be just as fatal to risk moving camp, for there was no real prospect of finding food anywhere in all the land. Halo's and Ootek's meeting with Charles and Fred at the Kazan cabin had made it clear that nothing could be gained by attempting to reach Windy Cabin. Yet it seemed to Owliktuk that there might still be one remote chance for their survival. Ninety miles to the eastward, at Otter Lake, a tiny outpost of a Churchill trading firm had operated spasmodically for some years past. There—if the people could reach the post—they might conceivably obtain some food. It was a slim possibility, made slimmer by the fact that a march of ninety miles, in subzero temperatures and on almost empty bellies, must tax the strength and endurance of the emaciated scarecrows who were Owliktuk's people beyond all limits.

Nevertheless Owliktuk saw it as the only hope, and when he had explained his intentions to the heads of the other families, they agreed to follow him.

That incredible march began about the 1st of April. The people took three sleds which carried the younger children who could not walk for any distance. The men hauled the sleds, and the women walked behind, some of them carrying babies in their parkas. The only food they had with which to begin that journey consisted of the flesh of three dogs which had died of distemper, and which Owliktuk had kept concealed against a last emergency. The only hope they had of obtaining food along the way lay in a rusty .22 rifle—a "spit gun," as the people call such a weapon—fit only for killing such small game as ptarmigan and arctic hares, and in seven boxes of .22 ammunition belonging to Miki. Their clothes were scanty and of poor quality for, due to the shortage of ammunition, they had not been able to obtain enough prime deer hides during the late summer to provide adequate winter clothing. They were as ill equipped in almost every physical aspect as they could possibly have been for such a journey. But they were well equipped in another sense. They were enduring, and they were indomitable.

They had much to endure. For five days they walked to the eastward and found nothing for their bellies. They were by then so weak that the women and the older people could no longer walk more than two to three miles in a day. At this juncture Yaha, plodding ahead of the straggling line, came upon the remains of a caribou that had been killed and eaten by wolves. There was not much left but bones, gristle and offal, but the find represented salvation for the band. They camped here for two days, and then they moved on there were not even any bone fragments left for the lesser scavengers.

On the tenth day Ootek saw and killed a single arctic hare with the .22 rifle—a morsel of fish amongst so many. But that hare, and the remains of the deer, comprised the total sustenance the people were able to extract from the frozen land during the entire trek.

It sufficed—almost. Near the end of the second week two of the little band reached the end of all their journeying. One of these was Epeetna, an old woman who was the wife of Elaitutna, and her journey had been long indeed, for it had spanned more than sixty years. The other was a baby less than a year old, who died at the dried-up breasts of its mother Nanuk, who was Ohoto's wife.

That any of the people could have survived that ordeal seems unbelievable, yet in the middle of April, when they were less than two days distant from the goal, all of them still clung tenaciously to life except for Epeetna, and Nanuk's child. They had come so far, but they could go no farther as a band. And so they camped—crowding together under some fragments of deer hides which served as tents—while three of the men, Oliktuk, Ootek and Ohoto, went on alone.

These three reached the tiny shanty which was the trader's home and they tried to make known their urgent need to him. But the trader either did not understand them (for they had no furs to trade) or he had no food to spare. He did accept some boxes of .22 ammunition in exchange for a small bag of flour, but that was all the help the people were destined to receive from him.

During the next few days all those who could walk or crawl to the post did so, and they tried in every way they knew to make their plight apparent to the trader. It did no good. Eventually they returned to the travel camp to await the inevitable end of their travail.

They waited almost until the end of April—but there were some who could not wait.

There was Elaitutna, Ohoto's father.

There was Nanuk's three-year-old son Aljut.

There was Uktilohik, the year-old son of Owliktuk and Nutaralik.

None of these could wait any longer, and so they died. The rest of the people must surely have followed in a little while, but in the last days of the month a single caribou, the forerunner of the northward migrating herds, appeared in the very middle of the silent camp where men lay dying. It was Ootek who found the strength to fire a shot from the despised .22 rifle—and it was he who killed the deer.

They ate that deer, even to its bones, and then they left their dead buried under the snow and turned westward on the terrible road they had followed from their home camps. It took them eighteen days to return, but they could not travel very fast, and they were often forced to spend a day or so in camp while the men hunted ptarmigan whose spring flocks were again coming back into the land. It was late in May before they reached the Little Lakes, and here they met Hekwaw. That good old man had at last obtained some ammunition from Charles, and had made a kill of the north-bound deer, so that he was able to feed the wanderers. For them that winter of torment was at an end.

Hekwaw had saved Owliktuk's band, but he could not bring his own dead back to life. In the long days before the deer belatedly returned to the plains, death had lived in Hekwaw's camp, and was only driven out at last when Charles took up the task that the authorities had laid down.

On March 21, the day after the plane had come a second time to Windy Cabin, Charles started north. His few surviving dogs were emaciated and they could only haul two hundred pounds of flour and lard, together with some oatmeal for dog feed. Even with this light load they moved very slowly and it was not until March 24 that Charles reached the first camp, that of Alekahaw. He found the family on the verge of death. He gave them food and hurried on toward the Kazan camp where he knew Katelo and Hekwaw had their tents. He did not stop at dusk, but urged his dogs forward into the darkness until they collapsed and could go no farther.

Early the next morning he reached his destination to find that death had long preceded him.

Death had indeed come early, and had stayed late amongst the two families who had waited here for help that never came. And the ones who had been unable to wait were these.

There was Oquinuk, who was Katelo's wife.

There was Homoguluk, a ten-year-old orphan.

There was Itkuk, the widow of Angleyalak.

There was Eepuk, who was one of the Hekwaw's wives.

There was Pama, a fifteen-year-old daughter of the dead Angelyalak.

Of those who still lived, only Hekwaw, Belikari, Katelo, and Katelo's son Iktoluka could stand upon their feet.

Charles camped with them for two days; scoured the country about with his team to find fuel for them; fed them and watched over them. On the third day he led them south to the Kazan cabin where they joined Alekahaw's family who had already come there on Charles's instructions.

Charles himself hurried south again, for he was aware that the food he had brought would not last for many days. Reaching Windy he instructed Fred to carry a second load of food north while he himself drove to the south end of Nueltin to freight back some of the supplies which the Norsemen had left there upon the ice.

From April 5 to May 31, Charles and Fred traveled more than twelve hundred miles behind their worn-out dogs, freighting supplies northward to the people in the starvation camps. They had no time to rest, no time to look at their own trap lines which had been abandoned since January. By the end of May both boys were drawn so fine that their high cheekbones seemed about to burst from the young dark skin. And it was in this condition that I found these two who had the will to do what no other human beings would do, to succor a people who had been savaged by adversity and doomed by our neglect.

4

The Drums of Hope

The deer came late to the inland plains in the spring of 1947.
During the final days of May the main herds swelled out of
the forests and streamed past Windy Post, directly driven by
a nameless urgency. The does came first, their swollen bellies
swaying as they breasted the softening drifts and climbed the
ridges where the last dwarfed trees clung in mute defiance of
the endless winds which strove to put them down.

Barely pausing to snatch a few mouthfuls of lichens
from the high crests where the snows had already vanished
under the harsh impact of the spring sun, the does streamed
northward seeking the fawning grounds before their time was
on them. Before the end of the month they were passing

through the country of the Ihalmiut and, for the first time in many months, children smiled and men went out to hunt knowing that they would not come back empty-handed.

So the turn of May brought the familiar visitation of the deer back to the land, but it also brought another, and a stranger, visitation. In the afternoon of June 3, a twin-engined Anson aircraft of wartime vintage came rumbling out of the east and landed roughly on the ice of Windy Bay.

When I climbed down from the plane and looked about me I thought that I had never seen such utter desolation. Under a gray and scudding sky the dark snows, the black lines of treeless hills, and the crouching back of an all-but buried and apparently deserted cabin sounded no note of welcome. There was a real temptation to clamber back into the old Anson and leave this place to its own abysmal loneliness; but I had worked too hard to get here, and I had made my decision and could not go back upon it.

The manner and the causes of my coming to Windy River have been described in detail in my previous book *People of the Deer*. It will suffice now to say that I was in flight from five years of war memories and that I was in search of a people whom I had no reason either to despise or fear, and of whose existence I was not even certain. A chain of accidents led to Windy River becoming my objective in that whole vast realm of the interior Barrens; and the con-summate skill of a man now dead—the pilot of the Anson—enabled me to overleap the barriers of the land.

During the first few days of my stay in the musty, frigid cabin, I was sure that I had made a blunder and that I would come no nearer to finding the people whom I sought. But after a week of gloom during which I cursed myself for my impetuous and almost completely uninformed venture into a land which seemed so desolate and hostile, the mood was shattered by the arrival of Charles. He came out of the north, driving a shrunken team, and returning from his fifth and final trip freighting supplies to the camps of the Ihalmiut.

The shock of discovering a stranger in his cabin was so great that it nearly robbed him of speech for a matter of several hours. That did not matter since, in my delight at finding him, I was loquacious enough for two. Slowly the barriers dissolved, and within a few weeks we had become friends. It was a friendship which was to grow with the passing months during which we traveled together on foot and by canoe for almost two thousand miles. And it was

44

through Charles that I found the people I had sought—the People of the Little Hills.

In the latter part of June we visited their camps, having half-paddled and half-carried our canoe up the roaring freshet named Little River; over the height of land, and down the small stream which the Ihalmiut called Tingmeaku—Goose Creek.

When we came amongst them, the People still bore clear evidence of their sufferings of the winter in every lineament of their faces—yet they were full of laughter and of an intense vivacity which perhaps belongs only to those who have escaped from what has seemed like certain death. They received a stranger from a race they had little cause to love, without restraint, and there was no limit to their hospitality.

During the journey north I had come to some appreciation of the gigantic proportions of that land, and I had felt a growing sense of unease at the absence of human life. Nor was this sensation much alleviated at the Ihalmiut camps, for there were only forty-nine of the People left, and this minute congregation seemed frighteningly insignificant in that limitless expanse of empty plain.

In June of 1947 the Ihalmiut were camped beside the shores of three little lakes which were first mapped—from the air—and named by us in 1954. They are now officially known as Calhoun, Stern and McCourt Lakes, but in 1947 they were still known to the people of the plains by the names Ootek, Halo and Pommela. These names have been obliterated now, for it is is our nature to obliterate even such ephemeral traces of those we have destroyed.

By the lake which bore his name lived Ootek, the young shaman, with his wife Howmik, and their daughter Kalak, who had been born just after the return from the starvation trek to Otter Lake. Kalak was born deaf and dumb, out of the sufferings of her mother, but the child was nonetheless dear to Ootek, for she was the only child surviving out of the four children to whom Howmik had given birth in the years of their marriage.

In a tent set cheek by jowl with Ootek's lived Halo and his wife Kikik. They had two surviving children out of the three which had been born to them, and this was a tribute to Halo's competence, for, next to Owliktuk, he was the best provider amongst the people, and the most indomitable man. He was a far better hunter than Ootek, yet these two were inseparable, for what the one lacked the other had. Ootek's abilities were of the mind and spirit and these were the perfect complement to Halo's competence with the hard realities of existence in the plains. They were so close, these two, that they were almost one.

The rest of Owliktuk's group—to which Ootek and Halo belonged—had pitched their conical skin tents a mile away by Halo Lake. The largest and the best-made tent of all belonged to Owliktuk, his wife Nutaralik and their four surviving children. Such was the determination and effectiveness of this man that he had lost only one child—Uktilohik—during the hungry years. Calm, reserved, yet incisive in a time of trouble, he had become the acknowledged leader of six families of the People, not by any overt domination, but solely by the power of his example. Yet leadership gave Owliktuk no pleasure, as it did Pommela. It had come to him unasked, and he bore it in the knowledge that no single man, nor yet a combination of all the men of the Ihalmiut, could forestall an inevitable end. Owliktuk had no illusions—he remembered the past, and he could understand the pattern it had made, so that he knew what the future must be. It was his tragedy that though he strove endlessly, he could find no sure avenue of escape. His dark reflections were not natural to the mind of an Eskimo, and it may be that they were a gift he had from the unknown white man who had fathered him. Yet, if he foresaw a hopeless future, Owliktuk never thought of bowing to it. He defended himself stubbornly and with such skill that it was inevitable that he should become the strong core of the decimated People.

Amongst those who looked to him for leadership were Yaha—an amiable and gentle fellow, but a good hunter for all of that—and Miki, who was a taciturn and withdrawn man given to moments of bleak fatalism. Miki's father had also been a white man, and he had abandoned Miki and his mother one bitter winter leaving the mother to die of starvation in her efforts to keep the boy alive. Miki survived only because he was accidentally discovered in the spring by Owliktuk's father, in the tiny cabin where he had lived for weeks with the dead and decaying body of his mother.

There was one other who belonged in part at least to Owliktuk's group, and he was perhaps the most tragic figure amongst the people. This was Ohoto. A squat and burly man, he was remarkable for his quick perceptiveness, his sharp intelligence—and his consuming sense of frustration. Years earlier, when he was still a boy, he had visited Reindeer Lake in company with his father, and out of that visit a steadily burgeoning desire to become one with the white man had been born within him. Like Owliktuk, Ohoto understood that his people, and their way of life, were doomed; but unlike the older man, Ohoto had never accepted the hopelessness of his position. He believed, with a blind and pitiful faith, that it would be possible to evade his fate if he could only transform himself into a white man; and through the long years he had labored toward this impossible objective. He no longer really belonged in the land of his fathers, yet he was unable to escape from it. He aped the white man and their ways in every possible manner. Several times he had accompanied Charles to Brochet, where he had even embraced Christianity at the hands of a missionary priest. For a while he had striven to obey the injunctions of the Church, but when he discovered that these would lead him not to equality and acceptance by the whites, but only to another kind of servitude, he angrily discarded them; and the words *Jesoosi Kristoosi* became a curse upon his lips.

In the summer of 1946 his wife Kekwaw, whom he had loved deeply, died of diphtheria. Ohoto took another wife, an aging widow called Nanuk, but she could give him no peace, and his restless, caged and rebel spirit continued to drive him so that he moved like a snow-ghost about the land, sometimes camping near Pommela, sometimes near Owliktuk, but more often by himself—except on those rare occasions when there was a white man within reach, and then Ohoto attached himself to the stranger like a veritable leech.

Only in Pommela's camp did I encounter any indication of hostility towards my own race. The old shaman had come through the winter with still greater certainty in his own powers, and with an increased contempt for the rest of the Ihalmiut who had submitted to his tyranny. Here, in his own land, he had no doubts as to my inferiority, and he made no secret of it—though later, when it became apparent that I could be of use to him, he changed his attitude.

His camp consisted of his own two tents and those of Katelo, Onekwaw and Alekahaw. Onekwaw was a wild-visaged, half-fey fellow whose shy smile and unbridled laughter could not hide the vast uncertainty which haunted him. He was childless (though his wife Tabluk had a daughter by another marriage) and he was Pommela's sycophant and totally under his control.

Not so Alekahaw, son of the great shaman Igluguarduak. He was a sly and clever opportunist and though he

47

adhered to Pommela's group, this was solely because he found it advantageous to do so.

Katelo, who was Pommela's younger brother, lived in company with his twelve-year-old son; and there was no longer any woman in their tent to cook and sew for them and to give comfort when they returned from the hunt. Katelo was a broken and lonely man who had all but lost the will to live. In his lifetime he had watched three wives and seven children die of hunger and disease and now he was old and very weary, and he no longer cared.

These, with Hekwaw's family, which lived apart from the two opposing camps, were the survivors of the People of the Deer when I first knew them.

At the time of that visit I had the most superficial knowledge of their history, even of their immediate past. It was not until nearly two months later, when Charles's taciturnity had melted and he had talked many a long night down, that I began to understand something of the nature of their experience. By then I had begun to be aware of the fearful want of humanity which we had displayed toward these people, and that awareness was brought into sharp focus by an event which took place in mid-August.

While the message that Charles had radioed to The Pas from Brochet had accomplished little for the Ihalmiut in an immediate sense, it had resulted in the first official recognition of the existence of the inland people by the government. Governments are notoriously ponderous and slow to act, but once having admitted that the Ihalmiut did exist the authorities were inevitably bound to display some show of interest in, and concern for, these long-lost people.

Consequently in mid-August of 1947 Tom Lamb's plane was chartered by an Indian Affairs representative. This plane made three flights to Windy Cabin. On the first flight it carried a doctor and a full load of aviation gasoline for the use of the pilot in future operations on the Barrens. The party went no farther than Windy Cabin, saw no Eskimos, and returned south. On the second flight the aircraft also carried the doctor's wives. The three visitors enjoyed a pleasant two-day visit at Windy River, caught some fish, and then flew south once more. They had still seen no Eskimos.

On the third and final trip they did much better. With Charles along, they flew to the Little Lakes and landed on Pommela Lake. The party remained with Pommela overnight, and the old man, recognizing their potential value to him, dispensed the full and fabled hospitality for which the Eskimos are commonly renowned. The doctor examined three out of the eleven Ihalmiut families and discovered that some of the children had head lice. The following day, after trading with the people for souvenirs and after removing sundry weapons and tools from the grave of Kakut, the mission to the Ihalmiut flew south and passed out of the land.

The three flights had cost the government about $3000 but, apart from the discovery of the head lice, had accomplished nothing. The mere fact that the flights were made was presumably considered to be an adequate safeguard against any further repetition of the years of our neglect. The report submitted by the inspecting official stated that the Ihalmiut were in good condition and that there was no need to be particularly concerned either about their future or their past.

This was not an opinion which I could share, and on my return to southern Canada that autumn I wrote a detailed account of what I had seen and heard, and mailed it to the Department of Mines and Resources which, at that time, was the federal agency nominally responsible for Eskimo affairs.

The following spring (by a series of rather remarkable coincidences which have no place in this book) I found myself heading back to the inland plains as an employee of that same government department. Together with a trained biologist, who was also an old friend of mine, I had been hired to assist in conducting a study of the caribou, for, though no one in authority showed the least alarm about the future of the Eskimos, there was a very real alarm about the future of the northern deer.

I spent a few days in Ottawa before flying north, and during this time I was able to talk about conditions amongst the Eskimos with several missionaries, Royal Canadian Mounted Policemen and government officials. These men represented the three groups which (with the addition of the traders) had ruled the arctic for half a century or more, and who had absolutely controlled the destiny of all Canadian Eskimos. The representatives of these groups assured me that the Innuit were a happy and contented people who wanted for nothing, and who were being well looked after. When I demurred, with the suggestion that this was too general a statement, I was instructed by the then Deputy Commissioner of the Northwest Territories—who was my superior—that I was not to interfere in, nor to concern myself with, Eskimo affairs. On that note I left Ottawa, by no means unwillingly, and journeyed north.

At Churchill I unexpectedly encountered Charles, and what he had to tell me roused my deepest apprehensions for the People. The autumnal migration of the deer in 1947 had been so scanty that, even with ample ammunition, Charles and Fred had been unable to kill enough meat for their own requirements. Nevertheless they attempted to operate their trap lines, only to find that the disease which had harried the dogs the previous winter had now almost eliminated the white foxes. They hung on as long as they could but not even the arrival of a charter flight sent in to them during December from Churchill with additional supplies could enable them to remain in the land. By March starvation had again become a reality, and the boys fled from the country by dog team—and did not return.

When he reached Churchill, Charles reported to the R.C.M.P. detachment that there was starvation amongst the Ihalmiut; but nothing was done about this report except to forward it to Ottawa. Ottawa, in turn, authorized a shipment of emergency supplies to be sent to the Ihalmiut when, and if, a plane happened to be bound that way.

These supplies, crated without labels, were still waiting at Churchill when I arrived there in mid-May, so I arranged to have them loaded aboard the aircraft which was to take us to Windy Cabin.

Before leaving the Barrens, Charles had told the People, and in good faith, that help would probably reach them by air within a week or ten days of his departure.

Consequently the Ihalmiut left their famine camps at the Little Lakes and made the long journey to Windy River. The place was deserted when they arrived but they settled down in the filthy outhouses to await the promised help. They waited through most of March, and all of April; and for sustenance they had the carcasses of the few wolves and foxes which Charles and Fred had been able to trap. They waited. . . .

One morning in the first week of May, Hekwaw's son Belikari struggled down from the top of the ridge behind the cabin crying out an electrifying phrase:

"The deer have come!"

Within the hour a band of does began to cross the ice almost directly in front of the cabin. They were met by a ragged fusillade. A few minutes later there was fresh blood upon the lips of the starving ones, and the famine was at an end.

When they had recovered sufficient strength the People left that place of broken hopes and walked towards their homes—but they were not yet secure. They had expended their last few rounds of ammunition upon the herd of does, and now no one, not even Pommela, had an ammunition left.

By the time they reached the Little Lakes they were surrounded by deer, but they had no means even of obtaining sufficient meat to last from day to day, let alone to put by against the summer months when the deer would be absent from their country. What was even more serious, they could not obtain the necessary skins to cover their kayaks so that they would be able to make an autumn kill at the water crossings.

There was no immediate danger of outright starvation, for they knew they could survive by snaring ground squirrels, by spearing suckers in the little streams, and by killing ptarmigan and small birds with slings. They could have stayed alive, if barely, while the summer lasted—but it was to the winter ahead that their thoughts turned.

Owliktuk and Pommela reacted to the crisis in their own ways. Pommela took two of his adopted children to serve instead of pack dogs, and set out on foot for the Hudson's Bay outpost at Padlei, some two hundred miles away by the route which he would have to follow. With him he took eleven fox skins, some of which had been caught by Onekwaw and by Katelo, and some of which he had taken, by threats, from members of the Owliktuk's band. These were all the fox pelts which the Ihalmiut still possessed—the only wealth they had. Pommela—who was, before all other things, a realist—was convinced that neither Charles nor a relief plane would ever appear at Windy Cabin.

Owliktuk was not so realistic. To him a promise remained a promise, and he believed that help would come. One day he took his carrying bag, empty save for a single fish, and set out for the south. He reached Windy Cabin on May 20, found it deserted still, and set himself to wait. He waited three days. On the third day he gave up hope and started on the long walk home; but he had not gone a mile when his heart leapt up within him, for he heard the unmistakable roar of the *konitaiu*—the white man's wings.

His faith seemed justified. He turned and came back toward the cabin at a trot, slowing to a walk only for dignity's sake as he topped the final ridge.

I shall not soon forget his face, nor the emotions with which he greeted us. Owliktuk was a proud man and a self-sufficient one, yet in this moment of greeting both pride

51

and self-sufficiency were momentarily forgotten in the relief which overwhelmed him. He shook us warmly by the hand, then hurried across the ice toward the cabin carrying a load of our supplies. Before we reached the snow-buried entrance he had already vanished up the river to collect firewood so that we might have a mug of tea.

By the time the brew was ready his emotions were again under control and he sat with us, in quiet dignity, and drank his tea; nor did he indicate in any way how serious the situation had become, and how badly worried he had been about the future. He mentioned nothing of his needs, and asked for nothing. After an hour or so he politely emptied the dregs from the tea-kettle into the dirty snow outside, and told us that he must return immediately to his camp. We saw him off, and we had no suspicion of how bad things were with him and with the rest of the Ihalmiut.

Months later it occurred to me to ask Owliktuk why he had been so reticent in a time of such great need; and his reply was:

"If you had wished to give me anything you would have done so. I could not ask for anything because I had no furs to trade. The five foxes that I caught in the winter I had left in the cabin in exchange for a file and some tea which I had taken, so I could not ask you for shells. I thought that when you were ready to give out debt [an advance on the next year's fur catch] you would do so; and I was no longer worried, for you said you would stay many weeks and I thought you had come as traders. I knew that when it was time you would give us debt so that we could kill many deer."

After Owliktuk had departed, my companion and I began to sort out the mountain of freight we had brought with us. Eventually I came to the boxes which were marked "Eskimo Relief Supplies" and I opened them. They contained six sheet-metal stoves, a bundle of fox traps, a dozen large axes and twenty galvanized-iron pails.

At first we thought that this was all some ridiculous mistake, and we chuckled at the mental image of the Ihalmiut men, each shouldering a great ax, and sallying forth to cut down trees for stove wood—in a land where no trees grew. But when we had consulted the accompanying correspondence, we discovered that there had been no mistake. The stoves, pails, axes and traps had indeed been intended to relieve the Ihalmiut's desperate situation. We laughed no more.

On June 4, all of the Ihalmiut men, except Pommela who was still en route from Padlei, arrived at the cabin. Ohoto, who had no inhibitions and no dignity to protect, told us the full story of the events of the preceding months, and the rest of the men confirmed the grim details. My companion and I had already begun to realize something of what had occurred from the evidence uncovered by the melting snows about our camp, and now it required only a close look at the emaciated faces of these people to know they spoke the truth.

Yet the activities of the visitors gave no indication of what they had suffered in the flesh and in the mind. Ohoto, quite unable to control his exuberance, capered about playing the clown, turning cart wheels and engaging in mock battles with the other men until even Owliktuk could not forbear smiling at his antics. That night we had a marathon tea party, and no one went to bed until the dawn had broken. There was more laughter, and more good-natured nonsense as we smoked and drank, than I have seen elsewhere in the world. It would have been easy to believe that these were indeed the "happy and contented people who want for nothing" of whom the missionaries and the police had spoken to me in Ottawa with such conviction.

Although we had been specifically instructed not to concern ourselves with Eskimo affairs, and had been told that this was a matter solely within the jurisdiction of the R.C.M.P., we nevertheless felt that the immediate crisis amongst the inland people was so serious that we should ignore our instructions. We had a small portable radio transmitter, and so we dispatched a message to Ottawa asking for emergency supplies of ammunition and food to be flown in at once. This message was acknowledged but it brought no action.

On June 4, there were still some deer in the country—the tardy stragglers bringing up the rear of the main herds which had already passed to the north of the Little Lakes. The Ihalmiut men had guns, and we had a fair quantity of .30.30 ammunition but, except in three cases, these did not match. Apart from Ohoto, Pommela and Owliktuk, who owned .30.30 carbines, the rest of the men were armed with ancient relics of .44.40 caliber. None of these weapons were fit for service, for they had been used so long and so hard that the barrels were worn smooth and the mechanisms functioned only spasmodically. It had been ten years since any Ihalmio, except Pommela, had been able to buy a new rifle from the traders.

We gave Ohoto and Owliktuk ten boxes of ammunition each and they undertook to hunt for all the People, though both they and we were aware that they could hardly hope to kill more than enough deer to meet the immediate need. Apart from the increasing scarcity of caribou as the herds moved farther north there was the fact that the best of marksmen, armed with these almost useless guns, would have been lucky to have made one kill for every ten shots he fired.

By the middle of June the last stragglers of the herds had passed out of the Ihalmiut lands, and Owliktuk visited us again. This time he threw off all restraint and admitted that hunger was coming perilously close to starvation. My companion and I distributed some of our own supplies to the Ihalmiut and then radioed Ottawa a second time. The message was hardly worded in the correct bureaucratic manner, for it contained a thinly veiled intimation to the effect that our third message—if one was needed—would go direct to the public press.

A reply finally arrived at the end of June. It authorized us to write off the supplies we had already given to the Eskimos against the Family Allowance payments to which the people had been entitled for the last several years but which they had never received. We were further instructed that we should register the Ihalmiut in preparation for a patrol by the R.C.M.P. which was to take place "in the near future." Finally we were instructed not to visit the Ihalmiut camps nor to become any more deeply involved in the situation.

But as to that, we had no choice. On July 2, Ohoto and Ootek arrived from the north to report that things were becoming increasingly serious since many of the women would soon be unable to feed the infants at their breasts, due to their own starvation. There were then twenty-two children in the camps, and upon these depended the whole hopes of the Ihalmiut for survival. These children had already experienced a protracted period of starvation, during the early spring, and they were in no condition to undergo another one. There was no deermeat left at any of the camps, and no prospects of obtaining any more until early August. No fish were running in the streams, where they might have been speared; and without kayaks or canoes it was impossible to set nets in open waters.

So we took the remainder of our supplies, set aside sufficient food to last the two of us for three weeks, and distributed the rest. It was very little we could give—less than six pounds to each of the Ihalmiut. And we were now helpless to do more, for our radio had ceased to function and we, like the Ihalmiut themselves, could only wait and hope.

When, on July 20, we heard the distant murmur of an aircraft engine, our excitement and relief must have very nearly equaled that of Ohoto, Ootek and Yaha who were at the cabin that day. We were convinced that the plane would be carrying a cargo of ammunition and essential food for the people, and perhaps a government representative as well; but we were wrong.

The Norseman which landed on the river below the cabin had indeed been dispatched by the Department of Mines and Resources—but by the Wildlife Section which employed us, and for the sole purpose of air-lifting us north to Angikuni Lake to continue the caribou study there. It carried supplies for us, *but nothing for the Eskimos*. Nor was there, amongst our official mail, any information concerning the government's intention on behalf of the Ihalmiut.

With some reluctance we boarded the plane and made the flight north; but when the Norseman left for Churchill it carried with it detailed reports of the current situation, and an urgent plea for immediate action. My companion and I believed that this would bring results, for we were still remarkably naive.

When we were flown back to Windy Cabin on August 14, we found, to our amazement, that nothing had yet been done. Nor was there any indication that anything ever would be done. My companion and I discussed the matter and concluded that I should return to Churchill with the plane and take direct action as a private individual.

In Churchill I accidentally encountered the official who, in his single person, was responsible for the welfare of the entire Eskimo population in the Canadian Eastern and Central Arctic. Although he was a busy man, he took time to listen to my account of conditions in the interior, and he promised that something would indeed be done. But I was no longer quite as naive as I had been, and so I visited the Canadian Army establishment at Churchill. Here, through the good offices of Lieutenant Colonel D. C. Cameron, I was able to obtain a dozen .303 army rifles in good condition, together with a thousand rounds of ammunition. Having listened to my story with deep sympathy, Lieutenant Colonel Cameron also suggested that I accept a supply of battledress trousers and jackets, for by this time the skin clothing which the Ihalmiut had been unable to replace was so far gone as to leave many of them almost naked.

On August 20, the long deferred patrol by the R.C.M.P. finally took place. A constable arrived by air; but he brought with him not one pound of supplies of any sort for the Eskimos. Near the completion of his visit this constable expressed it as his opinion that the Ihalmiut were simply shiftless, that they had not in fact suffered any losses from starvation during the preceding two years, and that, all in all, there was really nothing much to be disturbed about. He also made it clear that Eskimos were no business of ours, and that any supplies which they might need would be sent in, in due course, by the proper authorities, of which he was the official representative.

These supplies arrived on September 5. They included a drum of powdered milk, which turned out to be rancid and which made all those who attempted to use it very ill. The balance of the cargo consisted of some flour and lard, and two large bales of discarded service underclothing which had originally been destined for a cloth reclamation factory, but which had been diverted to the R.C.M.P. for distribution to the Eskimos.

The milk was destroyed. We examined the bales of underwear with some caution, for their state of cleanliness left much to be desired; and eventually we made a pile of legless, armless, torn and worn undergarments, in one of the outhouses. We did not offer these directly to the Eskimos, for we would have been ashamed to do so; but we left them to help themselves if they felt so inclined. We should have burned those rags, but our courage did not extend quite so far.

Nevertheless, we *were* able to issue every man with a new .303 rifle to replace the rusted antiques which had long outlived their period of usefulness, and with sufficient ammunition to ensure a good hunt in the fall.

They made a remarkable and strangely comic spectacle as they left us for the north, clad in the incongruous army battledress, and with service rifles in their hands. But they looked very different when October came.

On their first visit after the snow began to fall they came to see us, wearing fine new suits of skin clothing. They came with pride and assurance—and with full bellies. As he sat fingering his new rifle, Ohoto told me proudly that he had

56

already cached more than fifty fat deer against the winter, and that the other men had done as well, or better.

During my remaining time that season amongst the People I saw them, for the first time, as they must have been in the distant days when their camps stretched from Ennadai to beyond Yathkyed Lake; when the land was theirs, and when they were fulfilled within a land which gave them all things that a man might need.

With a resiliency which is not given to many people, they seemed to have recovered some of the substance of those ancient times. Hardly a day passed but a party of them came visiting to Windy Cabin, and these visits were without an ulterior motive. They were purely social events—though almost every group that arrived bore presents of one sort or another. One man might bring a bundle of caribou tongues, while another might bring two or three pairs of finely made deerskin boots. Ohoto, ebullient and irrepressible, undertook a mock courtship of my wife (who had joined us in late August), and on one memorable occasion he sneaked into the cabin during my absence to present her with an immense bouquet of marrowbones. When I selfishly refused to admit him to full cousinship, with all that this implies in Eskimo society, he brought the whole camp to a pitch of near-hysteria with a comic song which he sang to the accompaniment of a skin-drum, and which lampooned at great length the niggardly nature of the small white man called Skibby.

On another occasion Ohoto, Yaha, Miki, Owliktuk, Halo and Hekwaw came down to see us in a body, accompanied by half a dozen children. They arrived just at dusk, and after presenting us with a haunch of meat from a fat buck, they squatted on the floor of the cabin while we brewed tea for them in two-gallon pails. My wife had baked bread that day, and she distributed this with a lavish hand while she stuffed the children with cookies.

We two white men sat on the floor with our guests. As the cabin filled with pipe smoke, the tea-pails were emptied, refilled and emptied yet again until the night was well advanced and we had talked of all the important things—the numbers of the deer, their state of fatness, the hunt each man had made. Finally Yaha got to his feet with much assumed diffidence and took down the big hoop-drum which the people kept at the cabin for such occasions as this. For almost an hour he entertained us with a shambling dance while he sang long, lugubrious songs that told in detail of his shortcomings

57

as a hunter and even as a lover. We joined in the shouted chorus of *ai-yai-ya-ya* until the old cabin trembled.

After Yaha had collapsed in wet exhaustion, his place was taken by the youngest Innuit present—little Itkilik who was then six years of age, but who had nevertheless composed a song of his own which he danced and sang with deathly seriousness—for on this occasion he was *Inuk,* he was a man, and it behooved him to act like one. His performance was greeted with such enthusiasm that he was quite overcome by the applause, and had to retreat behind the stove until he could recover his composure.

We all danced, on that memorable night. We all sang and told stories until the food was eaten and the tea-pails bubbled with a throttled sound, for they were so full of tea leaves that there was hardly any room for water. When we became too exhausted to take the floor again, old Hekwaw got out a circlet of string and for an hour he wove flashing images in space; string figures of such complexity that the movements hypnotized the watchers into the conviction that we were living, in the flesh, the stories of old hunts, and olden times, which Hekwaw wove into the movements of the string.

The late dawn was breaking through the little windows in the shack when our guests, with obvious reluctance, at last began to straggle off to the tent which we had pitched as a sort of guest house for them upon the nearby ridge. It had been a night to remember, for we had all lived, during those brief hours, in a time that had vanished, and that could not return again except in such half-magic interludes as this had been.

It was a time for laughter and for gaiety, for all across the gravel ridges near the Little Lakes were mounds of gray rock under each of which lay the gutted carcass of a deer, already frozen. And each of these little rock piles was a fortress set against the winter months which lay ahead—a fortress against the sly approach of death.

It was indeed a good time to be amongst the People of the Deer; a good time to know them . . . and it was a good time to take our leave of them.

My wife and I said our good-bys one clear October day when the ice had already begun to form on Windy Bay, and the tundra ponds and lakelets were frozen over. Halo and Ootek came down to the shore to watch us paddle through the shell ice to the aircraft that waited impatiently with its motor roaring. They did not say good-by, for they have no word for farewell.

"So you are going now," Ootek called across the water. "But you will come back, Skibby—and there will be much to talk about when you come back."

I waved, and shouted that I would come back when the deer came; for I did not know that ten years must elapse before I would see the tents of the Ihalmiut; and I had no way of knowing that I would never see Halo and Ootek again.

5

Two Visitations

The early winter of 1948-1949 augured well for the People of the Little Hills. My companion of the summer remained at Windy Cabin until mid-December and he was well supplied, so that when an Eskimo needed a little ammunition, or some tea or tobacco, he could obtain it. There was nothing else the People needed, for there was meat and to spare in the camps by the Little Lakes.

There was meat in the camps, and therefore there was strength as well. Though the long winds mounted their ceaseless assaults through the shortening days and the lengthening nights, they could not reach through fur and flesh into people's bones as they had been wont to do in the years just past; for well-fed men could strive against the wind. They built high snow walls about the tents, and inside the shelters there was the comfort that comes only with full bellies, and which is proof even against the bitter arctic frost.

When the pale and shrunken sun rose in the mornings the women climbed out from under the thick robes on the sleeping ledge and lit the little fires of willow twigs in the cooking porch, while the older children, or perhaps the husbands, pulled on their double parkas and hurried down to the nearby lake armed with ice-chisels with which to open the water holes and fill the pails for morning tea. The day's first meal was meat, as were all the meals which followed, but with every meal there was hot tea. Only rarely could the women spare enough fuel to cook the meat, and for the most part it was eaten raw and frozen. Often it was accompanied by soft splinters of the rich white back fat taken from the autumn bucks, and sometimes there was a marrowbone to crack for the sweet frozen jelly which it contained. As long as there was enough fuel to brew a pint of tea, the frozen food represented no hardship—indeed to crunch the crystalline stuff between the teeth and to feel it melt against the tongue is a tactile pleasure far more satisfying than to mouth the flaccid foods which we are used to in the south.

The deer had been good to their People in the autumn, and they continued to be good to them as December passed. Several times a small herd of hardy bucks which had remained on the plains instead of seeking the shelter of the forests came within range of the hunters' new rifles. Then there was fresh meat to eat and, on rare occasions, soup of boiled meat, marrow and blood.

Hunger was banished from the camps that season. When the meat supplies stored in the cooking porch ran low, a man had only to take his light sled and his dogs (if he still had any) and travel across the faceless land to his nearest cache. The tracks of the great white wolves would be numerous around the little pile of rocks upthrust from the enveloping snows; and sometimes too there would be the prints of *kakwik*, the wolverine, who is the greatest robber of the plains. Then the hunter would anxiously pry away the heavy stones and cut down through the hard snow which had drifted between the interstices of the cache. Sometimes he would find that *kakwik* had forestalled him and there was little left but well-cracked bones and fragments of hair and skin; but that was a rare occurrence. Usually his cache would be as he had left it, and he would load the frozen quarters of deermeat on his sled and start contentedly for home as the early winter darkness settled somberly across the land.

The People did little traveling that winter. Though three or four bitches had survived the dog disease and had given

61

birth to litters of pups during the summer of 1947, there were still very few working dogs. But there was no need for extended traveling. There was ample meat close to the camps, and there were so few foxes in the land that there was no point in attempting to run trap lines. Even had the foxes been abundant, their pelts would have been almost useless anyway, for Charles had not returned to Windy Cabin, and there was no trader nearer than Padlei, two hundred miles away by the usual sled route.

Charles and his brothers had stayed on at Churchill with their father, for the old German seems to have concluded that there was more profit in putting his sons to work at the Army camp than in sending them back into the Barrens when the foxes were at the low point of their cycle. Nevertheless Charles did return briefly to the inland plains in January, as an employee of the Canadian Army, which was then involved in a remarkable venture that was to have a momentous effect upon the future of the Ihalmiut.

During the war the Royal Canadian Corps of Signals had been entrusted with the establishment of a string of radio and meteorological stations throughout the arctic. By 1947 stations had been built along the mainland coasts and on many of the arctic islands, but there remained the great expanse of the interior where the difficulties of transportation had made construction of such stations a seeming impossibility. The barriers which the inland Barrens posed were indeed so formidable that it was not until 1949 that our technical abilities could devise a method of surmounting them. In January of that year an audacious plan to establish a station at the north end of Ennadai Lake was put in motion.

Until this time Ennadai, and indeed the whole of the inland plains, had only been accessible (and barely accessible at that) to canoes, dog teams, and float- or ski-equipped airplanes. None of these would have sufficed to move the tons of supplies needed to establish a radio station, to carry in the huge power plant, and to stock the place. Nothing with less cargo-carrying capacity than a ship, or a train, could have done the job. Yet for many years a kind of train that did not run on railroad tracks *had* been operating inside the northern forest regions, opening up new mines in otherwise inaccessible locations, and freighting supplies into areas which could not normally be reached except by air. These were the so-called "cat-trains" consisting of giant tractors towing strings of sleds, and it was to them that the Army turned.

This was no simple innovation. No cat-train had ever operated on the open Barrens where the land becomes a gigantic frozen sea in wintertime, without landmarks; with no routes that can be followed by the eye; where gigantic combers of black rock or steep-sided eskers bar every path. No cat-train had ever attempted to operate in the abysmal winter temperatures of the Barrens where the unchecked wind can rage for days at velocities of eighty and ninety miles an hour and make the ground drift so impenetrable that all life becomes as blind as the lemmings in their dark and hidden tunnels.

Nevertheless the Army decided to send cat-trains overland to Ennadai in midwinter, across a snow desert, unmapped and largely unexplored, for a distance of three hundred airline miles, or more than four hundred as the tractors would have to pick their ways. There were no guides to be had, for no white man knew the intervening country between Churchill and Ennadai—but Charles was at least familiar with the immediate vicinity of that distant lake and he was therefore hired to accompany the expedition.

Early in January four huge caterpillar tractors, each towing a string of heavily laden freight sleds and a heated caboose for the crew to live in, ground their way out from Churchill. They crawled up the shores of Hudson Bay for almost a hundred miles and then they turned away from the known country into the white west.

For weeks they crawled tediously into the interior, charting their courses and plotting their positions by the use of sextants, like ships at sea. They were a lumbering argosy, sailing into an unknown world which had never seen their like before.

The people of that world had no warning of this new invasion until one day near the end of January when Yaha decided to make a journey south to the now abandoned cabin at Windy River, in the faint hope that Charles might have returned to it and brought some tobacco—for Yaha was an addict, and his usually amiable temper had begun to sour a little under tobacco deprivation.

Yaha never reached the post. One morning as he topped a long ridge near the headwaters of Little River, his quick eye caught a distant movement on the eastern horizon. He stared long and hard, for at first he thought it must be a herd of winter deer but, as he watched, his anticipation began to turn to rising consternation. The objects that crawled so slowly toward him were certainly not *tuktu*. They were something absolutely foreign to his experience and to his understanding. Then he remembered the old tales told in the camps of his father, of giant beasts which had once haunted the lands far to the northwest. That memory, and the sight of these mammoth entities crawling ponderously and implacably toward him, effectively nullified Yaha's longing for tobacco.

Yaha was afoot, and he wished fervently that he had many dogs to speed his departure from that place. At that it took him only half a day to retrace the full day's march to Owliktuk's camp. He was exhausted and somewhat wild-eyed when he burst into Owliktuk's shelter to report what he had seen.

Yaha was an imaginative man, and his story lost nothing in the telling. It was not long before all the people in the camp had squeezed into Owliktuk's place to hear the tale, and there were several otherwise calm and sensible men who became busily engaged in checking their rifles and counting their remaining ammunition, while the children stared at one another in half-delighted anticipation of the horrors which Yaha described so vividly.

The excitement and the apprehension which gripped the people could not be contained. Even the internecine tension which split the Ihalmiut camps was forgotten. Miki was sent posthaste to Pommela's camp for, though Pommela might be hated and feared, he remained a powerful shaman, and this seemed to be an emergency within his special province.

Pommela had not the vaguest idea as to what Yaha had really seen, but he immediately recognized an opportunity to make capital of the mystery and so he prepared to hold a spirit séance. All of the men (with one exception) and most of the women in both camps converged on Pommela's big shelter where they sat in an uneasy silence while the old man prepared to throw himself into a trance. His ritual was impressive, for he had had considerable practice, and it was not long before his shambling gyrations and his wildly inarticulate shouts began to have their effect on the watching people. Tension, and a gnawing foreboding, gripped the watchers as the old man collapsed on the dirty snow floor, went rigid, and began to foam visibly at the mouth as the spirits he had called upon began to enter into his body.

But Pommela's audience was not complete. Ohoto, the would-be white man and perennial skeptic, had listened carefully to Yaha's highly colored account and he had concluded that the visitation was somehow connected with the whites. He even had some inkling of *what* it might be, for long ago at Brochet he had seen small tractors hauling supplies along the ice road of frozen lakes and rivers which stretched southward to The Pas.

Thus, while the rest of the People were succumbing to Pommela's spell, Ohoto quietly borrowed Owliktuk's three dogs, hitched them to a small sled, and slipped off to the south.

He arrived back in darkness, and went straight to Pommela's camp where the séance was still in full swing. The shaman had been seized by three spirits in succession and all had prophesied a great evil entering the land. When Ohoto pushed back the deerskin flap and stomped in amongst the tense and frightened audience, he interrupted Pommela's impassioned interpretation of the spirit voices, but Ohoto could not have cared less. He was bursting with his news, and he gave no thought to the fact that he was about to earn Pommela's undying enmity.

Grinning from ear to ear, and as brash as a street urchin, he announced that the "things" were by no means supernatural, but that they were new and mighty machines of the white men hauling sleds which appeared to be laden with an enormous amount of trade goods. The séance broke up as fear gave way to a gathering anticipation and excitement at the prospects for the future. The traders had come back! There would be no more shortages of ammunition or of tea and tobacco. It was indeed exhilarating news.

The cat-trains made three trips to Ennadai that winter, and the mountains of material which they brought were unloaded on the shore at the north end of Ennadai, covered with tarpaulins, and left unguarded, against the return of summer and the arrival of the construction crews by air. When the trains were returning eastward after the completion of the second trip, they dropped Charles off at Windy Cabin with his dogs and his supplies, for he had not yet been entirely able to rid himself of the desire for his old way of life, and he intended to make one more attempt at living in the land. It was a brief attempt. After only a few weeks he found that he could no longer bear the lonely wilderness and he hitched up his dogs and left the Barrens, this time forever. His passing marked the final end of that chaotic and tragic period when the white traders and trappers had dominated the country of the People. Now the land was to come under the domination of a new kind of white man, motivated by inscrutable purposes which the Ihalmiut would never comprehend, any more than they were able to understand the meaning of the inexplicable objects hidden beneath their wind-whipped tarpaulins by the shores of Ennadai.

Within a few days after the departure of the tractors, most of the Ihalmiut men had followed the double line of tracks to the site of the new station and they had marveled at the immense quantity of cases, the piles of lumber, and the great steel sections of the aerial towers. They had marveled too that such wealth should be left unattended. The absence of a white man, and the inscrutable nature of the material, was to remain a mystery to them for months to come—but it was destined to be eclipsed within a few short weeks by a darker mystery which would bring terror to the camps, and which would fully justify the warnings given by Pommela's familiar spirits.

The story of the evil which came to the Barrens in the early months of 1949 began at Churchill the previous autumn when an Innuit from Eskimo Point visited the settlement. He was a young man and he had heard much of the wonders of the place, so that it was natural that he should wish to see them for himself. And the wonders of Churchill surpassed his expectations a thousandfold. Of all the fascinations that it held for him, none could approach the Army camp, with its great airport, its swarming vehicles of every size and shape, and the generosity of the many United States and Canadian soldiers. These men were equally fascinated by the young Eskimo, and they made much of him. They gave him many gifts, including one of which neither the giver nor the recipient was aware.

In October the young man started north, his sled laden with presents, and his mind overladen with stories to tell his people. A week after his departure one of the soldiers who had befriended him was hurriedly evacuated to a hospital in Winnipeg.

On his way north the Eskimo traveler could not resist the temptation to stop at every camp and talk about the things that he had seen. He stopped first at Nonalla, then at Thlewiaza River, and then at McConnel River, before finally reaching Eskimo Point. It was the Christmas season when he came home, and everyone for many miles about was gathered at the tiny settlement. There were even a number of Padliermiut from the interior, as well as some from the Maguse and Wilson Rivers. For many days these people visited their friends, whom they would not see again for perhaps a year, and they attended the hot and crowded religious services in

66

the Catholic and Anglican missions. It was well into the new year before the gathering broke up and the people dispersed to their many distant homes, each of them carrying within him a part of the young man's gift.

The unsuspected gift from Churchill had traveled widely, but it had not yet reached the end of its journeying. In January, a week or so before the first cat-train reached Ennadai, Pommela had driven his dogs overland to Padlei Post to beg or borrow some tea and tobacco. At Padlei he had met and stayed with men who had attended the Christmas festivities at Eskimo Point. He brought back more than tea and tobacco to the Little Hills; and the unseen gift which traveled with him must have been present at the crowded séance occasioned by Yaha's first sight of the cat-train.

Meanwhile, that gift—the name of which was poliomyelitis—had begun to display itself in the coastal settlements. In camp after camp men, women and children were suddenly seized by raging fevers and by agonizing pains in their muscles which presaged paralysis. Many of the victims died within a day of the first symptoms of disease. So savage and universal was the epidemic that by mid-March an area encompassing a hundred thousand square miles was given over to it. The efforts of the single doctor provided by the government to care for the health of the entire population of Keewatin District could do little to halt or to control it, even though in desperation he placed more than half of the huge district under quarantine. The combination of winter weather, lack of transportation, and the general oppression of his work prevented him from being of effective service to any of the stricken people except those in the immediate vicinity of his hospital at Chesterfield Inlet. In this one locality—the sole locality which had a doctor and medical facilities, and where adequate records could be kept—fourteen people died and there were 78 cases of permanent paralysis among 275 Eskimos.

Pommela's spirits had spoken truly.

At Padlei there was no record of how many died, but seventeen people were permanently crippled. They received no assistance until the epidemic had run its course, and even then only three of the crippled people ever received medical attention.

Nor was there a doctor at the Little Lakes when, one black February night, Ootek's wife Howmik woke her husband and her child with her fevered ravings. Ootek did everything he could to help his woman, but though he donned

67

his amulet belt and sang the sacred sickness songs known only to himself, which had been passed down to him through uncounted generations, they had no effect upon this alien invader. By morning both of Howmik's legs and both her arms hung limp and useless.

Halo, whose tent stood next to Ootek's, had risen in the night to help his friend, for Howmik's cries had awakened the whole camp. In the morning Halo stood with Ootek and looked at the wreckage of the woman Howmik, and his usually placid face was deeply furrowed. He glanced at Ootek seeking some reassurance or at least some explanation of the nature of this evil, but Ootek could tell him nothing.

They knew fear in that camp. And their fear bore fruit the following day when from Miki's shelter there came the wailing of a mourning woman, where Kahutsuak cradled the body of her youngest child.

The fear built to a crescendo as first one and then another of the People in Owliktuk's camp was stricken. There was a weird and terrifying capriciousness about the disease, for it struck some a mortal blow, others it crippled horribly, and others it touched with a gentle hand, and left unharmed. There was no pattern and no reason for it—there was nothing that a man could understand.

For a few days Pommela's camp escaped the plague, and the old man believed that this was the work of his guardian spirits; but in the event even they proved unequal to the struggle. Ikok, Pommela's youngest wife and perhaps the only human being for whom he felt affection, fell sick one morning and within two days she lay dead, contorted into shocking ugliness.

Death was the least of the horrors of those weeks. Worse than death was the paralysis, which marked men's minds even more heavily than it marked their flesh. They knew too well the sure and bitter fate of the hunter who cannot walk or hold his weapons, and of the woman who cannot cook and sew or nurse her child. And by early March it seemed assured that half the People would be crippled for their brief remaining days.

Even Hekwaw, the old bear, was crippled from the waist down. His grown son Ohotuk, a strong giant of a youth, lay almost totally paralyzed, and doomed. In Hekwaw's tent the one untouched survivor, Belikari, labored to be hunter and wife too.

Halo's wife Kikik was stricken while she was in Ootek's shelter caring for Howmik, but though Kikik was looked

68

upon as already dead by those who saw her, within ten days she had completely recovered from the disease, except for a slight limp which vanished in the months ahead. It was as well that she was spared, for a few days later Halo himself became insensible and raved the long night down. When he came to himself he had lost the use of his right arm.

Alekahaw was amongst those who were maimed for life, for he never recovered the full use of his right leg. But Pommela, who had again brought a plague upon the People as he had done once before in his youth, remained personally unscathed as always.

The many-pronged assault upon the People of the Little Hills, which had sunk into quiescence through the fall and early winter, had now been viciously renewed. The too brief armistice with fate was at an end. In the dark days of February, when the gales make no pause, and when the cold strikes into the very rocks until they split asunder; when the ice upon the lakes grows ten feet thick and contorts in the frost's grip until it cracks and thunders like a mighty cannonade, the crumbled fortress of the People was beleaguered once again, and men's hearts shrank within them. The fear of a known enemy can make men brave, but the fear of the unknown enemy is a succubus to drain the manhood from them. And there was no knowing this present enemy who thrust and cut into the fragile fabric of the People's lives.

This was the way of things when, in mid-March, men lifted their heads and listened to an unfamiliar sound—the roar of an aircraft coming to the Little Lakes. The plane landed on the ice of Halo Lake, and it disgorged two fur-clad members of the R.C.M.P. who had been dispatched from Churchill to discover if the epidemic had penetrated so far into the inland plains. The policemen saw at a glance that the disease had been before them, but they did not remove any of the stricken People from the camps. It was not their business. They left within the hour, but before they left they told the People that a doctor would soon come amongst them.

Two months passed before the doctor came, and even then he was only able to visit half the People. He had room in his aircraft for only two patients amongst the many in the camp, and he chose Ohotuk and Howmik. These two he flew to the hospital at Chesterfield, from which place Howmik was returned to her husband late in the summer, still partially crippled in both legs and arms, but able to be at least a semblance of a wife. Ohotuk did not return, but died in a foreign place.

So for the fourth successive year the Ihalmiut felt the scourge of hardship, and again they had no more than token help. They grew very hungry as the year advanced, for there had been no new supply of ammunition, and the deer were scarce. Nevertheless they survived the abrupt days of the spring transition when the snow melts like fat in a fire, and the rivers break out of their ice bonds almost overnight and go roaring to the distant sea. With the coming of the warmer weather they even made progress against the paralysis which still lay heavily upon so many of them, and day by day men and women began to recover some of their lost strength—though there were many amongst them who would never have the full use of all their limbs again.

In midsummer my biologist companion of the previous year returned to spend a month at Windy Cabin in order to complete his studies of the deer. The People came to him and told him the story of the spring, and once more he was able to provide them with a little ammunition. He was again amazed at the incredible resiliency with which they recovered from their adversities. They came to Windy Cabin in the gay and cheerful manner we had known the previous autumn; even the cripples came, though for them the sixty-mile walk from the Little Lakes must have been a grave ordeal. Once more the tea parties and the drum dances lasted into the dawn, and there was laughter.

But beneath the laughter there was a residue of fear and a great uncertainty. The People wanted one thing only, as they said, to make them content with their hard lot, and that was the permanent presence of a white man in their lands. Over the long years since the first white men had come to the plains, the People had been weaned away from their old ways into a vital dependency on such a presence, so that the supplies which they could obtain from the traders had become their shield, and now they knew no other. During the past decade that shield had rusted through and so they looked to the future with apprehensive eyes.

Ootek had expressed this ever-present concern to me in the summer of 1948 when he had said:

"Many strange things have come into our land that only the white men understand. If there was a white man here to whom we could take fox pelts, and who could tell us what to do when there was trouble of a kind that our own spirits cannot fight against, then we could keep ourselves safe and see our children live."

Ootek spoke for all the People, and I do not think they asked too much. Yet for many years their hopes had gone unrealized. It was not until the summer of 1949 that these hopes seemed about to be fulfilled.

In July, with the lifting of the poliomyelitis quarantine, a big amphibious aircraft of the Royal Canadian Air Force descended heavily upon the green waters of Ennadai Lake. The plane brought many white men, and as July passed into August that lonely place in a lonely land saw the slow transformation of the piles of materials left by the cat-trains into modern buildings and high steel towers. These made a curious and startling contrast with the dun-colored tundra that rolled away on every side, unbroken by any work of man's. When the day comes that we construct refuges on the face of the moon, we will only be enlarging upon such ventures as the one at Ennadai, for they also will be outposts of a familiar world upon an unfamiliar one. The radio establishment at Ennadai bore no relation to the earlier attempts of white men to establish themselves in the land, for the white trappers and traders had been in some degree a part of the new world they had invaded, and were at least partially dependent on it for food and fuel and shelter. The new intruders were dependent on it for nothing, and were no part of it. They brought their own world with them, and within its small circumference, shielded and protected from the unfamiliar, and therefore hostile, elements without, they lived almost exactly as they would have done in the homes that waited for them in the distant south. They were true aliens, and their thoughts and habits, and understanding, were alien too—and this is a vital fact, and one that must be kept in mind when their relations with the People are considered.

It was on the 20th of August that the Ihalmiut came to see the miracle that had been worked upon their land.

There were six men of Owliktuk's group led by Ohoto, and they had stolen a march on Pommela, who had not yet learned of the arrival of the strangers. They came with some trepidation, and not even that brash man Ohoto was immune to awe as they breasted a ridge and looked down upon the strange buildings, the mighty towers, the great piles of oil barrels, and the raw scars upon the tundra where a bulldozer snorted and bellowed like a wounded muskox bull.

It was a subdued and timid file that followed Ohoto down the slope and walked uncertainly toward the place where half a dozen white men had suspended work to stare in open curiosity at these grotesque visitors who seemed to have sprung directly from the bleak tundra which had given no previous indication that it had ever known men before.

If both sides were at a loss what to do next, Ohoto at least knew the form. Leaving his contingent grouped disconsolately some distance off, he ambled forward, seized the hand of a startled Signals sergeant, and shook it with such gusto that the man pulled away in frank alarm. Ohoto followed, grinning broadly, and after unlimbering his few words of English he formally presented a grubby letter of introduction written for him by my biologist friend at Windy Cabin.

The ice was broken, and now the visitors were royally received, for soldiers have the happy faculty of making friends wherever they can find them. It may be that in this little band of fur-clad, quiet people they saw some chance of an alleviation of the colossal weight of loneliness which the inland plains had laid upon them. There was, at any rate, a titillating sense of novelty about the meeting for, as one of the soldiers wrote, "We felt a bit like Columbus when he laid eyes on the first Indians. Only two of our gang had ever seen an Eskimo before, and they sure were a curious bunch."

Amongst the stores provided by a thoughtful quartermaster's department for the Ennadai post had been an English-Eskimo dictionary, and this was now hurriedly unearthed. All work on the site ceased, and the soldiers gathered about Owliktuk, Miki, Yaha, Ootek, Halo and Ohoto, and in a few minutes there was mutual laughter and much good fellowship. Cigarettes were freely proffered and gratefully accepted. The cook, happy to have guests, concocted a magnificent dinner, which few of the Eskimos could stomach, but which they gamely ate rather than offend their generous hosts.

On that first visit the Ihalmiut only stayed for a few hours, perhaps because they were uncomfortably confused by the multifarious impressions and by the astounding plethora of previously unknown and therefore inexplicable things they saw. Owliktuk in particular needed time to take it in, to think about it, and it was he who led the visitors away as night came down. They did not go empty-handed, for every man was laden with tins of fruit and other foods, with cigarettes and candy bars.

For the Ihalmiut it had been a momentous meeting, far more momentous than they knew. As they discussed the visitation amongst themselves during the succeeding days, they were unable to comprehend its real import. The barriers imposed by language and by the unbridgeable divergence in experience which gaped between the whites and the Eskimos made understanding totally impossible. The Ihalmiut could only interpret what they had seen in the light of their own very limited awareness of our activities and interests, and they could come to no firm conclusions. These things alone seemed certain: that the new white men intended to remain permanently in the land; that they were friendly, sympathetic and generous, and that they were incredibly endowed with material wealth. Perhaps because they wished so greatly to believe it, most of the People convinced themselves that the soldiers were in fact traders, and they took great comfort from this belief, seeing in it a protection against the years which lay ahead.

Only Pommela suspected that, whatever the real interest of these strangers might be, it was not trade. Once, during the war, he had accompanied Charles to Duck Lake where the United States Army had operated a meteorological outpost for a year or two. Pommela had fond memories of that visit. He particularly remembered the unparalleled generosity, or the stupidity, of those white men who had been willing to give away whole cartons of cigarettes and cases of tinned meat in exchange for such trivial things as a pair of skin boots, or the worthless pelt of an arctic hare, which no trader would have allowed to cross his counter. Pommela, alone of all the People, guessed something of what the arrival of the outlanders at Ennadai might really mean; but he kept his thoughts to himself so that he alone might profit by them.

If the Eskimos could not begin to conceive of what lay behind the white wooden walls of the station, then the soldiers were even less able to comprehend the life led by the Ihalmiut. They saw the People as a species of friendly local denizens whose every aspect was curiously outlandish. They had no idea how such people managed to survive, nor did they think about it much. They were busy men, and when a visiting party of Eskimos disappeared over the visual horizon they also disappeared beyond the horizon of the soldiers' thoughts.

In the autumn, after the snow had come and it was permissible once again for the women to sew new clothing, many of the Ihalmiut returned to the station carrying gifts which were a return for those they had earlier received. They

73

brought fine caribou-skin mitts, boots, and several complete outfits of double parkas and fur trousers. The soldiers were impressed and touched. One of them wrote:

"They seemed to take a proprietary interest in us and our welfare, regarding us evidently as a pretty feckless bunch who needed looking after. They pretty well outfitted us with winter clothes and showed us where the best fishing places were and offered to bring in meat when we needed any. They were a gay bunch, but they sure smelled high when they got inside the buildings . . ."

As winter drew on, the air of camaraderie which had been present at the earlier meetings between the white men and the Eskimos began to fade. Pommela contributed something to this, for he had made frequent visits to the station, and had attempted to establish the same sort of covert influence over the strangers that he had once held over Charles. His failure baffled him; but his attempts annoyed the soldiers, who came to look upon him as a confirmed scrounger, and one, moreover, who was not averse to theft.

Then, too, the general novelty of having these "stone age men" constantly about the place had begun to pall. As one of the soldiers pointed out, the Eskimos did not make ideal house guests, for they did not belong to the centrally heated living quarters amongst the easy chairs, the electric phonographs, and the general amenities of a different world. It was inevitable that barriers should begin to grow, and that the first happy contact should begin to solidify into something far less happy.

To the Ihalmiut, the change was inexplicable. They had done everything they knew to be as friends and brothers to the strangers, and their efforts had first been welcomed; but now were not. Pommela, and to a lesser extent Ohoto, who had seen the station as a port of entry into the white man's world, grew angry at the rebuffs which now became more frequent, but the most serious cause of perturbation amongst all the Ihalmiut was the gradual realization that the strangers were not traders, and had no real interest either in the land or in its inhabitants.

In describing that period, after the lapse of many years, Owliktuk gave some indication of the bafflement of his people.

"In the fall we started to come there to get things we would need and we asked for shells. Sometimes they would give us a few shells, but sometimes not. And there was never enough for what we needed. After that, when we began to catch foxes, we began bringing the pelts but the white men would laugh and say they did not want pelts; that other white men would not let them keep them. Sometimes they would give us some tea and tins of food, but what we needed was shells for our guns. They said they were not traders but they gave us some things even though they did not want our foxes."

The soldiers remained friendly, but in an offhand and guarded fashion which was inexplicable to the Ihalmiut. There seemed to be no way to make the white strangers understand how much depended on their help, and how much the People were prepared to offer in exchange. It was a deadly impasse.

That autumn, when the Ihalmiut waited the coming of the deer, they were almost out of ammunition, so that they had to trust to obtaining the requisite supplies of meat at the river crossings by the use of kayaks and spears. Unfortunately they had not expected to need kayaks after the arrival of the "traders" at Ennadai, and so they were not adequately prepared to make the sudden change back to the old hunting methods. Furthermore, the deer were very scarce that fall. The result was that the People began the winter with far too little meat put by in the caches, a situation which was made worse by the fact that more than a dozen of them still suffered from the paralytic effects of polio, and would be largely helpless and dependent on others for assistance during the months ahead.

Meanwhile, the soldiers remained unaware of the problems which beset the Ihalmiut. Had they known, they would undoubtedly have tried to help, for they were goodhearted men, as they demonstrated at Christmas time.

As the festival approached they decided that it would be worthwhile to have a party for the Eskimos. They thought in terms of a big meal; of presents for the children, and of offering the Ihalmiut a brief surcease from their world of bitter wind and endless snow—a world which appalled the soldiers as they gazed upon it through the double-windows of their living quarters.

They took a great deal of trouble with that party, for they meant well. The Eskimos came to it in response to a summons carried to all the camps by Ohoto. It was not easy for some of them to come, for already there were people who were weak from hunger, and it was not easy to bring the crippled, for there were still too few dogs to haul all the sleds. Yet they came, not knowing what awaited them, but hoping that the summons might presage an end to the terrible misunderstandings that had prevented them from obtaining what they needed to survive. Despite the earlier rejection of fox pelts, many of the men had continued to trap as best they could, not yet convinced that the soldiers had meant what they had said. Now they brought the pelts and when they presented them to the white men, they were overjoyed to find that at last they were accepted. The People of the Deer knew nothing of the white man's habit of exchanging gifts at Christmas time.

The party was held in the basement of the main building and to the soldiers it appeared to be a considerable success. There was much singing and laughter and impromptu dancing, both to the old music of the drum and to the surprising new music of a phonograph. There was much food too, though it was all eaten on the spot. And every Eskimo received a gift.

The soldiers were not aware of the undercurrent of strain amongst their guests. They did not know the Eskimo, and they had no reason to look beneath the placid surface, and so the fact escaped them that the smiling guests at that happy party were in reality desperately worried and, in some cases, starving people.

There was a bitter irony in that situation. It was as if an impervious yet partially translucent wall separated the Ihalmiut from the soldiers, but only the Eskimos were aware of its presence, and they had tried to break through it—but they had failed.

6

The Empires of the North

On the day after Christmas the Ihalmiut returned to their camps, having completely failed to make the soldiers comprehend their plight. There was now nothing more that they could do to help themselves. They could only wait beneath a growing apathy for what must come. They had no meat left, and again they were reduced to scavenging under the hard snow for bones and offal cast aside the previous fall. Their clothing was in pitiful condition, for they had managed to take only a few good hides during the preceding autumn, and most of these had been used to make the gift clothing for the soldiers. Scanty and dilapidated as it was, the clothing that they did possess was soon being taxed to provide food for their empty bellies. The dogs, whose numbers had only just begun to recover from the distemper epidemic, began to die of hunger. Some were eaten; but the tough, acrid flesh of an animal which has died from starvation is more poisonous than beneficial, and many of the People who ate the dog meat could not keep it down. Once more the men found themselves without the strength, without the warm clothing, without the ammunition, and without the dogs, all of which were vital if they were to help themselves. It was an old story to the Ihalmiut now. They sat silent in their frigid tents and waited.

Some of them knew a brief respite in mid-January when a cat-train arrived at the Signals station, and those of the Eskimos who had the strength for it were hired to act as stevedores. These men (there were only five of them) were well fed during the three or four days of their employment, and when they returned to their tents they carried gifts of canned goods and flour. For the members of their immediate families the inevitable was delayed a little while.

During the first week in February, 1950, the first death occurred.

In Yaha's snow-block shelter the old woman Kooyuk, who was Yaha's mother, came to the decision which only she could make. One night while the rest of the family lay uneasily asleep upon the ledge, she dragged her bony limbs from under the worn and almost hairless robes, stripped off her few remaining clothes, and crawled out through the entrance tunnel into the whining darkness of the night.

She was an old woman, and she had not long to live in any case, nor was life dear to her. For many days she had refused her own minute portion of the family food so that her grandchildren might have a little more; and it may be that she no longer cared to think of the warm spring days which might still lie ahead of her, for beyond them she must have seen the winters which were yet to come.

So she crawled, naked, out of the shelter and walked in the white wind until she could walk no farther. In a little while she sank to her knees and the snows rose over her. There was one less mouth to feed in Yaha's house.

A few days later death came to Pameo, who was the four-year-old daughter of Pommela's dead wife Ikok. While her mother lived, Pameo could live, but with her mother gone she had no hope of life, for she bore none of Pommela's blood, and she was a woman-child and worthless to him. He starved her systematically until her huddled little body no longer shivered underneath its ragged skins. This man who could sire no children of his own had scant love for the children sired by other men. He fed no useless mouths.

78

It was a strange irony that Pameo's death should bring the gift of life to the rest of the Ihalmiut, but this was what happened, for when Pommela—who had camped close to the station—visited the soldiers one day to beg for handouts, he casually mentioned that Pameo had died. When the soldiers wished to know how she had died, he sucked in his stomach and his cheeks in a gesture that needed no words to make it understandable.

The soldiers were immensely shocked. They had had no suspicion of the true nature of the crisis in the Ihalmiut camps, and the discovery that a child had starved to death almost within sight of their warm and comfortable oasis came as a dreadful disclosure. Their immediate reaction was to break out emergency supplies from their own stocks and to distribute these to the people within reach of the station. At the same time they radioed an urgent message to their headquarters at Churchill to the effect that the local Eskimos were dying of starvation and required instant help.

In due course of time this message was "processed" at Ottawa and orders were issued to the resident doctor at Chesterfield Inlet to charter a plane and make a flight to Ennadai to investigate the report.

The flight was made on February 26. The doctor examined some of the People and confirmed that they were indeed suffering from hunger. Unfortunately this was a disease about which he could do little, for he had not been authorized to bring in relief supplies, the issuing of which was controlled by the R.C.M.P.

It was food, not medicines, that the People needed.

There were a good many people in the inland plains who needed food that winter.

Throughout the whole of interior Keewatin the autumnal caribou hunt of 1949 had been a failure, and by February there were many starving Eskimos, not only at Ennadai, but at Padlei, Baker Lake and Garry Lake as well.

That all of the resident white men, the traders, missionaries and policemen in the country could have remained in ignorance of the seriousness of the situation does not seem credible. Nevertheless the first message concerning the famine to reach the outside world was the one dispatched by the soldiers at Ennadai. It was confirmed early in March when Richard Harrington, a free-lance photographer, traveled to Padlei by dogteam and subsequently gave the Canadian newspapers a horrifying account of the conditions which he had encountered there.

Although he was well equipped when he left Eskimo Point for the interior, and was accompanied by a competent Eskimo guide, Harrington soon found himself in dire straits. He lost four of his own dogs to starvation, and the drain on his supplies to feed the dying people whom he encountered in the Padliermiut camps was such that he came close to starvation himself. In his subsequent reports to the press he gave it as his opinion that some of the Padliermiut would indubitably perish, and that all of them might die if they should miss the spring migration of the deer, or if the deer should return too late. In the event, the deer did return in time, and in sufficient numbers to prevent a total catastrophe, but there were six known deaths from starvation amongst the Padliermiut that winter, and it is probable that many others died about whom no white man ever heard.

At Baker Lake conditions were not quite so severe, for those Eskimos who could reach the trading post received enough assistance from the local manager, a benevolent old Scot named Sandy Lunnan, to survive. Nevertheless there were eleven known deaths from starvation amongst the Akilingmiut on the Thelon River and amongst the Harvaktormiut on the lower Kazan.

Amongst the Hanningaiormiut at Garry Lake there was an unknown number of deaths. No official report of these was made, for Father Bulliard, an Oblate missionary who had recently gone amongst these people, was extremely anxious to protect them from contacts with any white man save himself, and he appears to have believed that his attempts at proselytizing might be prejudiced if he were to rouse too much interest in the plight of his self-chosen charges.

Bulliard need not have worried, for there was little likelihood that the responsible authorities would, in any case, have bothered themselves about the fate of such a remote group of people.

The government authorities were not particularly concerned about the plight of any of Canada's Eskimos, and the principal reason for their lack of interest is to be found in the nature of the unique situation which had resulted in the arctic from the continuing existence there of three white empires which exercised *de facto* sovereignty over the entire land and its native peoples.

The senior of the three empires was the Hudson's Bay Company which, until late in the nineteenth century, had legally possessed almost the whole of the Canadian arctic. In

1869, at the conclusion of a memorable struggle, the Company yielded up its exclusive charter, and its domains became a part of Canada. The transfer was almost purely nominal, however, for the Company continued to operate much as it had always done, and was not in the least hampered by the loss of paper sovereignty over its vast arctic holdings.

It was a good company, as trading companies go, though it was owned largely in England and had no particular allegiance to Canada or to Canadians. It was relatively benevolent as far as the Canadian native population was concerned. Most of its employees in the field were Orkneymen or Scots Highlanders, whose passionate loyalty to the Company almost transcended their own national loyalties, for to these men the fact that the Company was an empire in its own right seemed incontestable.

The Company's profits in the north were derived almost solely from the fur trade, which is to say, from the fur trapping activities of the Eskimos and northern Indians, and the policy of the Company toward these invaluable assets was therefore a practical one. As an historian of the H.B.C. wrote in 1932: "Common sense dictated the just treatment of an inferior people. Given fair treatment, and no opportunity to be dishonest, the native becomes a rather likeable chap. His very childishness is appealing and arouses a paternal instinct. The Hudson's Bay Company took an extreme care to select the protective type of post manager, and from that policy grew a relationship between the white race and an inferior people which for sheer beauty has not been equalled elsewhere on this earth."

The sheer beauty of that relationship, which bore marked resemblances to feudalism in medieval Europe, may be open to question, but there can be no doubt that many of the post managers sincerely tried to be good friends to the Eskimos, and that they often had what they conceived to be the best interests of the Eskimos at heart—though these interests had always, of necessity, to remain secondary to the purely financial interests of the Company itself.

It is not entirely fair to condemn the Company for its exploitation of the Eskimos, since it was, after all, a commercial firm, and it existed for the sole purpose of making money. It can hardly be castigated for making the most of its opportunities, for it never pretended to be a welfare agency. So long as Canada allowed it carte blanche to do what it pleased in the north, it was only to be expected that the H.B.C. would take full advantage of an effective monopoly.

From the point of view of the Company policy the Eskimo existed primarily as a source of marketable furs and it was therefore clearly to the Company's advantage to keep him in his aboriginal state and to discourage any attempts which might be made to enlighten him as to his rights and status as a human being of the twentieth century. It was equally to the Company's advantage to treat him moderately well, and to attempt to see that he did not starve to death as long as he was serving the Company interests—for a dead hunter traps no furs. Beyond this, the obligations of the H.B.C. did not extend.

Nor did the obligations of the second empire exceed those of the H.B.C. This second power consisted of two disparate elements—the Roman Catholic Oblate missions, and the missions of the Church of England. The great majority of the representatives of both were not Canadians, and they took their direction and instructions from Europe, not from Canada. While relations between the two organizations were by no means harmonious, they did subscribe to a common objective. The primary concern of both was the acquisition of Eskimo adherents to their respective faiths, and the Oblates at least were quite frank in their opinion that the physical welfare of the hoped-for converts was not of much importance, for it was the soul which was the priceless jewel. As an American-born Oblate priest succinctly put it in a magazine article published as late as 1957: "We figure the missionary goes before the doctor, first things first. It's more important [for the Eskimo] to get into heaven than to be cured of tuberculosis."

Yet the religious empire of the arctic was by no means built entirely upon things of the spirit. Physical possessions entered very largely into it, for there were scores of missions, and even a few schools and hospitals, not to mention a number of trading posts operated by the Oblate order. The schools and hospitals were heavily subsidized by the federal government and were, in fact, the only such institutions available to the Eskimos until the mid-1950's. The hospitals were completely (if it had not been such a tragic situation, one might have said farcically) inadequate. The schools were devoted almost entirely to religious instruction and they were of great assistance in implementing the general mission policy (which was identical in this regard with that of the Hudson's Bay Company) that the Eskimos ought to remain primitives, in enforced isolation from the outer world, and beholden in all important aspects to their guardians and mentors of the two empires. As for the larger aims of education these were, with rare exceptions, not considered to be of value to the Eskimos and were eschewed, with the result that in 1951— after some fifty years of mission control of arctic education— less than 3 per cent of Canadian Eskimos could speak, read or write English, or were in any real sense literate, despite the existence of a cumbersome syllabic script.

Despite the limitations imposed by mission policy, there were individual missionaries who were imbued with the honest desire to serve the Innuit. These were men of the best intentions, even though, it must be admitted, they were sometimes men of inferior understanding. Their sincerity is not open to question, although the ultimate results of mission activity in the arctic cannot argue for an equal immunity for mission policy.

The last of the three empires belonged to that renowned and prideful organization, the Royal Canadian Mounted Police. Initially the police had been sent to the arctic to show the flag and thereby to establish Canada's political suzerainty over the vast northern wastes. They remained, and prospered in the north, until the day came when they too possessed an arctic domain, complete with its own air force and nautical command, and a glowing legend, all of which were most gratifying to an empire-building higher echelon. Although their apparent role was that of law enforcement, there was remarkably little demand for their services in this capacity. So they became (perhaps partially to justify their own existence, and partially because there was no one else to do the job) a corps of colonial administrators—in so far as any real administration was ever undertaken.

The police established a reasonably amiable entente with the missions and the traders, and did not interfere with their activities. Indeed most members of the force wholeheartedly supported the view of the other empires that the "natives" (to this day the term is used by the police) should be protected as far as possible from contamination by our society—except for those particular benefits which could be brought into the Eskimo's life by these three chosen instruments of commerce, religion, and the white man's law.

It would be unjust to blame the police too severely for what happened to the Innuit in consequence of this attitude, for they were not fitted either by temperament or training to assist the Eskimos. They were, in theory at least, no more than the agents of the administration of the Northwest Territories, the Commissioner of which had been responsible for Eskimo affairs since Canada took her first official interest in the Innuit in the year 1927. Within the narrow limits of their ability and understanding, some individual policemen proved—as was the case both with the missionaries and the traders—to be wholehearted partisans of the Eskimos; while at the same time they subscribed to the general belief that *Inuk* would be best served by being kept isolated in his arctic limbo.

The Northwest Territories administration was a most intriguing body. In 1950 its Council consisted of the Commissioner (who was also the Minister of the Federal Department of Resources and Development), supported by the Deputy Commissioner (who was coincidentally the Deputy Minister of the Department of Resources and Development), and five appointed members, one of whom was the R.C.M.P. Commissioner. Nor were the rest of them all entirely devoid of special interest in the other empires of the north.

To guide the Council in matters pertaining to the Eskimos there was an advisory body, which came to consist of the Commissioner of the R.C.M.P., the Fur Trade Commissioner or the General Manager of the Hudson's Bay Company, the Anglican Bishop of the Arctic, and one, or sometimes more, Roman Catholic priests of the Oblate order.

The actual administrative machinery for dealing with Eskimo affairs consisted, according to a government memorandum dated 1950, of two officers and a stenographer employed by the Department of Resources and Development. This memorandum further stated that it was considered unnecessary to increase the size of the Eskimo administration section at that time since the commercial and religious organizations in the arctic, together with the R.C.M.P., were competent and willing to continue as executors for Eskimo affairs.

A somewhat cynical observer of this situation might have suspected that the federal government of Canada was happy to wash its hands of any real responsibilities for the Eskimos because, in the first place, it was cheaper and more politic to allow private organizations to deal with the Eskimos as they saw fit, and secondly, because the government and people of Canada felt themselves under no particular obligations toward the Innuit.

Nor would this have been such a gross canard against a modern and virtuously democratic nation as it might have seemed. While the fate of the Eskimos remained, to all intents and purposes, in the hands of the three empires, Canada's voice was often heard championing the cause of the world's underprivileged peoples. We Canadians looked askance at the South African exponents of *apartheid*, at the segregationists in the southern United States; and we gazed with holy horror upon the inhumanities which we were told were being perpetrated on primitive peoples under the rule of Communism. Indeed we looked virtuously in all directions; except northward into our own land.

For most of us, this was not conscious hypocrisy. Through many generations we had been carefully conditioned to accept a myth in place of the real Eskimo. The myth had become stereotyped into the figure of a happy, skin-clad little fellow, living in a white and shining igloo, carefree and contented; not quite human perhaps, but lovable for all of that; and asking no more of us than that we leave him to his prehistoric pleasures and his outlandish pastimes. Some of us even envied him his atavistic freedom from the complexities of modern life.

Believing that this was the real man, we felt conscience-free to leave him under the aegis of the three empires, which were themselves a vital element in the northern myth. We had long since acquired strong mental images of the dogged, persevering Mountie driving his dogs through howling blizzards, that justice might be done, and that his Eskimo brother might be served; of the paternal fur trader who treated the Eskimo with the kindly forbearance of a good father toward a rather feckless child; of the self-sacrificing missionaries who gave themselves up to searing frost and cruel hardships so that the immortal soul of the poor pagan might come safe to Heaven when he died.

Men believe that which they wish to believe, and most of them prefer to believe that which gives solace to their consciences. Who is to blame us if we chose the myth?

Even had we so desired, it would have been extremely difficult to ascertain the true reality, for this had been so carefully and thoroughly obscured that it was almost totally lost to the public view. The Hudson's Bay Company and the missions kept a close tongue in their heads. The R.C.M.P., a notoriously close-mouthed organization at best, reported secretly to the Minister of Justice (if indeed it reported to anyone save God) and its records were never profaned by public scrutiny.

As late as 1954 it was virtually impossible to uncover sufficient information with which to assess accurately the situation in the north. It was not until 1958 that the terrible nature of the reality began to be fully apparent. In 1958 it became known, for instance, that one out of every eight surviving Eskimos had a history of tuberculosis. It became known that the life expectancy of an Eskimo was only slightly more than twenty-four years. It became known that the infant mortality rate stood at more than 260 deaths for every 1000 births and was still rising. It became known that more than three-quarters of all Canadian Eskimos suffered from chronic malnutrition. By 1958 the carefully constructed myth was at last becoming threadbare; but in 1950 it still remained intact. Indeed in those not-so-far-distant days the government, and the R.C.M.P., did not even know how many Eskimos were under their protection—the figure was thought to be about 8,000 though it was probably much nearer to 12,000. But honest facts were unimportant in 1950, for the myth still flourished.

All of this must be kept in mind in order to provide some understanding of how little the brutal disclosures which Harrington made to the press were able to accomplish.

His charges were, of course, officially denied but, what was worse, they were slurred over by the appointed guardians of the old order who in their posture as the expert authorities on Eskimo affairs had, and held, the public ear. By the end of March the accounts of famine amongst the Padliermiut had been forgotten in the south, where men fed well and slept warmly through the winter nights.

Apart from the visit of the doctor, no further action was taken to assist the Ihalmiut until mid-April. Meanwhile, they survived as best they could.

On April 6, Ohoto arrived at the Signals station in a state of near-panic to report that some kind of disease had smitten all the children. The sergeant in charge was aware of what sickness might do to the emaciated and weakened youngsters, and he immediately radioed Churchill with a request for a doctor—but this time no doctor was forthcoming. Instead the authorities referred the problem back to Ennadai.

The soldiers thereupon resolved to organize an expedition to the sickness camps. They had no means of transportation other than their caterpillar tractor, which was unreliable at any time; and the Ihalmiut only possessed three dogs amongst them, so that any relief expedition had to be made on foot. Considering the unfamiliarity of these white men with the land, the journey which they contemplated called for courage, and vividly demonstrated the reality of their concern for the Eskimos.

The sergeant and one other soldier set out, with Ohoto as a guide, and after trudging twelve miles to the nearest camp—it was Alekahaw's—they were exhausted. They were also frustrated by the discovery that the sickness camps lay thirty miles farther off at the Little Lakes, a distance which might as well have been three hundred miles. Nevertheless there was work for them in Alekahaw's snow shelter, for his wife Kaluk was suffering from a paralysis of her right leg which was slowly spreading to include her whole right side. Her condition was obviously serious, though neither she nor her husband had made any complaint nor had they asked for aid.

The soldiers returned to their base and again radioed Churchill. They were instructed to have the woman at the station by April 11, when a military inspection party was scheduled to arrive at Ennadai by air. Getting her to the station was no light task—in the end it was accomplished by cranking up the recalcitrant tractor and making a harrowing journey to Alekahaw's and back, bringing Kaluk in upon a makeshift sled.

The aircraft arrived on the 11th, carrying as an extra passenger an R.C.M.P. sergeant from Churchill, together with some emergency food for the Eskimos. The policeman did not visit the outlying camps from which the sickness had been reported, but he agreed to take Kaluk back with him to the military hospital at Churchill.

For Kaluk and for Alekahaw this posed an anguishing dilemma. Their youngest daughter, Ookala, was only two years old and was still being breast-fed in the usual Eskimo fashion. There was no other woman at Alekahaw's camp with whom she could be left and, deprived of her mother, it did not seem unlikely to the Eskimos that she would die. Alekahaw and his wife pleaded that the child might be allowed to accompany Kaluk to Churchill; but the request was refused on the grounds that the child was not ill. It is possible that the sergeant did not understand the situation.

So Kaluk vanished from the land where, in the distant camps, the disease continued to run its course.

The policeman's visit to Ennadai does not appear to have been concerned with the present plight of the Eskimos, but was primarily intended to apprise the station personnel of a plan to move the Ihalmiut to a new location "nearer a trading post." The police sergeant asked the soldiers to have the Eskimos assembled at the station in readiness for the move as soon as possible. He gave few further details.

It could not have been that he did not have these details, for the police detachment at Churchill had been intimately concerned in the development of a most remarkable scheme.

Its genesis went back to 1948 when plans for the establishment of the Ennadai station were first made public in Churchill. News of the project aroused considerable interest amongst some of the local businessmen. They wasted no time in preparing a useful-looking scheme, and by late in 1948 they had already put the wheels in motion by submitting elements of their plan to the Department of Resources and Development for approval.

According to their submission, what they envisaged was a commercial fishery at Nueltin Lake, whose produce would be sold to the military establishment at Churchill. This operation—so they said—would be able to offer wage employment at $150 a month to the men of the Ihalmiut band who, "as everyone was aware," were having a hard time of it at Ennadai. Furthermore, the Eskimos would be provided with nets and the rest of the requisite fishing gear at no cost to themselves. Since the fisheries would not occupy all their time, they would be able to hunt caribou as of old and, conceivably, do considerable fox trapping as well. All that was required to realize this utopia for the Ihalmiut was to have the authorities consent to moving the Eskimos from their present home to the proposed fisheries site at Nueltin.

To cinch their case the fish company enthusiasts pointed out that the otherwise prohibitive cost of flying the fish three hundred miles to Churchill would be offset by the use of aircraft belonging to Arctic Wings (a small airline in which, incidentally, the fisheries entrepreneurs shared an interest with the Oblate order). Arctic Wings, so the planners claimed, firmly expected to receive a contract from the Army to make regular supply flights to the new Signals station at Ennadai. On the return flights the aircraft could stop at Nueltin, take on a load of fish, and proceed to Churchill.

The Department of Resources and Development received the plan with unalloyed enthusiasm, but with a naïveté which was astonishing even amongst the bureaucrats. No one seems to have bothered to examine the details with any care, for if they had done so they would have wondered why it was necessary to go three hundred miles from Churchill to catch fish which were more easily obtainable at half that distance. And they would have discovered, had they investigated, that the Army had no intention of chartering civilian aircraft to service Ennadai, since the bulk of the annual supplies were to be taken in during the winter by cat-train, while any summer flights which might become necessary would be made by service aircraft of the R.C.A.F. These oddities in the proposal were not immediately apparent, and the authorities were too enamored by the prospect of the Ihalmiut becoming not only self-supporting, but positively rich, to be particularly critical.

The R.C.M.P. who, as the administrative representatives in the field, should have been more closely in touch with reality, were consulted, and they gave the plan their full approval. After the lifting of the polio quarantine in the late summer of 1949 the requisite permits were therefore issued to the fisheries company, even though it was *known* by then that they would not have any contract with the Army, and would therefore have to cover the entire freight costs on the fish themselves.

The permits were issued, even though a fisheries biologist employed by the federal government had visited Nueltin and had reported that, while there were indeed fish in the lake, his studies had convinced him that transportation costs made commercial fishing at a profit, under any existing circumstances, a most unlikely possibility.

Neither did anyone pay any attention to the confirmatory evidence of a professional fisherman who explored Nueltin's possibilities during the early winter of 1949–1950, and who reported that, without the payment of heavy transportation subsidies, the operation would never be commercially feasible. This man's report contained other information, of an even more revealing nature, for he pointed out that—by himself—he had been able to catch up to a ton of fish a week, and that the catch of two or three fishermen would be enough to swamp the limited market available in Churchill. It was his considered opinion that the employment of numbers of native fishermen at Nueltin would be economic nonsense, even assuming that any way could be found around the transportation difficulties.

For that matter, no one paid any heed to the known fact that the Ihalmiut had never been fishermen, did not like fishing, and had always avoided it, having discovered in antiquity that fish was a starvation diet in a land where only meat and fat could adequately sustain human life.

The most generous view which can be taken of the authorities' refusal to face these facts is that they must have believed the fisheries company was quite prepared to lose formidable sums of money while engaging in a charitable enterprise on behalf of the Eskimos and Indians—for the Chipewyan Indians had been brought into the scheme too.

When the operation got under way in November of 1949, the fishery company persuaded a considerable number of Chipewyans from the Brochet area to come north and share in the good thing. It was intended to add the Ihalmiut to this labor force in early spring of 1950, by which time there would be enough Eskimo and Indian fishermen on hand to supply a market the size of Winnipeg—if such a market had been accessible.

It was no doubt mere coincidence that the owners of the fishery company also operated trading posts in Keewatin in competition with the Hudson's Bay Company, and had in fact run the post at Otter Lake near which five of the Ihalmiut had starved to death in the spring of 1947. It may have been quite coincidental that the Ihalmiut were not, after 1948, working for any trader, and that they were eligible to receive Family Allowance payments (as were the Chipewyan Indians). Certainly it was a fact that these payments, which would total a considerable sum every year, would have to be spent somewhere.

It may also have been coincidence that the new company closed down its trading post at Otter Lake and brought the manager to Nueltin to take charge of the new project.

The rest was inevitable. During the winter of 1949–1950 a trading post appeared in conjunction with the fishery, and its operations soon bid fair to eclipse the fishery itself.

All of this was, of course, known to the R.C.M.P. at Churchill, but had no effect upon the decision which had been already confirmed, to give the Ihalmiut into the control of the fishery company.

The move itself was conducted in secrecy as far as the Ihalmiut were concerned. They were given no indication of what the future held in store for them other than the statement of the R.C.M.P. sergeant that "they were to be moved nearer to a trading post." They were *not* told in advance that they were to be employed as fishermen. They were *not*, of course, permitted to make their own decisions as to whether they should move or not. Perhaps the police realized that the Ihalmiut might refuse if they were given such an opportunity.

Ohoto was the first to hear of the impending move, when he arrived at the station on April 12, to inquire whether the white men had forgotten about the sick children in the camps by the Little Lakes.

In telling Ohoto of the R.C.M.P. plan, the soldiers did their best to soften what even they realized would be a stunning blow, and they are to be forgiven for intimating that the chosen land for which the Ihalmiut were bound was a place where the deer were always numerous, where no man ever went hungry, and where the Eskimos would receive nothing but benevolence at the hands of the white men they encountered. Yet they must have felt some compunction, for one of them wrote:

"The Eskimos are primed to go to a land of plenty. Heaven help us if any of them ever find their way back here . . . !"

This, at least, was an honest comment on a situation about which there seems to have been all too little honesty.

At first Ohoto reacted to the news with bewilderment which rapidly became stubborn resistance. He refused to act as a messenger to persuade the rest of the People to gather at the station preparatory to the move. But in the end the visions of personal propinquity with white men seduced him, and he went out to gather the Ihalmiut. They were instructed to abandon all their belongings, except what they could carry on their backs, for there would be no room in the aircraft for anything but human freight.

At those camps where hopelessness was greatest, Ohoto had little trouble; but at Owliktuk's camps he ran into resistance. Owliktuk staunchly refused to obey the summons until several days had been spent in discussion, and until his wife had reminded him that two of their children were still sick (the six-month-old son of Yaha and Ateshu had already died), and that there might be help for the surviving children at the Signals station. Subjected to these pressures, Owliktuk eventually agreed to the move, but only because he had convinced himself and the others that the "trading post" referred to by the soldiers must mean Padlei—a place many of the Ihalmiut had visited and where they had relatives. The People were not adverse to being taken there, for they knew that if they did not like it, they could walk home again; and in the meantime they would be able to visit friends, and perhaps obtain ammunition and supplies "on debt" against next winter's furs, from the Hudson's Bay post manager.

On April 19, 1950, the first of the deportees began, in the words of one of the soldiers, "to straggle in; and a more tattered and discouraged rabble it would be hard to imagine.

91

All were in poor shape, no food, no dogs, and precious few belongings. When asked what they had been eating they replied that they had kept going by boiling and eating old caribou robes and parkas."

It was April 22 before Ohoto arrived with Owliktuk's group, but he had not yet located Pommela nor Hekwaw and so after a night's rest he was sent off again.

There were now thirty Eskimos at the station and they were ordered to build snow shelters for themselves while rations were being prepared. In order to ease the administrative problems, the soldiers began by distributing three days' rations at one time; but they soon realized that this procedure would not serve, for the entire amount was wolfed down by the starving people in a single meal.

On the 24th, a military aircraft carrying an Army doctor from Churchill arrived at Ennadai. The doctor had been instructed to examine the people preparatory to the move— rather, one suspects, as cattle are vetted before being sold to a new owner. However, this particular doctor was an Army man, and he cared nothing for political expediency. He was horrified by the condition of the Eskimos, and when he returned to Churchill he issued a statement to the Canadian Press news service to the effect that the Ihalmiut were on the verge of starvation. He added that, lacking any authority or facilities himself, he could do no more for them than to send in drugs and medicine.

His visit had not been wasted, for he had quickly diagnosed the sickness amongst the children as influenza, and he had provided sufficient drugs to stamp it out.

Pommela was one of the last of the Ihalmiut to reach the station and he came in alone. His dependents, so he explained, were so weak from hunger that they could not travel. On the strength of this he was issued with a considerable supply of food to take to them but, being Pommela, he did not make any attempt to rejoin his family. Instead he camped a mile or so away, and ate the food himself.

His wife Onikok (who was dying of cancer, though no one knew it then) and three of his remaining adopted children staggered in two days later, in the last stages of exhaustion. Onekwaw, who went to help them, was the first to realize that the ten-year-old boy Alektaiuwa, the son of Pommela's dead brother Kakut, was missing. Word of this spread quickly amongst the other Eskimos, but such was the fear in which the old man was held that no one dared to question him about the disappearance of the boy. It was not until Ohoto nerved himself to tell the soldiers, who thereupon demanded an explanation of Alektaiuwa's absence, that Pommela deigned to speak. The boy, he said, had simply lagged behind the rest and would arrive within a few more hours—Onikok had assured him that this was so, and there was really no need for anyone to worry.

This explanation was sufficient for the soldiers, but not for Onekwaw, who knew Pommela far too well. Quietly and unobserved, Onekwaw took the back trail, though he was himself so weak that he could hardly travel.

He found the boy early the next morning, some ten miles from the station, where he had collapsed in a drift and lay unconscious. Onekwaw endeavored to carry him to safety, but he had not the strength. He covered the child with snow and then dragged him back to the station where he told his story to Ohoto, who promptly told the soldiers. A rescue party was organized, and by late that night Alektaiuwa lay on a bed in the basement of the station.

He appeared to be quite dead, but when he had been stripped of his frozen garments and covered with heated blankets the soldiers were able to detect a pulse. One of them wrote later that "the sight of that poor undressed body took my breath away for he had been starved to the point where we despaired of saving him." Nevertheless they worked all night to save him, and by morning they had succeeded in restoring him to consciousness.

As Alektaiuwa began to recover from his ordeal the outrage which the soldiers felt on his behalf was vented on Pommela. They searched the shaman's travel sled and when they discovered a hindquarter of caribou meat (though there was not a scrap of meat in the rest of the encampment) their anger knew no bounds. With Ohoto's help they then interrogated Onikok and she told them, hesitantly, that Alektaiuwa had been systematically starved for weeks on Pommela's orders, and that neither she nor the children had been allowed even to share their own meager rations with him.

Some of the soldiers were in favor of beating Pommela up physically, but they did not dare to go so far, so they beat him instead with angry and contemptuous words. They did this in full view of all the Ihalmiut, and Pommela, who had never been bested by any living man, was forced to endure the assault without recourse. He who had terrorized his people for so many decades was stripped of his armor and mercilessly castigated as if he had been an erring child. He was shamed, and proven helpless in his shame, before the people. He, the great *angeokok,* was chastised with impunity, and not all his magic or his fearsome spirits could aid him or protect him. Pommela had brought tragedy to many people in his time, but the fate which overtook him in this hour was almost commensurate to any he had meted out to others. For an Eskimo there could have been no crueler punishment. It was a deserved punishment; but it is a measure of how little the men of the one world understood those of the other that the soldiers were bitter in the belief that Pommela had escaped unpunished for his treatment of Alektaiuwa.

7

Journey into Fear

As April, 1950, drew near its close the soldiers at Ennadai found themselves harassed to distraction by this mass descent of the Ihalmiut. They had neither the knowledge nor the time to cope with the situation which had been thrust upon them. When they were able, on April 29, to notify the R.C.M.P. that the collection was complete, they were heartily delighted at the prospect of ridding themselves of their unwanted dependents.

"It was not," one of them wrote, "that we did not have any affection for them; but the work details, the ration details, the sick calls and the courts of human relations simply snowed us under."

An Arctic Wings Norseman arrived on the morning of May 1, carrying the policeman who was in charge of the move. This man spoke no Eskimo, and had no interpreter with him. He was unable, had he so desired, to explain to the assembled people what was in store for them; and he was in a considerable hurry. Stripped of all their possessions except the small bundles which they could carry on their backs, the first batch of Eskimos was ordered into the plane and it immediately took off into a clear spring sky, circled once and then headed, not northeast for Padlei, but almost due south.

The rest of the People, clustered forlornly on the shore, watched it go with increasing bewilderment—and when it had vanished into the southern horizon they looked at each other with a mounting apprehension.

The plane flew a long way south, passing over the tenuous edge of the forests and penetrating deep into the black spruce and jack-pine scrub. There were sixteen Eskimos jammed so tightly into the cramped cargo space of the small single-engined aircraft that only one or two could crane their necks to see where they were going. They saw nothing which they recognized; instead they saw the forests thickening beneath them. The sight was terrifying. Below the plane was a foreign and forbidding world—the world of trees which had belonged through all time to their ancestral enemies, the Idthen Eldeli Indians.

Eventually the aircraft landed on the ice of south Nueltin Lake. The policeman swung open the door and the Ihalmiut looked out upon their promised land.

They saw the trees, marching almost to the shore, but what held their vision—filled it—was a row of waiting Indians, their faces lean and unfriendly in the hard spring sun.

The sixteen deportees were unceremoniously herded up the beach and turned over to the fishery manager, while the aircraft swung up the lake to fetch another load.

The next group did not enter the aircraft quite so resignedly. Some of the women wept. Owliktuk was with this group, and he hesitated briefly until a shouted order which he did not understand decided him. He could not resist the inscrutable design of the police. With a blank face he clambered into the cramped space.

It required three trips to carry the forty-seven Ihalmiut to their new home—two on May 1, and the third the following day. And then the land was empty. The People had gone; had abandoned their camps, most of their possessions, the graves of their dead, and the places of their memories. They had been taken from the one place in all the world where, even in the most tragic times, bedeviled by hunger and disease, they had at least been solaced by the familiarity of remembered things.

It may be felt that this is laboring the emotional and physical effects of this upheaval in the People's lives but, on the contrary, it would be impossible for a white man to do full justice to it. This was an unbelievably harsh uprooting of a people who possessed a most limited understanding and experience of anything beyond their own immediate frontiers; it was literally an expulsion—and none too gentle a one at that—from their known world into one that not only was peopled by men whom they still thought of as their blood enemies, but which was also the domain of hostile spirits over which the Eskimos could exert no control, and against which there was no defense. It was, for the Ihalmiut, a virtual hell on earth.

It was also—by decree—their new home. And this is what they found. They found themselves camped on an island where, when the thaws came, they would be cut off and unable to escape. They found themselves in the midst of a band of Idthen Eldeli Indians who wasted no time in making the Eskimos understand that they were not wanted, and that it would be better for them if they departed quickly to their own country. They found that they were not even wanted by the white man in charge of the fishery.

They were issued with some nets, tents, and a little flour and lard (for all of which the government was later billed), and told to get busy and fish—not for the company, but to support themselves. The fantasy of a commercial fishery had already vanished and, since it was now almost spring, and there would be no fur trapping again till fall, the Eskimos were in fact a useless encumbrance—or would have been had it not been for the fact that they had Family Allowance credits (which were a complete mystery to them) that could be spent at the company store.

Since they had not been told of the $150 a month salary they were to have received, they did not note its absence. But they did miss, and desperately too, the land from which they had been taken.

Not many details of that time of exile are known with certainty. The records are very scanty. But in June an itinerant American gospel preacher arrived at the camp in his small airplane and spent some days with the Ihalmiut. He was distressed at their pagan state, though their physical condition does not seem to have concerned him overmuch. He attempted to evangelize them, but elicited no response, for the Ihalmiut were in no receptive mood toward white men.

It is also known that, in this period, there were several deaths. Katelo, that lonely man, was one who died; and another was Kielok (Kala) who was Hekwaw's wife. The death of these two is shrouded in mystery. According to the official records the first died on July 1, and the second on August 1 of "old age and pneumonia." They were fifty-one and fifty-two years old respectively, and when they were examined by the doctor in April they had both been in good condition. Their bodies were not examined by a medical man nor by the police, who made out the death reports some time later. It is unlikely that the true causes of death will now be known, for the surviving Ihalmiut do not speak freely on this matter. Nevertheless there is reason to believe that these two died primarily because they no longer wished to live. They had no reason to desire life in exile.

There is much which will not now be known of that black interlude in the history of the Ihalmiut, and this may be as well, for what *is* known cannot sit easily upon the consciences of those white men who were involved.

On May 25, just twenty-three days after the transportation had been completed, the soldiers at Ennadai were amazed to see an Eskimo accompanied by three starving dogs come walking slowly up the shore toward the station. They recognized him from a distance. It was Pommela.

Mindful of his past history the soldiers questioned him as closely as they could, and with particular reference to his family. Pommela told them that his people were still at Nueltin and that he would go back for them when he had established some summer meat caches on the land—but the old man lied, for he no longer had a family.

His wife Onikok had been ill for many months and when she was examined by the doctor in April he suspected what the trouble was and requested that she be evacuated to Churchill when the Nueltin move was completed. At Churchill the doctor confirmed his early diagnosis. Onikok had cancer. She died a few months later, and never saw the inland plains again.

During the first few days at Nueltin, with no woman in his tent, Pommela's family disintegrated rapidly. Alektaiuwa had never returned to him but, after his recovery from the ordeal in the snows, had gone to live with Yaha. Now the three remaining children abandoned the old man whom they had come to hate and fear, and placed themselves under the protection of other families of the Ihalmiut.

Even his former followers, Onekwaw, Alekahaw and Katelo, avoided the shaman, for his defeat at the hands of the soldiers was fresh in memory. Pommela was quite alone, and this, together with his growing resentment of all whites, decided him that he at least would no longer submit to the arbitrary orders and actions of the police.

Old and discredited as he might be, Pommela was still a man. One night he stole three dogs from the Indians, fled in darkness across the lake ice, and vanished into the thin forests beyond. The wooded lands did not hold the same terrors for him that they did for the rest of the People, for he had traded south to Brochet through this country in the old days. Nevertheless he did not linger under the shadows of the trees, but drove the three dogs north, each with a small pack upon its back, until the plains were reached. It was a long journey and it took him two weeks to walk to Ennadai.

In reply to the questions of the soldiers Pommela stated that the new place was no good, that the deer could not be hunted there because of the thickness of the forests, that the white men were no good, that the Indians had threatened the People, and that he—for one—had had enough of it. He planned to stay at Ennadai just long enough to build a kayak, before proceeding down the Kazan to an area where he could intercept the migratory deer herds, and make a summer kill.

With the old man's departure ten days later (it took him just eight days to build a kayak out of scraps of lumber and the skins of some deer he had killed on the way north), the soldiers saw no other Eskimos until November. They assumed that the rest of the People had remained at south Nueltin Lake—but they were wrong.

For some time after the arrival at the fishing camp the majority of the People were too dispirited and too disoriented to contemplate any attempt at escape. They were afraid of so many things: of the white man into whose charge they had been given; of the police who had brought them here; of the forests which surrounded them, and, not least, of the Indians. Left to shift for themselves, they clustered close together forming a little enclave of despair. They fished a little—for they had to do so in order to exist—while the Indians became bolder and more overt in their dislike of this invasion by their ancient enemies into the Indian lands. The Ihalmiut found that their nets were being interfered with and that their possessions were being stolen, and, in the eyes of the Eskimos, the Idthen Eldeli began to assume a dangerously menacing stature. Fear of the Indians began to approach panic, and this fear eventually overcame the other fears and became the key with which the People liberated themselves from servitude.

Things came to a head on June 17, when a nine-year-old girl called Ahto, who had been one of Pommela's adopted daughters, was shot and killed. No details of this affair have ever been made public. The R.C.M.P. have refused to elaborate upon the brief report which they subsequently made to the administrative officials, and which simply stated that Ahto died "accidentally from gunshot wounds." It is probable that they are unable to enlarge upon the affair for, if an investigation was ever made, it could not have been undertaken before mid-December when the police again patrolled to the interior, and by that time it would have been most difficult to discover the truth, since all those who were concerned were by then scattered far and wide.

If the Ihalmiut themselves are to be believed, the killing was no accident, and the Idthen Eldeli were involved in it.

In any event, the shock of Ahto's death released some of the People from the bonds which had held them prisoners, and a few days later—while the melting ice would still carry human traffic—Owliktuk, and those who chose to follow him, vanished from the fishing camp.

Once begun, the exodus continued through the summer until everyone had abandoned the moribund fishing enterprise, including even the white man who had been in charge of it. He appears to have moved his supplies to the old cabin at Windy River and there he retained some of the Eskimos—notably the families of Alekahaw and Onekwaw—by virtue of the fact that he was able to dispense rations to them against their Family Allowance credits.

The rest of the People had already fled the district. They went slowly, on foot, and they did not go near Ennadai, for they believed that if the police found them they would once more be herded south to the place of terror from which they were so desperately anxious to escape.

Yaha, Ohoto and Hekwaw, with their families, bypassed Ennadai and the Little Lakes and continued north until they reached the northwest bay of Hicks Lake, where for the moment they felt themselves secure against discovery. They had a little ammunition, and they were able to kill a few deer from the late-summer herds; but these herds were very much dispersed and small in size, so that they were unable to lay up sufficient meat to see them through the winter. Nevertheless they did not dare to visit the Army station until mid-November, when hunger broke down their resolution to remain in hiding and brought them to the station to plead for food.

Pommela seems to have wandered widely and alone during the summer, but not even a man of his tough and independent character could withstand the isolation of the land for long, and in late fall he appeared briefly at Ennadai to claim the three dogs which he had left there. Using these as pack beasts, he traveled south to Windy Cabin where he joined his old adherents, and slowly began to re-exert his influence over them, even to the extent of reclaiming one of his remaining adopted children, a boy eight years of age called Angataiuk.

The fragile fabric of the Ihalmiut society, which had been so overstrained for many years, had now given way completely. The events of the spring and summer had rent it into fragments and the People had fled as fugitives to the far corners of the inland plains. They could no longer even face their common fate as one, nor draw upon the essential strength of the community—that strength which is the very essence of Eskimo existence. Each small fragment of the band was now alone and isolated from the rest, harried by the fears and uncertainties which had arisen from the shattering experiences at Nueltin, and bludgeoned by the hard blows of famine against which there was no real defense left to them.

With this disintegration of their social structure there came an inevitable withering of the spirit within each human being. The weakest of the People succumbed first. These were the ones who had remained at Windy River and who now gave up all pretense of struggle and became no more than beggars, utterly dependent on the charity of Family Allowance, while Pommela preyed upon them with a restored and strengthened arrogance.

The small group at Hicks Lake was made of sterner stuff and held out longer, but in the end the frightful oppression of a land wherein they lived divorced from all other living men, combined with the effects of famine, proved too much to bear. So they struggled back to Ennadai, where they remained until early in the spring, becoming increasingly dependent on the bounty of the white men.

Only in Owliktuk's band did a semblance of the vital unity and strength of purpose which had marked the People in the past remain alive. This group had shrunk until it consisted only of the families of Owliktuk, Halo, Ootek and Miki. Nevertheless, it remained a unit, for the inner fortitude of Owliktuk was still proof against the forces of dissolution. There was a quality of basalt in his spirit.

He was deliberate, and courageous too. When he led his little band away from the nightmare of Nueltin, he chose a path that none of his people had ever walked before. It was a difficult route, but purposely chosen to avoid any contact with those who had banished his people to the fishery camp. The route avoided the known lands of the Ihalmiut, even the Little Lakes beside which the People had pitched their camps for generations. Owliktuk knew that the airplane is a mighty seeker, and that there was no safety in the old familiar places.

So he and his followers walked to the northeast, passing over the interminable rock ridges which lie like titanic slag heaps to the west of Nueltin, and which even the deer avoid, for they have a quality of lunar desolation about them that is unrelieved by any living thing save the gray moss and the black and blood-red lichens that cling to the shattered rocks. They walked very slowly, for the sharp stones cut their skin boots to shreds and the children could only maintain the slowest of paces. Although they had almost no ammunition, Owliktuk had thoughtfully taken some of the fishing gear from Nueltin and, though the People might frown on fish, he made them understand that in this time of danger and of flight, they must eat fish or die.

They were more than a month en route, and it was not until late in the summer that Owliktuk called a halt. The little travel tents of canvas which they had made from the wall tents issued to them at Nueltin were finally pitched beside the shores of Otter Lake about twelve miles to the south of the now abandoned trading post. There were no white men nearer than Padlei, as far as Owliktuk knew, and here he felt his people would be safe.

The omens for the approaching winter were very dark. The little band of exiles had seen few caribou during the long walk, and Owliktuk guessed that for the second year in succession the deer would not come through the land in any numbers. It did not matter much, for the men possessed only about two dozen rounds of ammunition for their four rifles.

Owliktuk therefore prepared to meet the winter in a manner completely foreign to his people's past.

Under his direction two nets were set, and for the first time in their history the Ihalmiut became fishermen in earnest. Until the ice formed they caught fish enough to eat in the nearby rivers though, since they had no kayaks or canoes, they were forced to set the nets by wading shoulder deep in the frigid waters. When the ice became firm enough to bear, they moved the nets out to the lake, setting them through holes in the ice. At all hours of the shortening days, when there was no other work to do, Owliktuk set the children, and even some of the women, jigging for more fish with hand lines.

They made good catches, for this lake had not been fished for many years, if indeed it had ever been fished before. The drying fish hung from crude scaffolds, swaying in the autumn winds; and as winter came hard and white, the piles of frozen fish began to mount like cordwood beside the little tents.

Yet food was not everything. Despite hard hunting by Halo and Owliktuk, less than a dozen deer were obtained before the last caribou vanished to the south. There were not nearly enough hides to provide warm clothing for all the people. Consequently most of them faced the approaching winter wearing only torn and ragged summer garments which did not suffice to keep the waters warm even in the early days of autumn.

The omens were dark enough for the four families by Otter Lake—but they were much darker for the Padliermiut, who were their nearest neighbors. The Padliermiut hunters had rifles, and an adequate supply of shells, and so they had relied entirely upon the deer. But the depleted caribou herds did not come to the Padlei country in the fall of 1950.

It was an ironic turn of fortune that Owliktuk's fugitive band should have survived that winter because they had so little ammunition, while their cousins, who had plenty of shells, were doomed to starve. Owliktuk had not been able to place a dependence on the deer, and so he had turned to fish. But when the Padliermiut understood that the deer would not be coming to them, it was already too late for them to seek a substitute.

The Padliermiut, who then numbered about one hundred and seventy people, and whose camps were scattered within a hundred-mile radius of Padlei Post, had begun to starve

103

before November ended. Their dogs died quickly—those that had survived the preceding winter—and the men began to come in to Padlei on foot seeking food to keep the women and the children in the distant camps alive. The post manager radioed to the police at Eskimo Point, explained the gravity of the situation, and asked permission to begin issuing relief rations. Permission was granted, but he was instructed not to allow the Padliermiut to come in off the land or to congregate about the post.

The constable in charge of the R.C.M.P. detachment at the coast firmly believed that the tough official policy of making the Eskimo scratch their own living from the land was the only salvation for the "natives"; and he was a rigid man who—like most policemen—would choose to adhere to policy in the face of any eventuality. In normal times this particular policy was not entirely a bad one—but these were not normal times.

Only one white man in the area seems to have sensed the true magnitude of the approaching disaster. He was the Hudson's Bay post manager at Eskimo Point, a man who had spent thirty years amongst the Innuit and who both knew and loved them, but who could never have been accused of "spoiling" the Eskimos by accustoming them to dole, for it had always been his business to show a profit on his yearly outfit, and there is no profit in Eskimos who sit around the post.

Nevertheless, when he smelled death in the offing near the end of November, he acted in a manner directly contrary to the policy which the policeman was determined to implement. He dispatched messengers to the camps of all the People who traded to Eskimo Point, and the gist of his message was simple and direct: abandon your camps, load your families on your sleds, and come in to the post at once.

They knew him, and they obeyed without hesitation. Within a short time nearly two hundred Eskimos had converged on Eskimo Point, and their igloos stretched in a solid line along the shore for half a mile. When they arrived some of them were already too weak to walk and had to be carried by their relatives and friends. Hunger had already eaten savagely into the strength of almost every one of them.

The policeman at Eskimo Point seems to have been outraged by the trader's action. He ordered the People to return immediately to their starvation camps; but for once they would not heed the voice of authority. They were deaf to him, and listened instead to the trader who told them, quietly enough, that they were to remain where they were until the famine ended. Perhaps irritated by this defiance, the policeman not only refused to authorize the payment of relief vouchers, but he also held back the Family Allowance credits (monies which belonged to the Eskimos by right of law) until the People would agree to leave the post and go back to the land—to the hungry, empty land.

The People did without their Family Allowance until after Christmas had come and gone. They were fed for three full months out of the Hudson's Bay warehouse, and not one of those who had come to the trader for assistance died.

But at Padlei, twenty-two men, women and children died directly or indirectly of starvation.

They died almost entirely because they were not allowed to bring their families to the post and to remain there until the crisis had passed. Only the men were allowed to come, and on each visit they were issued two weeks' relief supplies of flour and lard and baking powder, and sent away again. Some of these men had taken a week to reach the post, and needed a week to regain their camps—by which time the rations which they carried on their backs (they had no usable dogs remaining after November) were sadly depleted. The inevitable came to pass. After three or four such journeys the men either became too weak to face another journey, or they put it off until it was too late.

The deaths of these people were almost solely due to the inflexibility of the policy which the police, in their capacity as administrators, had determined was the right and proper one. It was no doubt the same policy which prompted the Commissioner of the R.C.M.P. to make this statement before the Northwest Territories Council in January of 1958: "I feel it is just as bad for an Eskimo hunter to become a scavenger and a beggar as it is for him to starve or freeze to death."

Owliktuk's people all survived the winter, but it was no pleasant life they lived. In their small tents, walled around with snow blocks, they huddled in abject misery. They were never warm, for they had no suitable clothing and there was no deer fat with which to stoke their bodies' furnaces. They were always hungry, for the human stomach cannot contain sufficient frozen fish to satisfy it when the thermometer plunges to 40 degrees below zero, and the gales thunder down from the far distant arctic ice whirling the sharp snows before them until the particles cut like driven sand.

Once in January, Owliktuk accompanied by Ootek and Halo walked north to try and obtain some deer fat from their cousins of the Padliermiut. They visited two camps in which men and women were already dead or dying; and they returned hurriedly and gratefully to their own daily diet of lean fish.

It was about this time that their sanctuary at Otter Lake was invaded. Two white men appeared and reoccupied the empty cabin. One of these was the ex-manager of the fishery at Nueltin Lake who had later run the trading post at Windy River. This latter post had now been finally abandoned, and the manager had left the service of the trading and fishing company to revert to his original profession as an independent trapper. He and his companion brought no trade goods to Otter Lake, but they did bring a woman of the Ihalmiut, called Ootnuyuk, who had borne three children to one of the white men.

Despite Ootnuyuk's presence and her assurance that the white men meant no harm, Owliktuk was deeply disturbed by these intruders. While he preserved courteous relations with them, he kept his group at a distance. He soon concluded that his people must abandon Otter Lake and find a safer sanctuary as soon as travel conditions and food resources made this possible.

In March, Owliktuk and Halo made a trip to Padlei Post bringing with them a number of fox furs which they traded for ammunition. This visit involved a calculated risk, for Owliktuk realized that it would undoubtedly result in news of his presence in the area reaching the police. Nevertheless, it was vital that he and his people have ammunition before they set out to the west, for he envisaged a period of many months during which there would be no further contact with the whites and no way to obtain supplies from them.

Convinced as he now was that the only hope of survival lay in isolating himself from the activities of the white men, he was confronted by an insoluble dilemma, for he knew that the Ihalmiut could no longer exist without access to certain of the white man's goods.

He did what he could to balance these two conflicting factors. As soon as he returned from Padlei, his people struck their camps and vanished toward the west.

Through the April days when the sun began to melt the

snows a little in daytime, and the frosts hardened them again at night, Owliktuk's people walked westward into the great plains in search of a place where they could be at peace. Their journey took them near the Little Lakes and here they encountered Yaha who had walked to the Little Lakes to pick up a cache of equipment which he had abandoned there before the transportation to Nueltin.

Yaha was delighted to find his friends, for neither he nor they had known if the others had survived. He told Owliktuk of the Hicks Lake site, and Owliktuk concluded that this would be at least as safe a sanctuary as any other, and so he led his group northward, to be followed a few days later by Ohoto and Yaha.

Meanwhile, the abysmal failure of the Nueltin fishery plan had not gone entirely unnoticed in the outside world. As early as November of 1950 rumors that all was not well seem to have reached official ears, and on December 11, a chartered plane was dispatched to fly to the interior from Churchill and investigate. It carried a policeman, a federal government official, and one of the directors of the now defunct fishing company. The plane visited Windy Cabin and Ennadai, where the official heard that other Eskimos were living to the north somewhere near Hicks Lake. No one knew, apparently, that almost a third of the band was then far to the east at Otter Lake.

The report submitted by the official was, in general, a cheerful one. He reported that the people had lots of fish, and that they seemed perfectly happy and contented. He also had something to say about the failure of the fishery plan, but he was careful to ensure that no shadow of blame should be cast on any of those who had been responsible for it.

By spring of 1951 the shattered fragments of the Ihalmiut had drawn together once again within the boundaries of their remembered lands. To the north, at Hicks Lake, Owliktuk's group had been reunited and now embraced the families of Miki, Yaha, Ohoto, Ootek and Halo. Near Ennadai, Pommela's reconstituted group was living at the Little Lakes, for their fear of another transportation was outbalanced by their increasing dependency upon the radio station, which they visited at frequent intervals. Hekwaw was living at the station itself with Belikari, his remaining son; for the old hunter was very ill that spring and he could not travel even to join his friends to the northward.

Thus, to the superficial, and official, eye, it must have seemed that all was well again in the interior plains, and that the whole shameful episode of the Nueltin fiasco could now be safely buried and forgotten.

8

The Rusting Rifles

By the spring of 1951 the R.C.M.P. had evidently begun to feel that administration of the Ihalmiut was becoming too great a burden. The Churchill detachment had its hands full with local obligations, and the distance between Churchill and Ennadai made it awkward to maintain even a semblance of supervision of the inland Eskimos. The suggestion was therefore made that the Army personnel at Ennadai should be given administrative charge over the Ihalmiut.

The Department of Resources and Development and the Northwest Territories Council (they were really almost one and the same thing) appear to have agreed to this proposal without hesitation, for it suggested an easy and convenient way of disposing of the minor problems of what to do with, and about, the Ihalmiut.

In 1951 the Ihalmiut represented only a very small aspect of a much greater problem, for as everyone connected with the north was by then becoming uncomfortably, if belatedly, aware, the entire economic basis for Eskimo existence throughout the Canadian arctic was disintegrating with frightening rapidity.

The second catastrophic collapse in fur prices, which had brought the average value of a white fox pelt down from about $40 to as low as $3.50, had seriously affected the trading companies—so much so that they were already preparing for the day when their arctic operations would no longer depend primarily upon the fur trade. Many of their posts in Eskimo territory were already running at a loss—a situation which no commercial organization could tolerate for long.

Meanwhile the government's expenditures for Eskimo relief were rising sharply, though the total amount involved still remained a bagatelle compared with other expenditures such as those involved in the caribou study, which had already cost more than a quarter of a million dollars. This survey had at least served to show that the caribou herds appeared to be inevitably headed for extinction—taking with them those Indians and Eskimos who depended on the deer for their survival.

Even the Commissioner of the R.C.M.P seemed to have been aware of the general situation, for in his annual report for the year 1950 he wrote as follows:

"The necessity for relief of destitution amongst the Eskimos has been increasing in the past few years on account of the scarcity of game mammals in some districts, including sea mammals, and the scarcity of fur and low prices [for fur] . . . it is believed that the economic situation amongst the Eskimos is bound to deteriorate from year to year."

This was a masterful understatement. By 1951, Eskimos throughout the Canadian arctic were already dying of malnutrition and its attendant diseases at an unprecedented rate. In those few areas where the incidence of tuberculosis was known with any certainty, as many as 48 per cent of the population were afflicted. Outright starvation was known to have killed at least 120 Eskimos between January of 1950 and the middle of the following year. Except for some Eskimos in the Mackenzie delta who were able to trap muskrat, the average income of most Eskimo families had shrunk to a cash value of less than fifty dollars a year—a sum which had a purchasing power in northern trading posts equivalent to that of about twenty dollars in southern Canada.

This was a stiuation which we had deliberately created by our destruction of the aboriginal Eskimo way of life in favor of the white-fox trapping economy, and which we had intensified by discouraging the Eskimos from turning in any direction other than toward the trapping of foxes, in their search for a substitute way of life. We, and not the Eskimos, were responsible for the decimation of the food resources—the caribou, walrus and even the seals—for we had put the means for massive destruction into the hands of the Innuit, and far from attempting to show the people how to use their new killing power wisely, we had encouraged the wholesale slaughter of game animals.

There were no two ways about it. The hideous dilemma in which the Eskimos found themselves in 1951 was the direct result of the interference and intrusion of primarily selfish white interests into the arctic.

Despite this obvious fact, and despite the full knowledge of it possessed by the officials of the Northwest Territories administration, no steps were being taken in 1951 to enable the Eskimos to escape their obvious fate. It does not seem to have occurred to the men whom we had elected, hired, or appointed, to deal with Eskimo affairs, that the Innuit deserved any better fate at our hands than would semi-domesticated animals which had outlived their usefulness. There never had been any real policy directed at assisting the Eskimos to help themselves, and 1951 evidently did not seem to be a suitable time to formulate such a policy. Instead, the responsible authorities turned blind eyes upon the north and sought for an expedient way to avoid the entire problem.

They found it by a facile reversal of the principle which had been enunciated on their behalf by the police—that at all costs (even if it killed them) the Eskimos must be prevented from becoming dependent on handouts and relief.

The official solution to the problem of Eskimo survival now became the dole. Family Allowance payments and outright relief became the chosen instruments for the resuscitation of a stricken people.

On April 1, 1951, an R.C.M.P. patrol plane arrived at Ennadai carrying the sergeant in command of the Churchill detachment. The sergeant had not come to see the Ihalmiut. The purpose of his visit was to make arrangements with the soldiers to act as the distributors of Family Allowance and relief supplies and in effect to become the guardians and supervisors of the local Eskimos.

111

The soldiers were not pleased; but they had no choice in the matter, for arrangements had already been concluded between the Department of Resources and Development and military headquarters in Ottawa. Unwillingly the handful of Signallers now found themselves the arbiters of the Ihalmiuts' fate.

Their discontent did not stem from any lack of desire to assist the Eskimos, but from the honest realization that they were completely untrained and unprepared for such a job. As one of them wrote: "Most of us were signals technicians hailing from all over Canada. We would get moved from station to station at frequent intervals, and wherever we happened to be our main job was *inside* the radio shack, so we never got to know much about conditions outside. Most of our fellows knew no more about Eskimos than what we could pick up from casual meetings when they drifted in to one of our stations. Sure, we would have liked to have been grand-daddies to them, because they were a likeable people and in a tough spot. But what did we know about their problems?"

That was a frank and fair appraisal. The good will was there, but good will alone could not provide the required insight into the problems the People faced—and with which the Eskimos themselves were unable to cope. The situation at Ennadai was doomed to become a case of the blind leading the blind, and the results were inevitable.

In the event, the soldiers had few duties in their new role that spring and summer. Until an R.C.M.P flight brought in a load of Family Allowance supplies on July 30, they had nothing to give the Ihalmiut. Owliktuk's band, still wary, remained at Hicks Lake where (with the help of the ammunition they had obtained at Padlei) they had been able to kill a few of the late-spring deer so that they had some meat on hand that summer.

Oddly enough, it was the small group which lingered near the white men that suffered most, for they had no ammunition, and there was none for them at the station. Eventually Onekwaw and Alekahaw were forced to take their families back to the Little Hills, where the fishing was better than at Ennadai.

When the policeman arrived on July 30, he saw only Hekwaw and Belikari. Hekwaw was being treated for his sickness by the soldiers, and Belikari was repaying the white men by assisting them in the general chores about the place. The policeman interviewed these two and then departed for

Churchill where he reported that all was well with the Ihalmiut.

Two weeks later the land was visited by another white man, and what he saw and reported was in direct contradiction to the optimism of the policeman.

The stranger was M. J. P. Michea, an anthropologist from the Centre National de la Recherche Scientifique, in Paris. Michea had previously spent five seasons with various Eskimo groups and was a responsible and accurate observer. In 1951, when he determined to visit the Ihalmiut, he went first to Ottawa where the Northwest Territories administration told him that the people he sought were still at Windy River. In Churchill he was told the same thing by the R.C.M.P. Acting on this erroneous information he chartered an aircraft and flew to Windy Cabin.

It is hard to know why Michea should have been misdirected, for unless the authorities kept their records in a worse state of confusion than is normal even in government organizations, they could not have helped knowing that the Ihalmiut had not been near Windy River since January. Conceivably someone may have felt that it would be as well if Michea did not encounter the People at all.

In any event Michea was duly deposited at Windy Cabin and the chartered plane departed, with orders to return and pick him up in three weeks' time.

Michea found no Eskimos, and no one else, at Windy River. Only a few tattered nets whitening on the nearby rocks remained as a last memorial to the ill-fated fishing enterprise, and it was clear to the visitor that there had been no Eskimos about for many months. However, he was not a man to be easily daunted. He had brought with him a collapsible kayak, and taking this upon his shoulders he set out to the northward across the plains, intent on finding Eskimos if there were any to be found.

Without a guide, without even a map, he walked sixty miles, ferrying himself across rivers and lakes as he encountered them, and eventually fate smiled upon his stubborn search. He came at last to the shores of Halo Lake and in the distance he saw the squat conical silhouettes of two small tents.

The tents belonged to Onekwaw and Alekahaw and their families, and according to Michea these people were living in a state bordering on starvation. They had no reserve food of any kind, and they had barely been able to survive upon the fish they had been able to catch, supplemented by birds and small mammals. Michea was distressed by the low morale of these two families, and by the dependence which they placed upon the issue of supplies from the radio station. Only the fact that the station had no supplies for them during July had forced them to return to an approximation of their old life, but they had done so most reluctantly, and with no real initiative.

They told the visitor a good deal about the fishing enterprise at Nueltin, and they were able to give him a list of the surviving people, including those who were living near Hicks Lake. The total came to forty-two: twelve women, eight men and twenty-two children of all ages.

Michea could not stay with them long, for he had insufficient food. Reluctantly he said good-by to this miserable little group of human beings who seemed so utterly alone and isolated in the vastness of the land, retraced his steps to Windy River. In due course he reached Ottawa again, and there he submitted a report of what he had seen. In a letter written in November of 1951 he concluded his description of the Ihalmiut situation with the remark that he was very uneasy as to what would happen to the People during the winter of 1951–1952.

No other white man seems to have shared his unease; but the Ihalmiut did.

Shortly after Michea's departure the two families from Halo Lake returned to Ennadai, where Pommela joined them, and they all settled down to spend the winter within sight of the radio station. The cold months were approaching, the months of darkness and the months of hunger; and these three families had determined that they would never again attempt to face those months without the bounty of the white men at their backs.

At Hicks Lake there were also people who looked to the approaching winter with a deep foreboding, and who were prepared to abandon their freedom and to take their chances at the radio station. Owliktuk argued against this, pointing out that the Ennadai station was a poor place to intercept the migrating herds, and that any who went there to live would forfeit their chances to lay in enough meat to last till spring. He reminded the waverers of what had happened to them the previous spring, and he was able to balance their fear of a hungry winter against the possibility of another transportation. Eventually it was agreed that Halo and Ootek alone should travel south to the station and there attempt to obtain

114

enough ammunition for all five families at Hicks Lake. Meanwhile, the rest of the men would make a hunt of the late-summer deer using kayaks and spears at the water crossings.

Halo and Ootek reached Ennadai in the first days of September. They found that the station had been stocked with goods intended for the Eskimos—with new tents, flour, lard, oatmeal and tea. But they also found that *no ammunition whatsoever* was available.

This was a tremendous blow. Halo and Ootek were unable to make up their minds what to do, but eventually they decided to wait at the station through two precious weeks in the hope that an aircraft might answer the urgent radio requests of the soldiers, and bring in the vitally needed ammunition. By mid-September, when the first migrating deer had begun to pass Ennadai bound southward, and no aircraft had appeared, Halo and Ootek realized that it was now too late to make a hunt at Hicks Lake, even if the shells arrived at once. Reluctantly they turned northward, empty-handed, and carrying with them only the assurance that the winter which was already almost upon them once again bore the shape of nemesis.

At Hicks Lake the last pathetic remnants of the true People of the Deer faced the approaching winter together, as their own masters still, but with empty rifles and with the knowledge that they were almost helpless to defend themselves against approaching famine.

They did what they could with two kayaks which they built, but these little boats had been covered with skins reclaimed from old sleeping robes (for it had been impossible to obtain any new late-summer hides). The reclaimed skins were thin and rotten, and the kayaks were dangerously unseaworthy. Nevertheless, they offered the sole hope of survival for the five families in Owliktuk's group.

With Ootek and Halo away, the onus for the spear hunting at the water crossings devolved on Owliktuk, Yaha and Miki. They were assisted by the elder boys, although none of these had ever previously taken part in the ancient spear hunts of their ancestors. Two of these boys, Mounik—who was now seventeen and a man to all intents and purposes—and sixteen-year-old Iktoluka, the orphaned son of Katelo, took to the kayak hunts with enthusiasm. Iktoluka in particular was passionately enamored of the business, and whenever a kayak was not in use he would claim it and paddle away on a hunt of his own.

During the last days of August and the early weeks of September these hunts were distressingly unproductive. There did not seem to be any large herds passing south, and the small groups of deer which were to be seen here and there were wary and elusive. Had they been armed with rifles, the hunters could probably have procured a fair number of these scattered animals, but the whole technique of successful kayak spearing demands heavy concentrations of the deer so that, when they take to the water, their own numbers will prevent them from dispersing and escaping from the attacking kayaks. There had been no such concentrations up to the day in mid-month when Iktoluka took one of the cranky craft and paddled six miles westward to a narrows between two small lakes which lay athwart the traditional caribou migration routes.

What follows is a reconstruction of the probable events of this fateful voyage.

It was a brilliant September day, with the rolling plains flamboyantly beautiful under the orange flames of the dwarf willow leaves which had already been frost-turned to their autumnal colors. Immeasurably high in the pallid sunshine a raven or two hung like flecks of wind-swirled soot—and the presence of the great black birds was a good omen, for Iktoluka knew that the ravens are the outriders of the migrating herds of deer.

When the boy reached the narrows, he carefully drew his leaking kayak to the shore under the concealing loom of a mass of frost-riven rocks. Gingerly he squeezed out of the tiny cockpit and, climbing the black rocks, he found a sunny niche where he could squat and watch the white horizon to the north.

All that day he waited, and he saw nothing living except the ravens and flocks of summer birds that drifted past him to the south. Then, as dusk came near, and the sun filled the western sky with a great gout of color, his quick eyes saw at last what they had been seeking all that day. Atop a distant ridge, Iktoluka beheld the branching forest of a myriad antlers, and he knew that a great herd was bearing down upon him.

In an instant he regained the kayak. He drew the spear from its skin scabbard on the deck, and tested the edge of the polished steel point against his lips. And then he waited, frozen into tense immobility, until the herds should suddenly appear upon the farther shore.

It must have been a marvelously exciting moment when

116

the wind brought a faint clatter of hoofs on rocks to his aching ears, and when suddenly the ridge upon the other shore grew horns, than vanished under the flood of beasts that topped it and swept down toward the water's edge.

This was a truly great herd, of a kind that was not often seen in the years when Iktoluka approached his manhood. The deer were almost all fat bucks. There was meat enough within the hunter's reach to feed not only the family of Yaha—his adopted father—but all of the People in the Hicks Lake camp for many months. Iktoluka must have felt his heart swell with the knowledge that he, a boy in years, an orphan and alone, was to have this chance to do so much—to prove so much—to be a man in truth.

He waited as the leaders of the herd came to the shore and milled irresolutely, until the pressure of the beasts behind became irresistible, and they were forced into the cold, clear water.

He waited motionless until half the herd had plunged into the narrows; each great beast floating high with its antlered head thrown back, and striking strongly for the opposite shore.

Then Iktoluka came to life. His double-paddle dipped and flashed and the kayak shot out upon the broken surface of the water with the speed and lightness of a waterfowl.

The stream of caribou did not break as the kayak struck against its flank. There was no room for the individual animals to swing away, and in the instant that the fragile craft spun broadside to the herd Iktoluka's spear arm rose and fell. He felt the iron bite into the back of a fat buck. A quick twist, and a withdrawal, and then his arm ran red with blood as it was raised to thrust again, and yet again. Maneuvering his kayak with his left hand, he sent it twisting and turning amongst the now panic-stricken beasts while his spear glittered dully in the setting sun.

Exalted beyond any conscious thoughts, or beyond any experience that he had ever known, the boy had become one with his forebears.

It was Yaha who found the kayak two days later, where it had drifted up against the shore. One of the old skins with which it had been covered had burst like a wet paper bag, and it had filled and overturned. Yaha searched all of one day, but Iktoluka was never seen again.

Yaha and Miki recovered more than a score of deer which the boy had killed, and these they carefully preserved beneath rock piles near the shore. Iktoluka's had been the most successful hunt that the Ihalmiut were destined to make that fall, for in the succeeding weeks the best efforts of the men, using the remaining kayak, only accounted for a few more caribou. There were far too few to form a barricade against the winter famine which would come.

With the return of Halo and Ootek to Hicks Lake it became obvious to all that they could not remain in the present camps and still hope to see the spring again. Yet such was the respect in which Owliktuk was held, and such was the general distrust of the white men, that no one chose to leave the group and travel south until the time came when there would be no other choice.

Meanwhile, all through September and the first half of October, the soldiers who had become the official guardians of the Ihalmiut had been sending increasingly urgent radiograms to Churchill asking for ammunition. But the R.C.M.P. aircraft must have been very busy on other duties, for no time could be spared for a flight to Ennadai. It was not until October 14, when a Dakota aircraft of the R.C.A.F. was dispatched to air-drop a side of beef to the soldiers, that an opportunity was found to deliver some ammunition for the Eskimos. The delivery came far too late. By mid-October most of the deer had vanished from the land.

In November, as the lakes froze deep and the snow wraiths danced on the wind-swept ridges, a small two-seater aircraft on skis came to Ennadai with something for the Eskimos. It brought the promise of salvation and of eternal life to fill men's stomachs and to warm their flesh. The plane was piloted by the American evangelist who had visited the people at Nueltin the previous summer. The new arrival was coldly received at the Army station, but undeterred he flew off to visit the camps at Hicks Lake. To his chagrin he found that the already hungry members of Owliktuk's band did not seem overly interested in his proffered gifts. They were, in those bleak November days, more practically concerned with the salvation of their own flesh than with obtaining the approbation of the blood-and-thunder God of the evangelist. The little plane departed somewhat hurriedly for the more cheerful climes from which it had made its sally into the winter plains.

At Hicks Lake the cold grew more and more intense. Very soon Iktoluka's deer were eaten, and the deer which had been killed by the men were eaten too. Before the end of the month Owliktuk acknowledged that he was beaten. He and his little band gave up the hopeless struggle. They abandoned their last free camps, and began to straggle south toward the radio station.

It was no easy journey, for they had only a few dogs left, and both they and the dogs were already weakened by the hungry weeks. Men and women hauled the sleds, while the younger children rode, and the older children followed in the narrow tracks. It was a slow and miserable progress, made bitter for Owliktuk by the knowledge that, after all, there was no escape for him or for his people; that, in the end, they were still ensnared as certainly as if they had remained in exile at Nueltin Lake. For a year and a half he had struggled mightily to regain a measure of the freedom that had once belonged to the Ihalmiut, and it had been a useless struggle. Now he traveled, with the others, to beg for food from the hands of the white men, the *kablunait*—without whose help neither he nor any of his people could continue to survive.

It was a long, sad march, and there was tragedy near the end of it. They were only a day out from Ennadai when a full blizzard struck the attenuated line of people and sleds, enveloping them suddenly in swirling vortices of snow. The ground drift lifted higher than their heads and each of the fugitives became isolated in his own white universe. They did not halt, for they were afraid to stop in the open without shelter, and they were already so hungry that they did not have the strength to pitch a proper camp in the teeth of the storm. They plodded on, barely moving now, and each alone.

Halo's eight-year-old son Noahak was following his father's sled—the last in line—when the blizzard struck. He was not missed for a long time. When at last Halo understood that the boy had vanished, he turned back and fought his way into the maelstrom of wind and snow until his legs buckled under him; but he never found his son. Noahak had gone down before the weight of wind, and his own weakness, and the snows had buried him.

Noahak's death was to be the last overt sacrifice to the land which had once nurtured its People, and which had now become their nemesis. It was to be the last such death for many years; for from this time until almost the end of their tale the Ihalmiut ceased to be a part of their land, ceased to be the People of the Deer, and became, in common with so many thousands of Eskimos scattered across all of the Canadian arctic, the People of the Dole.

The last of the Ihalmiut reached Ennadai on the 27th day of November; the soldiers saw that they were starving and at once issued them with food. The five families built their shelters within sight of the station, and close to those of Onekwaw, Alekahaw, Hekwaw and Pommela, so that for the first time in many months the People were again united. They were united all that winter: united in passive and indifferent acceptance of the weekly dole which kept them living—barely. One and all they had at last become part of the same pattern.

This was no longer emergency relief they were receiving, this was the beginning of a continuing charity—a stone-cold and bitter charity, which was the easy solution to the problem of what to do with a race of men who had been deprived of their way of life, and who could find no other.

It was during the long winter of 1951–1952 that something of the true nature of their situation began to be borne in upon the minds of men like Ootek, Owliktuk, Yaha and Halo. They began to understand that the old pattern established by the traders had now been permanently supplanted by another. The deer were gone now, and the fox no longer mattered. All that men could do to save themselves was to pitch their camps in the shadows of the white men's houses, and hold out their hands for food.

Ayoranamut! There was no help for it.

There was no other choice: yet no man of the Ihalmiut conceived of the magnitude of the price that he would have to pay in order to endure a precarious handhold on a continuing existence.

There had been other men, in other times and other places, who could have told them what it costs to take the dole.

9
People of the Dole

The ability to make capital out of the misfortunes of others had always been a major element in Pommela's character. As the fabric of the Ihalmiuts' lives grew more tenuous through the years, he himself had grown stronger, fattening on their tribulations, and expanding his domination over them as their increasing uncertainty weakened their ability to stand against him. When fate turned upon him in the matter of the abandoned boy Alektaiuwa, and in the death of his wife Ikok, this was a double blow which would perhaps have permanently shattered the pretensions, and stilled the strivings, of a lesser man; but Pommela seemed able to throw off the effects of this dual disaster with an energy and resilience which belied his age, and which must have been almost unique amongst his People.

Even before the winter of 1951 began he had recouped much of his lost power and prestige. When, in the autumn of that year, the Signals staff was changed and a new group of white men, who did not know him or his reputation, took over the Ennadai station, Pommela made the most of the opportunity and ingratiated himself with the newcomers to such good effect that they soon came to accept him as the "chief" of the local Eskimos, and to work through him in their dealings with the People. Even before this event, he had re-established his hold over his one-time sycophants Aleka-haw and Onekwaw, and to this little group under his personal control he was able to add Hekwaw and Belikari, for the old hunter now no longer cared what happened to him, and was content to sit in silence in his tent and dream of the days when he had been a man amongst men.

When Owliktuk's band came straggling into Ennadai in November, starving, and subservient in their need for help, Pommela thrust himself into the position of intermediary between them and the soldiers, and thus, for a time, he was able to exercise effective authority over the whole of the surviving People. This was a temporary suzerainty, which only lasted until Owliktuk's people had recovered their strength, and their desire and ability to resist the shaman. Nevertheless, it must have seemed to Pommela that, with luck and cunning, he could at long last hope to achieve the total domination over the Ihalmiut for which he had hungered all his life.

That it would be a hollow victory to become the over-lord of a people who had been reduced to an ineffectual handful of despairing individuals seems to have had but little bearing on the strange and contorted design which had long been the most important motivation for Pommela's whole existence. Yet, from our viewpoint, there is a terrible pathos in this striving of an aged man to direct his final years to the achievement of a goal whose very substance had now become nearly as ephemeral as the snow ghosts which danced upon the wind-swept plains.

Although the summer of 1951 had seen his grip upon the Ihalmiut partially restored, Pommela still lacked one vital adjunct before he could hope for full success in his design. He lacked a family of his own. For almost two years there had been no woman in his tent, and consequently he had been forced into a humiliating dependency upon the wives of

Onekwaw and Alekahaw for the essential services which a man cannot provide for himself without much loss of face. This, in itself, was intolerable to him; but there was still another consideration, for no Eskimo achieves, or can maintain, full stature in the eyes of his fellows unless he heads a family, and preferably a large and vigorous one. A man's dignity requires such a circle of intimate dependents, since the ability to provide for many mouths has always been a major yardstick against which an Eskimo hunter's worth is measured.

Pommela was fully aware of these things, but there was no woman for him in the Ihalmiut band. He pondered long upon this problem, until in December of that year he took the only course open to him and set out to find a wife elsewhere.

He was then sixty-six years of age, and ancient by the standards of that land. Yet such was his resolution and his compulsion that he set out alone, in midwinter, with almost no dog feed on his sled, to travel the two-hundred-mile route to Padlei.

He reached Padlei Post just before Christmas time, gaunt and hungry, but still vigorous. Having traded a few fox skins for food and tobacco, he then spent two weeks visiting the outlying Padliermiut camps, talking little, but looking hard. And eventually he found what he was after, in the person of the woman named Ootnuyuk.

At thirty, Ootnuyuk still retained something of the beauty which had once made her famous, and which—in combination with her competency—had brought her a strange and complex history. The daughter of that famous man Igluguarduak, she had been born a Padliermio, at Hicoliguak. In her childhood she had come south with her father to join the Ihalmiut near Ennadai, and there she reached womanhood. She remained there when her father journeyed north to die in solitude in his ancestral lands, and since she was a woman she became the ward and responsibility of her elder brother, Alekahaw.

When she was sixteen Alekahaw married her to a Padliermio hunter, and she went to live with her husband near Ameto Lake. It was a short-lived marriage, for a white trapper saw her, desired her, and took her for himself.

She lived with the white man for several years and bore him three daughters, but in the spring of 1951 this man left the country and sent Ootnuyuk back to rejoin the Padliermiut. There she met Oolie, an Ihalmio widower who had

123

taken part in the starvation trek to Otter Lake in 1947, and who had later emigrated to Padlei.

Oolie was in need of a wife, for women were scarce in the Padliermiut country too. He talked to Ootnuyuk, who was anxious to obtain a father for her children. She was agreeable to marriage, so Oolie sent a message to her brother Alekahaw, to the effect that he would give a new rifle, six dogs, and some tobacco in bride payment. This message was carried to Ennadai by Ootek who visited Padlei with Owliktuk in the early spring of 1951.

But 1951 was no year for an inland Eskimo to pay his debts. The foxes were scarce and the famine which swept the country made it almost impossible for Oolie to keep his new family alive, let alone pay off a bride price. These were facts of which Pommela was fully aware when he returned alone to Ennadai in January of 1952. He had said nothing of his intention to Ootnuyuk, nor to anyone at Padlei; but now he called Alekahaw to him, reminded the younger man that his sister's bride price had not been paid, and demanded that Ootnuyuk be given to him. Whether Alekahaw had any right to do so did not matter—he agreed.

Meanwhile, Owliktuk and the families who followed him were finding that life at Ennadai was becoming more and more unpalatable. Although they were receiving enough food to keep them living—mainly flour and lard—they were being treated with a restraint which made it obvious that the soldiers considered the extra tasks of administering relief and Family Allowance to be a considerable nuisance. The Eskimos were reaping first fruits from their attachment to the dole, for no matter how sympathetic the giver of charity may be initially, he eventually comes to feel a growing contempt for the recipient. It was so at Ennadai, and Owliktuk was quick to sense the change in mood and it served only to make him more bitterly aware of his own helplessness. Now it was he and his People, and not the intruding white men, who were the incompetents, unable to survive without assistance. The knowledge burned within him.

Things were made no easier by Pommela's assumption of the role of intermediary, and by the fact that much of the relief supplies which were distributed with his assistance inevitably stuck to his hands and got no farther.

By late January the situation had become intolerable and so one day Owliktuk struck his camp and moved away. The remainder of his group was torn between a desire to follow him and the fear that, if they did, they would only starve the

124

sooner. Eventually Ootek took up Owliktuk's trail and prevailed upon his friend to pitch his tent near the Little Lakes, where the rest of the People would join him, and where they would still be close enough to the station to be able to obtain their ration issues.

The departure of Owliktuk's band took some of the savor out of Pommela's life, and after a few weeks he ordered his followers to pack up and move with him to the Little Lakes. Pommela had decided to dispatch Alekahaw to Padlei in early March to fetch Ootnuyuk, and he intended that the arrival of his new wife should be witnessed by all of the Ihalmiut.

Alekahaw duly did as he was bidden, and drove Pommela's team to Padlei, ostensibly to visit his sister and her husband. It could not have been a pleasant meeting for any of them. Ootnuyuk was happy with Oolie, and he with her; but the influence and reputation of Pommela was widely known and feared even amongst the Padliermiut, and when Alekahaw reluctantly explained why he had come, Oolie was unable to muster even a show of resistance. He knew that he was in the wrong about the bride price, and he also knew that Pommela was believed to have killed many men, even from a great distance, by his spirit power. So, in the end, Ootnuyuk and her three daughters joined Alekahaw on the long road back to the Little Lakes.

The effect of their arrival on Pommela's ego can hardly be overestimated. At one stroke he had not only acquired a new, young and desirable wife who had slept with a white man for many years and knew all the *kablunait*'s intimate secrets, but he had acquired a family as well. It was a tremendous coup, and one made even more effective when Pommela bluntly demanded that his adopted sons Kaiyai and Alektaiuwa, who had taken refuge with Yaha during and after the Nueltin debacle, be returned to him. Yaha dared not refuse this demand and so by the early spring of 1952 Pommela was the master of a wife, three daughters, and of the three boys Alektaiuwa, Angataiuk and Kaiyai.

So it came to pass that once again the Ihalmiut lived at their old camp sites by the Little Lakes. They remained here for the rest of the winter; but it was hardly an improvement over Ennadai. There was literally nothing to do but sit in their snow-banked tents and wait for the release of spring. Most of the men had no dogs, or too few to enable them to engage in any serious attempt at trapping, even had there

125

been any incentive—and there was none. Once every week or so the men would walk to Ennadai to receive their handouts; but they were not welcomed any more, except on those rare occasions when their services were required. Twice during April they were ordered to the station to serve as stevedores in the unloading of aircraft; once for the soldiers, and once for a party of government geologists who intended to use Ennadai as a base for an aerial survey of the mineral resources of the inland plains. The Ihalmiut men were employed briefly to do the heavy cargo-handling for this project, which was designed to open up their ancestral land and its potential riches for exploitation by the intruders.

In humping freight the Eskimos were presumably fulfilling the intentions of a spokesman of the Northwest Territories Council who had just announced to the Canadian public that "Wherever possible the Eskimos will be made full sharing partners in the development of the arctic, and will benefit fully from the development of our natural resources."

For the rest, 1952 was a year of deepening apathy for the Ihalmiut. They remained at the Little Lakes, and at intervals the men appeared at the radio station to receive their Family Allowance issues. A deadly stupor seemed to have settled over most of them. They did not live any more, they simply waited out the endless days.

The children too were at a loss. Imitative by nature, and by training, they found little enough to imitate about these lethargic camps. They had no incentive to imitate the hunters and become hunters themselves, for the hunt was ceasing to have much meaning. Even their games were being metamorphosed into queer combinations of the new and imperfectly understood experiences of the present and the half-forgotten memories of the past. The boys made crude models of aircraft instead of model dog sleds, but having made these toys they could not give them any meaning in terms of their own lives.

Even the women were no longer dedicated to their special tasks—the feeding and clothing of their families. The casual and listless hunting expeditions of the men yielded little meat and very few good hides for clothing; and in any event there seemed to be an inexhaustible supply of castoff white men's clothing to be had for the asking at the Army station. Now the people who only a few years earlier had dressed in well-cut, neatly turned out *attigi, holiktuk,* and other deerskin clothing, wore ragged and filthy denim trousers, raveled sweaters, and tattered jacket coats.

The pilot of an aircraft which visited Ennadai late in the summer of 1952 described the Eskimos he saw as "a sleazy, stinking bunch of bums, wandering about like so many lost curs." He was not an unfeeling man, and at heart he was sorry for the people. His problem was that he could not repress the very human urge to disassociate himself, and the way of living which he represented, from a group of beings who were a frightful reproach to him and all of us.

This disintegration did not of course all come about within a single year—but it was in 1952 that the Ihalmiut as a group reached the next-to-bottom level of the abyss that we had dug for them.

The wellsprings of desire were drying up. There was no reason any more to seek accomplishment.

Yet there were still men amongst the People who blindly strove to find an avenue of hope, and of escape.

There was Ohoto, who still believed with a kind of insensate stubbornness that he might yet become a white man and enter a new world. He was impervious to the inevitable and constant rebuffs that his attempts to cross the barrier elicited from the whites with whom he came in contact. He simply would not face the knowledge that there would be no acceptance of him in his new guise by those he sought to emulate. To them he remained a rather pathetic, but at the same time rather obnoxious, native, who clearly did not know his place. When his importunities became too much to bear, they suppressed his pitiful endeavors with a brutality of which they were totally unconscious.

And there was Ootek who, as the years passed, seemed to become less a tangible human entity, and more of a thin ghost. His great eyes stared into places that no other man could penetrate, as he searched the lonely darkness where unknown spirits dwelt, for understanding of the inexplicable design of which he was a part. For hours, and sometimes for days, he spoke to no one, not even to the patient cripple, Howmik, who was his wife; but sat in silence, lost in time—tormented by his inability to bring some comprehension out of the groping chaos of his thoughts.

There was Owliktuk, too. His was perhaps the greatest struggle, for he alone of all the People seems to have had the ability to see clearly the certain shape of the future which awaited himself and them. He seems to have known, even then, that there was no way out for him; but he also seems to have been supported and impelled to struggle by a belief that his sons and daughters need not share the parents' fate. He and his wife Nutaralik, almost alone of the People, were resolute in their determination to preserve some of the substance of their pride. Owliktuk still hunted, and hunted hard. He sometimes refused the Family Allowance issues, or gave them away. He provided his wife with meat and skins, and she in turn provided food and clothing for her children. Between the two of them they preserved at least an outward semblance of a life which was not yet utterly bereft of meaning. And this they did for their children's sake. Owliktuk believed that someday there would be a bridge across the gulf which separated the Innuit from the white men, but, unlike Ohoto, he knew that the bridge was not yet built.

What would Owliktuk's thought have been had he known that, in this year when the Ihalmiut had almost ceased to be, some twenty thousand Eskimos in a nearby land had crossed the bridge and had entered into a new world?

It was in 1952 that the Danes announced the penultimate step in the development of an Eskimo nation in Greenland. After long years of careful guidance, the Greenland Eskimos were taking over their own internal government and were almost ready to emerge as full-fledged citizens of the modern world. But Owliktuk knew nothing of this, nor did any other Canadian Eskimos. There were few Canadians of any race who gave much attention to the announcement from Denmark, although the event did not go entirely unremarked in Canada, for in July an editorial appeared in a Toronto newspaper, which said in part:

"What should strike thoughtful Canadians most forcefully is Denmark's determination to give a native population every possible political, social and economic advantage. . . . Canada has no such policy . . . are we to see a prosperous and advancing segment of Eskimo population flourishing just across our northern frontier while on our side we continue a policy of sentimental paternalism?"

No one rose to give an answer to that question.

The gentlemen of the Northwest Territories Council might have answered had they chosen—though their reply would have had to be an unqualified affirmative. Within the Council, the R.C.M.P. Commissioner was easily able to convince his hearers that the police were doing a magnificent job, and needed no assistance; while Mr. Louis Audette, who had been an appointed Council member since 1947, and who held the Oblate missionary order (which had given him much of his education) in high esteem, was equally convincing with his contention that the missionaries had the situation well in hand.

The old order still stood firm. In speech after speech, and statement after statement, the members of the Northwest Territories Council extolled the kindly virtues of the missionaries, the police and the traders, and appeared to evade any suggestion that the Eskimos of Canada were not living the best of lives in the best of all possible worlds.

Fortunately for all our consciences, it was still possible for us to ignore the realities of Eskimo existence; for no compilations of facts and statistics yet existed which could prove the Council wrong—there were only the jovial, if vague, assurances of the constituted authorities in the arctic that all was well. As for the Eskimos themselves—they had no voice.

What was happening at Ennadai in 1952 was happening also throughout the rest of the Canadian arctic. In the igloos and tents of most of Canada's eleven or twelve thousand Eskimos there was slow starvation, and a slow death of hope.

Meanwhile, across the Davis Strait things were not the same. Denmark, a small country, with only a fraction of Canada's wealth to work with—but with a standard of moral rectitude which Canada did not appear to possess—had poured its efforts and its money selflessly into a land from which it could never hope to draw a commensurate financial return; and it had done this because it felt a duty and an obligation toward a native race.

As far back as 1860 the Danes had eliminated illiteracy in Greenland, whereas in 1952 only a few score Canadian Eskimos were in any sense literate.

As far back as 1900 Denmark had begun to give a measure of self-government—a voice—to the Greenland peoples, and had taught them how to use that voice in their own interests. In 1952 the Canadian Eskimo still had no voice, but was restricted to the status of a mute dependent who was expected to give unquestioning obedience to the traders, the missionaries, and the police.

In the early days of Danish interest in Greenland, laws had been passed which effectively curbed purely selfish commercial penetration by white men, and the only trading posts which were allowed to operate were run by the government— often at a loss to the Danes, but with much gain to the Eskimos. Only one religious denomination had been allowed to proselytize (also under state control), so that there had been none of the internecine strife between opposing faiths which stigmatizes the history of Christianity in the Canadian arctic.

Indeed things had been done differently in Greenland, and it was now a far greater distance from the little villages on Greenland's coasts to the tent camps of the Ihalmiut than could be measured in mere miles. It was, in fact, the distance between a morally insensible, and apparently calculated, indifference towards the Eskimos on the part of one civilized nation, and the deliberate acceptance of full moral obligations with all their consequent and costly physical involvements, on the part of another such civilized nation.

In the summer of 1952, an unbiased observer was able to write as follows in a Canadian newspaper: "The Danes have pursued a policy to which those who object to the exploitation of native populations must extend endorsement. What they have done to date for Greenland has been almost exclusively on behalf of the Eskimo population, which has doubled in numbers within a generation and whose income per capita has also doubled."

In the spring of that same year the Canadian press recorded the results of a two-day conference on Eskimo affairs called by the Commissioner of the Northwest Territories, and attended by the Anglican Bishop of the Arctic, the Roman Catholic Bishop of Mackenzie District, the Commissioner of the R.C.M.P., the General Manager of the Hudson's Bay Company, and sundry civil servants.

"The conference was told that Eskimo relief had risen from $11,000 in 1945 to $115,000 in 1951 ... knowing that there is always Government aid to fall back on, the Eskimo in some parts of the north has lost a certain amount of his interest in hunting and fishing for a living ... reports indicated that the spread of tuberculosis was increasing seriously ... the conference was generally agreed that the present measures for the care and advancement of the Eskimos are sound [and] that the Eskimo should be encouraged to live off the land and follow his traditional way of life."

In the country of the Little Hills and in a hundred other places throughout the Canadian arctic, the Eskimos were to be encouraged to live off the land and to follow their traditional way of life. The incontrovertible facts that the land was rapidly becoming a land of death, and that the traditional Eskimo way of life was already dust and ashes, were not acceptable to the missionaries, the police, the traders and the administrators, for they were convinced that the present measures for the care and advancement of the Eskimos were sound. Nor can they be accused of dishonesty in this. They believed what they said; though as to why they chose to believe these things—they alone must answer.

When the summer of 1952 ended and the plains once more burned with an orange flame as the frosts swept over them, only a few of the Ihalmiut men went out to meet the south-bound deer. There were several reasons why they did not go. For one thing Pommela, whose lust for domination had by now become insatiable, seized the ammunition which had been issued both to the men of his group and to Yaha and Ohoto as well. He apparently had also hoped to intercept the share due to Owliktuk's band, but in this he had been frustrated for Owliktuk and Halo had gone early to the radio station, and had quietly but resolutely refused to leave until they obtained their quotas.

Perhaps Pommela had intended (once he had cornered all the shells) to dole them out again to those who came as supplicants—but having failed in his intention he seems to have determined to revenge himself at least upon those whom he controlled. At any rate he steadfastly refused to give away any of the ammunition he had amassed.

In the event it did not matter much. Apart from Halo and Owliktuk, no one was very anxious to go hunting anyway. In order to stand a chance of finding enough deer to ensure a decent hunt, the men knew they would have to travel to crossing places on the Kazan, two days' journey from Ennadai, and that they would perhaps have to stay away a month. This would mean missing at least one ration issue from the station—and they had become so habituated by this time to the regularity of the dole that few of them were anxious to leave a certain security for an extremely uncertain opportunity of killing caribou.

Thus it was that only two men visited the old killing places that autumn. They were Owliktuk and Halo, whose wives had given birth to the only two children born in the Ihalmiut camps that year. Both these men knew that a nursing mother cannot make good milk on a diet of flour and lard. So they went hunting, and they succeeded in killing enough deer between them to last their two families through the first part of the winter.

They might have saved themselves the trouble. When, in December, the ration issue from the station was considerably reduced, the Ihalmiut turned—as they had always done in ancient times—to the hunters who had meat. Owliktuk and Halo gave freely of their stocks, for it would have been unthinkable for either of them to refuse. In this respect, at least, things had not changed in the Ihalmiut way of living; for the automatic generosity of the successful hunter toward his less successful neighbors was too deeply ingrained to be easily destroyed.

The reduction in the Family Allowance issue had not been caused by a shortage of supplies at Ennadai, but seems to have resulted from a new ukase of the police to the effect that the Ihalmiut were now to be persuaded to take up active trapping once again. The plan envisaged by the authorities was that the Eskimos would trap, then turn the pelts over to the soldiers, who would in turn ship them out to the R.C.M.P. detachment at Churchill as opportunity allowed. The R.C.M.P. would subsequently sell the pelts and purchase those supplies which they felt were best for the Ihalmiut. Meanwhile, the police were authorized to hold back Family Allowance and relief in order to force the Eskimos to trap.

Apart from its flavor of coercion—something which was by no means unusual in the dealings of the arctic authorities with the Eskimos—the plan had merit. But like so many plans formulated by unthinking men at a distance from the problem it would not work in practice. In the first place the Ihalmiut had no dog feed and therefore could not trap far afield. In the second place, the very existence of a relief and allowance issue had ensured that they would all cluster close to the radio station, and therefore would all be forced to trap over much the same ground. Finally, men who lived day in day out on the flour pancakes known as bannocks had barely enough energy to stay alive, let alone walk great distances afield in winter weather in pursuit of foxes.

The outbreak of a distemper epidemic in late December and the consequent loss of most of the dogs ensured that the trapping efforts of the Ihalmiut would lead to no more than token results. Once more the People huddled in their shelters and hoped only to outwait the winter, and to be alive to see the return of spring.

By this time the soldiers were becoming alarmed by the lethargic depths into which most of the People had descended, and they notified the police that the Eskimos appeared to be increasingly unwilling to do anything to help themselves. The police responded by ordering that all the Ihalmiut should be gathered at the station on January 12, at which time a patrol would visit them and, presumably, breathe new vigor into them.

Docile, and dull-eyed, the people duly gathered at the station, but, though they waited a week, the patrol did not come. They were sent back to their camps, only to be recalled on February 2; but again the aircraft did not come, and once more they drifted apathetically back to their cold and hungry camps.

By this time they were obviously starving, and the soldiers arbitrarily increased the ration issue and again radioed to the police. It was not until the second week in March, however, that the patrol at last arrived. The aircraft carried additional relief rations; but the policemen were not able to stay long enough to see the Eskimos.

In May the cumulative effects of a winter of severe malnutrition made themselves felt, when an epidemic of pneumonia swept the camps. Within two weeks more than three-quarters of the people, of all ages, had been stricken. Had it not been for the prompt and vigorous action of the soldiers there would undoubtedly have been many deaths; but the new sergeant in charge acted with decision. He radioed military headquarters, and an R.C.A.F. Norseman flew in at once bringing sulfa drugs. Ten days later, in the middle of breakup, the plane returned, and, though unable to land, it air-dropped further drugs to the hard-working sergeant and his men. By the end of June the epidemic was at an end and there had been no deaths. It was a considerable personal victory for the Signals sergeant, but it was in reality only one more delaying action in a battle which was already lost.

During the summer, all of the people remained within easy reach of the Army station. They fished a little, but primarily so that they could barter fresh fish to the soldiers for tea and tobacco. Then one day they were all summoned to the station where a rather apologetic sergeant informed them that, on orders from Ottawa, they were to begin earning their keep by carving pipe bowls out of soapstone.

In Ottawa, at the same time, a spokesman for the administration had released a statement to the press to the effect that "A new program of economic endeavour for the Eskimos has recently been implemented and there are considerable hopes that within a very short time all the Eskimos will be gainfully employed."

There is a photograph extant which shows the beginnings of that new economic endeavor at Ennadai.

One bright September day, when the ravens hung high to mark the approach of the deer herds, Pommela, Hekwaw, Alekahaw and Onekwaw sat in a row upon the ground outside the radio shack. Each man had a knife and a piece of soapstone in his hands, and they were busily engaged in carving pipes.

They knew how to do it, for through innumerable generations they had made pipe bowls from soapstone after an oriental fashion which is still popular in Siberia. But the pipes they had once made had been for their own use and were a part of their lives. Now, most mysteriously, the white men had ordered them to manufacture pipes en masse. Who for and what for? No one knew. It did not matter. So they sat in the pale sunlight and worked slowly at their tasks, while beyond the most distant hills *tuktu*, the deer—the heart and spirit of the land—pursued their own inscrutable destiny unhindered.

10

Madness and Denial

While the struggles of the Ihalmiut against their common fate became progressively weaker and less effective, the personal struggle between Owliktuk and Pommela mounted in intensity. The conflict between these two had become almost the only emotional reality left in the People's lives, and they watched its development with a sick fascination.

Although he was now completely obsessed by, and engrossed in, what was to be his climactic effort to dominate the People, Pommela had still been unable to make any real impress upon the stubborn resistance of Owliktuk; and until Owliktuk was overwhelmed, those who followed him remained beyond Pommela's reach. For his part, Owliktuk could not completely free himself or his followers from the old shaman's influence, for he lacked Pommela's magical abilities and therefore could not meet his enemy on equal

135

terms. Although he had Ootek's support, this was not enough to enable him either to give battle or to break clean away.

It was an uneasy impasse, and from Pommela's point of view an insufferable one. But during the early months of 1953 the old man apparently devised a means of ending the stalemate.

In early April a frightening rumor began to spread amongst the People. It was said that the troubles of the Ihalmiut, and the miseries from which they suffered, stemmed from the presence in their midst of a particularly inimical devil hiding within a human body. The rumor gained strength with each passing day, for those who heard it were in no condition to resist the terrors of the supernatural, nor to look for rational explanations of their own pitiful condition.

Although the rumor undoubtedly originated with Pommela, there is some possibility that it may not have been entirely contrived. Perhaps it was so at first, but as it grew and took on form, Pommela may have come to believe in it himself. In any event he gave ample substance to it, as far as the rest of the Ihalmiut were concerned, by pronouncing that his guardian spirits had confirmed the presence of a devil in the camps. He waited a few days for this to do its work, and then he announced that he would hold a séance to unmask the evil one.

On a night in late April the entire adult population gathered, unwilling and yet directly driven, in Pommela's snow-block and canvas shelter. Most of the women, and many of the men, were in a state of near-hysteria before they arrived, and the mouthings and wild gesticulations of the shaman as he entered his trance did nothing to pacify their leaping fear. As silent as the rocks without, the people squatted in a compact mass that stank of panic while, by the dim flicker of a single candle, Pommela worked himself into a frenzy; to fall at last upon the snow floor where he lay writhing like a wounded beast, his eyes rolled up until only the discolored whites showed beneath his flickering lids.

His familiars began to come to him, and one by one they muttered and screamed unintelligible noises through the shaman's twisted lips. The tension mounted until the watchers, even Owliktuk among them, began to know the palsy of outright terror. For more than an hour the unseen spirits yammered and muttered in that confined space and when at last Pommela lay silent and to all appearances unconscious, there was not one of his audience who retained a grip upon reality.

Pommela recovered slowly from his trance, dragging out the long minutes while the people waited in intolerable suspense to know the verdict of his guardian spirits. But Pommela did not immediately give them what they waited for; instead he turned upon Ootek—the competing shaman in the enemy camp—and roughly demanded that the younger man interpret what the spirits had said.

It was a totally unexpected, and remarkably astute, move, and one with which Ootek was incapable of coping. How could *he* understand the words spoken by another man's guardian spirits? It was an unheard-of suggestion, yet in their present mood the people who waited rigidly for the evil in their midst to be identified would not consider this. Ootek must have realized that he was trapped in an impossible position and, had he been less honest, or less of a true priest, he might have given rein to his imagination and mumbled something which would offer an escape. But Ootek spoke no word. He sat in silence while Pommela turned to the others and incontinently derided his opponent. Then, while the impression of Ootek's failure remained strong, Pommela told the People what the spirit voices had said.

They had spoken grim words; words that appalled the listeners and filled them with a cold apprehension. For if Pommela was to be believed, his spirits had told him that the evil entity dwelt in one of his own adopted children, Ootnuyuk's daughter who was called Akagalik. Furthermore the spirits had also said that only the death of the little girl would banish the devil from her body, and its influence from the Ihalmiut camps.

Akagalik was then seven years of age. She was half white, for her father had been the trapper who abandoned Ootnuyuk and her children in the spring of 1951; but the only link which she now bore with her father's people was the nickname he had given her—he had called her Rosie. Rosie had been born clubfooted, and it was this deformity which had enabled Pommela's spirits to identify her as the repository of a devil.

There followed two nightmare weeks in the camps by the shores of the Little Lakes. Pommela insisted that the child must die and, furthermore, that it was the will of his familiars that she die by Ootek's hand. There was no overt resistance to his dicta, since reason had all but vanished from that unhappy place. Only a few individuals, with Owliktuk paramount amongst them, had kept a grip on sanity. The temporary effect of the séance upon Owliktuk had been abruptly dissi-

137

pated by Pommela's shocking announcement that a child must die. Yet not even Owliktuk dared openly resist Pommela in this matter, for the fear which the shaman had generated throughout the camp had by now become so real that it was almost tangible.

Ootek was shattered by events. The one sure thing to which he had clung desperately through the tragic years—his steadfast belief in the immutable infallibility of the unseen being who ruled his world—was now being strained to the breaking point; and if it broke, Ootek would perish. He knew that Pommela had tricked him, and he must therefore have guessed that there had been a falseness to the whole séance. Yet he had always believed that Pommela was a true mouth-piece of the spirits. He did not dare accept the possibility that the whole affair had been a travesty; but there was at least one thing of which he was quite certain—it would not be his hand which struck down Akagalik. And so one night in early May he vanished from the camps beside the Little Lakes.

With Ootek's flight, Pommela had achieved a partial victory, for the younger shaman was now completely discredited. Nevertheless, Ootek's disappearance posed a difficult problem. Pommela had said that the child must die, preferably at Ootek's hands, and he could not easily commute the sentence without grave risk of weakening the hold he had established on the People. He may also have been counting upon some kind of moral blackmail against Owliktuk's group if he had been able to force Ootek to commit murder. He was certainly wise enough to know that the child's death might be avenged by the police, and Pommela had no desire to taste the white man's vengeance. For a time after Ootek fled he seems to have tried to persuade Alekahaw to shoot the girl, but Alekahaw had no stomach for this kind of thing.

The execution could not be indefinitely postponed or Pommela's hegemony of fear would disintegrate. The old man was at last forced to compromise. He announced that, during a second visit from the spirits, he had been told that it would be enough to amputate the child's clubfoot, wherein the devil dwelt.

But Pommela had already delayed too long. Ootnuyuk had managed to free herself of the web of terror put upon her by her husband, and one day she took her three daughters and fled to Owliktuk's tent, where she sought sanctuary.

With Pommela's long-dreamed-of victory almost in his grip, the flight of Ootnuyuk now bade fair to undo all that he had accomplished and to leave Owliktuk stronger than before. The old man's rage at the new turn of events became so ominous that even Alekahaw began to avoid him, and passed a warning to Halo that Pommela was contemplating the murder of Owliktuk and all within his tent. This may only have been intended as a threat to force Owliktuk to send Ootnuyuk and the children back. Pommela could not openly demand their return, for this would have betrayed a weakness, and would have cost him much prestige. Or perhaps he really had become almost berserk enough to murder his opponent; and it may only have been the knowledge that his finger might not be the first to squeeze a trigger which deterred him.

He waited, closeted in his tent, and after three days Owliktuk still had not sent the woman and her children back to him. Pommela must have been aware by then that the frenetic passions he had fired were now rapidly cooling, and that more and more people were drifting back to sanity, and to Owliktuk's side.

Nevertheless he stayed sequestered in his tent and spoke to no one until a week had passed. By then the people of the camp had recovered from their frenzy, and life had begun again to move in its accustomed ways.

Then Pommela emerged. He came out at dusk one evening, and ordered poor, dull-witted Onekwaw to follow him. Behind a ridge which backed against Owliktuk's camp, he found Rosie Akagalik playing with some of Miki's children and he called her to him. Still with Onekwaw's uncomprehending help, he took the girl to a valley some three or four miles distant, and there he hacked her foot off with his knife.

It was an act of madness.

A wild-eyed and gibbering Onekwaw brought the news into the camps, and Yaha, Miki and Owliktuk accompanied him back to that place of blood and madness. They found the child mercifully unconscious, and they brought her home. Shocked, and uncertain what to do, they attempted to deal with her wound themselves, but when it began to fester they carried her to the Army station. An urgent radio message to Churchill soon brought a Norseman roaring to the scene, and a few hours later the mutilated girl was in hospital.

Although many of the details of the incident were recorded by the soldiers at Ennadai, it does not seem to have been investigated by the police or, if it was, no action seems to have resulted. Pommela went unscathed as far as our justice was concerned.

139

But there was justice for him in his own land. The shaman himself was never seen again, for he had vanished, leaving in his place only the restless hulk of an old man who was despised by all, and feared by none. Pommela, the man who had displayed the tenacity and the strength of twenty men in his fateful and ruthless pursuit of a useless and unattainable ambition, had ceased to be. Yet, because this was an Eskimo society, the living image of the vanished man was tolerated in its decay, and no one took outright vengeance on him.

While the conflict between Owliktuk and Pommela drew to its conclusion, the Ihalmiut were unwittingly involved in still another conflict. But this new struggle was being waged far from the Land of the Little Hills. It had its origins in 1952, when I published my book *People of the Deer*, dealing with the Ihalmiut and their plight as I had seen it in 1947 and 1948.

It was a heated book, and it had its share of faults and frailties, for it was written with too much subjectivism, and with too few statistics. Vilhjalmur Stefansson had these prophetic words to say of it in a review published in the *Dartmouth Quarterly:*

"Like many another book written at white heat, this one is vulnerable in that it has errors which are readily detected and handily useful towards discrediting the whole on the basis of 'let's see how right it is on a few points we can check' following with the conclusion that since a, b, and c are demonstrably wrong, we are justified in dismissing the whole as a tissue of misinformation and wrong conclusions ... this reviewer wants to plead against that attitude toward 'People of the Deer.' "

Stefansson's plea went unheeded, at least by the Hudson's Bay Company, the Oblate missions, the Northwest Territories Council, and the Department of Resources and Northern Affairs (as the former Department of Resources and Development was now called). All of these organizations displayed markedly hostile reactions toward the book; and the editor of *The Beaver,* a magazine published by the Hudson's Bay Company, made space available to Dr. A. E. Porsild, a long-time employee of the Department of Resources and Northern Affairs, to speak out on behalf of the indignant empires of the north.

Dr. Porsild's contribution duly appeared in *The Beaver,* as a book review, and quite the longest one *The Beaver* has ever run. Despite its length, however, no space was wasted on literary matters, for Dr. Porsild's forthright and declared objective was to discredit me personally, and thereby discredit what I had said about the Eskimos and their unhappy fate. With rather awesome thoroughness the Doctor ran the gamut from accusations of illegal trading and flagrant and malicious prevarication to the suggestion that I had probably never even been to the interior Barrens anyway. From the pinnacle of his authority as a senior government official, he further stated that the Ihalmiut had never exceeded more than a few score in numbers, and rather surprisingly he went on to claim that there were no more than 5,600 Canadian Eskimos extant—a piddling number of people about which to raise such a hue and cry, even assuming that there was a grain of truth in what I had written. But, as Dr. Porsild vehemently assured his readers, there was *no* truth in the book anyway, and precious little in Farley Mowat either. The review concluded with the bestowal of a pseudo-Eskimo title upon me: that of *Sagdlutorssuaq*—Great Teller of Tall Tales.

Publication of the review was only a preliminary step. Copies of it were mailed to all the major Canadian newspapers, together with a covering letter suggesting that I had perpetrated a hoax upon the Canadian public. Some libraries were even asked to withdraw the book from circulation, and *The Beaver* very nearly gave me apoplexy by consistently refusing to publish my rebuttal of Dr. Porsild's charges, or even to reply to my impassioned letters on the subject.

The storm eventually blew itself out in the House of Parliament in Ottawa, where a brief but revealing rear-guard action was fought on January 19, 1954.

The exchange which took place that day on the floor of the House between the Hon. Jean Lesage, Minister of Resources and Northern Affairs (aided at one point by Mr. Adamson), and an opposition member, Mr. Knight, has its revealing overtones.

MR. KNIGHT: I do not know whether the Minister will remember the last time this subject [Eskimos] was under discussion I brought to his attention certain allegations that had been made in "People of the Deer" by Farley Mowat. I think that at that time the Minister said he would look into the subject and see what he could tell me about it ... If the allegations in the book are true it is a terrible indictment of neglect upon the part of somebody and I do not know anybody better to blame than the Department of the Dominion Government that handles these affairs.

It is true that some of Mr. Mowat's allegations were denied publicly and to that denial he has replied in terms which I see no reason to disbelieve. His allegations were that a certain tribe of Eskimos have been allowed, through various circumstances, to disintegrate and that in fact their numbers were decreased and depleted through starvation. The theme of the book is that the natural way these people live is through the use of their natural food, the caribou... Now the allegation is that these people were separated from their ordinary means of livelihood. I should like to know if the Minister has anything to tell us about it. It is a rather serious business. It involves the lives of people. It involves their extermination by starvation...

I made some inquiries of the Minister in the last Parliament. I have to say that the answers I received were not adequate. I would not like to call them evasive, but they certainly were not satisfactory. I am informed now that this tribe is subsisting largely on the charity of the members of some military expedition in that north country... What are the comments of the Minister upon the whole situation, and the allegation that this particular tribe was allowed to be starved and separated from their natural means of livelihood?

MR. LESAGE: I said, and I do not believe I can say anything more, it [the book] is false, the allegations are false. If the Hon. Member wishes to have a detailed criticism of that book [Dr. Porsild's review] indicating the extent to which the information upon which the book is based is false, I am sure that my officers and especially my Deputy, would be delighted to send it to the Hon. Member... there is nothing more false than that part of the book which says that a certain tribe was allowed to perish by starvation. There is no grounds at all for that allegation.... As I said, I do not have in my mind all the facts concerning the allegations in this book, but I shall be delighted to have an officer give the Hon. Member all the information he

142

requires in order that his soul, as a Member of this Parliament, may be at peace, and that he will not believe he has been at fault in allowing starvation to occur in this country without any measures being taken against it.

MR. KNIGHT: Since the Minister has said categorically that these things are false, I should like to say that I, too, have information from what I consider to be a fairly competent authority stating that such allegations are largely true. . . .

MR. LESAGE: At the time the book was written and the events occurred to which my Hon. Friend has referred, I was not very well versed in either northern affairs or Eskimo affairs. However, I am now informed by responsible officers in my Department that the information in the book is false, and that the statement just made by the Hon. Member would not be exactly correct. My officers are in a position to satisfy him that there was no delay by the proper officers in doing what was necessary to cope with an emergency.

MR. KNIGHT: I think it would be wise if the information which the Minister asserts his officers can give, were to be given publicly to the whole country.

MR. ADAMSON [for the government]: Would it be possible to have Dr. Porsild's monograph on the subject given to those Members who may be interested in it?

MR. LESAGE: I thank the Hon. Member for his suggestion . . . and I will see to it that Dr. Porsild's monograph is mimeographed and distributed to them. This would be one of the best answers to the allegations in the book "People of the Deer."

MR. KNIGHT: Let me suggest that in all fairness . . . if Dr. Porsild's statement is to be made public [here] then the reply by Mr. Mowat should be made public so that Hon. Members can come to their own conclusions . . . If the government is going to mimeograph Dr. Porsild's reply at public expense, then I suggest that it should mimeograph the other at the same time. Does not the Minister consider that this would be the fair way to handle the matter?

MR. LESAGE: I do not want to enter into this controversy and I can see no reason at all why we should perpetuate it. And, under the circumstances, since the Hon. Member objects, nothing will be mimeographed.

So this struggle, too, came to its conclusion; but not before Dr. Porsild had fired one conclusive shot to mark the end. Late in 1953 an award was made to *People of the Deer* for its "contribution to better human understanding." When the news reached Dr. Porsild, he wrote a letter in his capacity as an official of the Department of Resources and Northern Affairs, addressed to the chairman of the awards committee. "I am sure," wrote Dr. Porsild, "Farley Mowat is pleased with the award and perhaps a little amused too—for he has a keen sense of humour—that his 'plea for the understanding help without which these people will vanish from the earth' has been heard. What worries me is that the Ihalmiut people never did exist except in Mowat's imagination."

11

A Dawn Extinguished

The distance from Ottawa to Keewatin remained immeasurably great. Almost at the same time that Mr. Lesage was denying the fact of starvation in the arctic, a band of Eskimos at Perry River, including three Hanningaiormiut families who had been forced to abandon their inland homes at Garry Lake due to hunger, were being driven to eat their dogs to keep alive. In early February the R.C.A.F. made a mercy flight to Perry River with a supply of meat; and if this meat was unfit for normal human consumption, it was at least adequate for Eskimos, and the Perry River people survived into the spring.

Those of the Hanningaiormiut who had remained at Garry Lake, where Father Bulliard had now established a minute church-state, were not so lucky. Four starved to death that spring, and one more died of what was euphemistically

145

called "exposure." The rest barely endured until the starvation season ended and the priest returned again to minister to them.

Things were not quite so desperate amongst the Ihalmiut, for no one died directly of starvation that winter. But at the end of February, Ohoto's wife Nanuk, who was big with child, became so ill that the soldiers demanded and obtained a rescue flight, and she was flown to Churchill. Ohoto had hoped and dreamed that the child would be a boy, for he had never had a son and this was a part of his personal tragedy. This child was indeed a son; but it was stillborn, and the reason given by the doctors was a state of advanced toxemia in the mother, brought about by severe malnutrition.

The caribou migration came late to Ennadai in 1954, and when it came there were no hunters to meet it and to take their toll of it. Almost every adult Eskimo was sick, stricken by a virulent form of influenza which was then raging throughout most of Keewatin. In the interior it went unchecked, except at Ennadai where, once again, the soldiers became doctors and nurses. They labored to such advantage that there was only one death amongst the twenty-two adults who contracted the disease. But at Baker Lake and Garry Lake a reported total of eighteen Eskimos died during this epidemic, and no one will ever know how many actually succumbed.

By early June, largely as a result of their failure to make a kill of caribou, the Ihalmiut were again starving since the stocks of relief supplies at Ennadai had early been exhausted. Despite the dispatch of a whole sequence of urgent radio requests for emergency help, no assistance was to be had from Churchill. The Signals sergeant *was* authorized to issue flour from his own stock but, as he was unhappily aware, the small amount of flour, lard and baking powder which he could spare was no more than a gesture to a people starved by a long winter, exhausted by sickness, and starved again throughout the spring.

During May, June and most of July, the diet of the Ihalmiut was limited to an inadequate ration of flour, lard and tea. By this time the people had become so physically debilitated that none of them, not even Owliktuk, had the strength or the ambition to venture more than a mile or so away from the relative safety of the radio station. They did not even have sufficient initiative to fish successfully. Throughout July there was a constant sequence of sickness, which the soldiers attributed in their reports: "Mainly to poor diet."

In early August an epidemic of mumps swept through the camps and two of the children who contracted the disease became so ill that a military aircraft had to be summoned to evacuate them to Churchill.

By this time the soldiers had become frantic. They were dispatching almost daily messages to their own headquarters, to the police, to the civilian authorities, asking for new supplies of food. But no food came, despite the fact that there were five tons of foodstuffs in storage at Churchill destined for the Ihalmiut. This huge stock of food had been purchased with the Eskimos' own Family Allowance credits and with money from the sale of the few furs they had been able to trap during the two preceding winters; but the R.C.M.P. aircraft was too involved in other tasks to deliver these supplies to Ennadai.

On August 18, Mr. Lesage's officers at last took action, and on that date a plane load of buffalo meat arrived from Fort Smith. It elicited the following message from Ennadai:

ONE AIRCRAFT LOAD OF BUFFALO MEAT SENT HERE BY DEPT. RESOURCES AND NORTHERN DEVELOPMENT FOR STARVING ESKIMOS STOP THIS IS THE FIRST MEAT TRIBE HAS TASTED FOR MONTHS STOP CONDITION OF PEOPLE PARTICULARLY CHILDREN IS PITIFUL MAIN DIET FLOUR AND A FEW FISH STOP DOGS ARE JUST A BAG OF BONES AND HAIR AND HAVE BEEN TURNED LOOSE TO FEND FOR THEMSELVES STOP ALL OLD BONES AND CARIBOU HOOVES IN AREA HAVE BEEN GATHERED BY ESKIMOS TO MAKE SOUP STOP THE GENERAL HEALTH IS POOR AND THEY ARE CATCHING ALL SORTS OF DISEASE STOP TO DATE TWELVE ESKIMOS EVACUATED TO CHURCHILL FOR HOSPITALIZATION.

The entire course of events through the spring and summer of 1954 seemed to indicate that the Departmental officials were in full agreement with their chosen spokesman, Dr. Porsild, that indeed the Ihalmiut did not exist at all. And had it not been for the efforts of the handful of soldiers at the radio station, there is considerable likelihood that Dr. Porsild's contention would have become truth indeed.

It had been no happy time for the soldiers, who were humane men, and it was with relief that they heard the news that the radio station was to pass from military control to the control of the Federal Department of Transport, in the early autumn of 1954.

The soldiers may have been glad to leave, but their departure was a severe misfortune for the Ihalmiut. Through the terrible years since 1949 the soldiers had done their best, within the limits of their own experience and authority, to assist the people. To them, and to them alone, must go the credit for the physical survival of the last remnants of the Ihalmiut; nor can they be blamed in any way for the spiritual disintegration which took place during those years. They were good men all, and they did the best they could at a time when no other Canadians appear to have been more than academically concerned with the fate of the People of the Deer.

If 1954 brought little or no improvement in the fortunes of the Ihalmiut it did at least see the beginnings of what appeared to have the makings of a revolution in Ottawa. During this year the department responsible for Eskimo affairs again changed its name, becoming the Department of Northern Affairs and National Resources and, for the first time in Canada's history, a government agency began to display a nascent sense of responsibility towards the Eskimos.

On October 21, Mr. Lesage, still Minister of the Department, gave the outline of a new Eskimo program to the press. He explained that, for the first time, the civil authority would have its own men in the field in the shape of six Northern Service Officers who had been chosen to go to the Eskimos, to live with them, and to lead them to a new and better way of life. These six were to be responsible for "approximately 9,500 Eskimos" (no accurate census of their numbers yet existed), scattered over an area equal in size to that occupied by about two-thirds of the United States.

"This is a work with a rare kind of challenge," said Mr. Lesage with tactful understatement. "Canada is now turning in earnest to the development of its northland. The Northern Service Officer will have a great responsibility for the lands and the people who live there."

Those Canadians who were startled by the government's suddenly awakened interest in the Eskimos did not have far to seek for an explanation. They noted the order of precedence in the words "the lands and the people who live there" and they must be pardoned if they accepted Mr. Lesage's protestations of concern about the Eskimo with a degree of skepticism.

The fact was that Canada was indeed turning in earnest to the development of its northland and of *all its potential resources* there. Since 1950 Canadians, most of whom had traditionally considered the arctic to be a useless and sterile waste, had been undergoing a change of heart. It was becoming increasingly obvious that the arctic held a good many economic opportunities, particularly in the field of mineral exploitation. Furthermore, the rapid development of military activity throughout the Canadian north, most of it under the direct aegis of the United States, had aroused some belated anxiety amongst Canadians that, if they did not take it on themselves to possess the broad northlands in full reality, they might find that they no longer possessed them even in name.

So Canada was looking north; and in 1954 she began to recognize the existence of the Eskimos in the context of her own ambitions and desires. She did not see them as a minority that had been callously disregarded for half a century. She saw them instead as a potential asset which could be of service in the fulfillment of her own ambitions and economic hopes. The words of Mr. Lesage's press release made this quite clear:

> As the tempo of activity steps up in Canada's far north there will be an increasing demand for skilled and semi-skilled labour. The supply of qualified white men who can endure life in the bleak and cold arctic wastes is, however, extremely small. To the Eskimos, on the other hand, the hardships of the north form a part of everyday life. In addition it is the opinion of many who have worked among them that they can be trained to meet the need for labour that is bound to arise. It is a common misconception [and, the release did not add, one that had been assiduously fostered as long as it suited us] that the Eskimo has the mentality of a child, but to those who know better he is a highly intelligent person who possesses many capabilities, most particularly an aptitude for all things mechanical. These natives of the north know no greater joy than driving a truck, running a boat, or caring for a machine. . . .

Here, then, was the crux of the matter. Nevertheless, whatever Mr. Lesage's—and the government's—real motives may have been, some of the changes which his release portended seemed, at first glance, to be to the Eskimos' advantage.

The concept of employing Northern Service Officers would indubitably have been a good one if it had meant a change from the haphazard and incompetent administration of Eskimo problems under the R.C.M.P., the traders and the missions, to a vital and intelligent approach under the direction of well-trained and competent field men who were free of the pressure which could be exerted by the old empires of church, police and trader. But with the announcement of the actual appointment of the first six N.S.O.'s, it became tragically obvious that no real change was intended. One of the new N.S.O.'s was a serving R.C.M.P. officer seconded from his force for temporary duty. Another was an ex-R.C.M.P. officer. Two had served for many years in the arctic as traders. Furthermore, it was apparent almost from the start that these men were not to be encouraged to interfere with the existing patterns of white domination of the Eskimo.

The task of the N.S.O.'s, as defined by Mr. Lesage, fell into two categories, the flagrantly impossible and the deliberately nebulous. The first was perhaps designed to impress the general public; the second were probably intended to quiet any anxiety which the old empires might feel at this intrusion into their preserves. In the actual words of the Department officials as these were recorded in the press release of October 21:

"The Department is approaching the new undertaking with extreme caution. When the N.S.O.'s are first dispatched to their posts, for example, they will be under strict instruction to tell no one why they are there, or what their jobs involve. If asked, they have been told to say they don't know why they have been sent or what they are supposed to do, one official explained ... this attitude illustrates the healthy respect the Department has for the dangers which lie in tampering with the ancient habits and customs of primitive peoples."

The release could not add that the new emissaries to the Eskimos had also been instructed that under no conditions were they to interfere with R.C.M.P. activities amongst the Eskimos, and that they were *not* to consider that they had any authority to effect changes contrary to the desire of the traders, missions, or police in their areas.

Without putting too fine an interpretation upon the N.S.O. scheme, it was inevitable that some observers should jump to the conclusion that these new government employees were intended to serve primarily as labor recruiters; and that in fact the government had not suffered any real change of heart about the Eskimos at all.

Those who believed that this was the case were not slow to make their opinions known, and five days later Mr. Lesage made a new speech, in which he said very little about the role of the Eskimo as a truck driver, but soared instead to heights of oratory in an endeavor to show how disinterested and altruistic the government's program really was.

It was the government's sincere hope, said the Minister, to see Eskimo settlements across the north governed by councils of their own people and, before many years had passed, it was hoped to see, not only self-governing Eskimo settlements, but Eskimo men and women trained and serving as teachers, nurses, craftsmen and, in fact, in every activity in the Canadian northlands.

He continued, "We hope to see such Eskimos as are interested in doing so, enter into the life of Canada as workers in fields of their choice—in public service, the professions, in business."

But even while he was propounding this magnificent fantasy, Mr. Lesage could not wholly refrain from returning to more practical matters, for he concluded:

"It is the task of the Government at once to protect the aboriginal Eskimos from the ill-effects of civilisation and on the other hand to create the conditions which will enable them to take their places in the expanding economy of Canada with particular reference to the fact that they are already dwellers in the arctic, not only used to the country and competent to live there, but loving their country as men the world over love the land they live in."

It is an unhappy truth, as Mr. Lesage soon became aware, that compromise decisions seldom please anyone. Even before the N.S.O.'s went north to take up their appointments, there were undercurrents of suspicion from the old empires. No amount of assurances from the Department could entirely quell the fears of the missions that the days of church domination, particularly in the educational field, might be threatened.

Nor were the police particularly happy about the change. Although they retained their hegemony intact, and although they were actively represented amongst the N.S.O's, they were, nevertheless, disturbed for the future; and the attitude of their staffs in the field toward the interlopers was, to put it rather mildly, uncooperative.

The traders alone seem to have had the intelligence to realize that things were changing. Although the Hudson's Bay Company can have hardly welcomed the new intrusion into its traditional domains, it made no overt resistance; and in fact it was by then very busy reorienting its entire approach to the arctic. It had accepted the obvious conclusion that the day of the fur trade, as a major industry, was done; and it had formulated and was implementing a new policy which was intended to turn its network of trading posts into retail merchandising stores which could take advantage of the economic exploitation of the arctic which was now about to start.

Despite Mr. Lesage's anxious and sincere desire to allay the fears and suspicions of the police and the missions, there were in fact some grounds for the unease of the old orders. Even at this early stage there were a few men of integrity and humanity in Canada who were deeply concerned about the future of the Eskimos and who had concluded that their only hope of accomplishing anything was to associate themselves with the Department of Northern Affairs. One or two of these men had become N.S.O.'s and several others had obtained positions within the Department at Ottawa, where they could eventually hope to assist in shaping a new official attitude which would result in real and enduring benefits to the Eskimos. These few were to know frustrations and defeats, at the hands of the old orders, which must have been well-nigh unendurable. Still they persevered, though it was to be a long time before their efforts came to anything.

The People of the Little Hills meanwhile remained insensible to the brave new world which Mr. Lesage envisaged for them, and through the winter of 1954–1955 they existed much as they had done for many years. The only external change apparent to them was in the attitude of the new white men who now manned the radio station. These were civilians and, for the most part, they were highly trained specialists in communications, whose lives were bounded by the confines of their jobs. At first they were mildly interested in the Eskimos as curiosities, but when it became apparent that they were expected to concern themselves with the problems of these primitives, their interest rapidly waned. They seem to have felt, and with justification, that Eskimo administration was no affair of theirs, and they appear to have harbored some resentment of the fact that they were ordered to carry out duties which clearly lay within the province of another government department.

Consequently their contacts with the Ihalmiut were largely limited to those things which they could not avoid—the issuing of Family Allowance supplies, relief rations, and the receiving of such furs as the Eskimo hunters might manage to obtain. The result was that no bond of human intercourse or understanding could be established between the new white men and the Ihalmiut, and the contacts which did exist were unpalatable to both parties.

This change was momentarily to the benefit of the people. Those who still retained some pride of race and person reacted to the atmosphere of barely concealed hostility and disdain by withdrawing as far as possible from contact with the whites. Owliktuk's group, which had regained a considerable amount of its cohesion as a result of Pommela's downfall, returned to the Little Lakes where it became more self-sufficient and vital than it had been for two long years. The older men, Halo, Ootek, Owliktuk, Miki and Yaha, together with the younger men, Kaiyai, Anoteelik and Mounik, even managed to make something of a deer hunt during the late autumn of 1954, and were consequently able to do some trapping.

It was indicative of their relations with the radio station personnel, and of a nascent resurgence of independence and pride, that they chose to take most of the furs to the distant post at Padlei, rather than to the station where, in due course, the pelts would have been picked up by the R.C.M.P., sold in Churchill, and their value returned to Ennadai in the form of supplies arbitrarily chosen by the police.

In January of 1955, Ootek, Halo and Owliktuk made the long journey to Padlei, and Owliktuk remembered that trip as being one of the happiest of his life. They had barely sufficient dogs to haul their sleds, but they had lots of meat for men and dogs. They traveled well and hard, knowing the satisfaction of being free men in harmony with their own land once more. As they neared Padlei they encountered outlying camps of their cousins of the Padliermiut who had almost made a good autumn hunt and so had lots of meat. The visitors were welcomed in the all-but-forgotten fashion with drum dances and song-feasts that lasted the long night through, while the woman kept the meat trays and the soup pots full.

At Padlei Post the travelers traded their furs for the

things *they* wished to buy—tea, tobacco, ammunition, thread and duffle cloth for the women, and oddments of equipment needed in the hunt. They bought little food, for they *had* food—the kind of food they needed.

Nor did they have food for the stomach alone. The relative abundance of the deer in the autumn had provided food for men's spirits too. For the first time in many years the herds had seemed almost as numerous as in the good days of the past; and the presence of the deer had revitalized both the land and the men of the land. At Ennadai, at Padlei, on the Thelon and at Garry Lake, the inland Eskimos had witnessed the return of *tuktu* with an upsurge of hope, and they had taken it as a sign that the hard years were done.

They could not know that what they had beheld was an illusion; that accident alone had directed almost the entire surviving Keewatin herds along a narrow path leading past the Eskimo camps. They could not know what the more enlightened biologists or the Dominion Wildlife Service already knew—that the caribou were doomed.

This winter of 1954–1955 was to be the last winter when the Ihalmiut, the Padliermiut, the Akilingmiut and the Hanningaiormiut would know a degree of certainty; when they would eat to repletion and could forget the evils of the preceding years.

There was light in the long nights that winter.

When Owliktuk and his friends returned from Padlei in early February they were met by cheerful women, and by contented children; and there was a great round of tea-drinking parties while the travelers recounted the Padlei gossip to the stay-at-homes.

There was hope in the dark months when hope is hard to hold.

In February, Arlow, Owliktuk's fifteen-year-old son, was formally betrothed to Miki's daughter Kugiak, and the two youngsters slept together from this time on, alternating their nights between the tents of Miki and Owliktuk. Furthermore, one of Owliktuk's daughters, Akjar (who had married the youth Anoteelik a year earlier), was now expecting her second child. Since their marriage, Akjar and Anoteelik had lived with Owliktuk but now the time seemed ripe for them to become an independent family. All the men contributed fall-killed deer-hides, and the women went to work in concert to cut and sew until, in the early days of March, a new tent stood by the shores of Halo Lake. It was a stirring sight. For the first time in a decade the number of the Ihalmiut tents had increased—instead of shrinking year by year.

Nor was this all. In mid-March Owliktuk's oldest son Mounik married Yaha's daughter Ookanak, who had just turned fourteen, but who was a woman in all ways. There was hope now that before another spring, new tents for Mounik and Ookanak, and for Arlow and Kugiak, would join that of Anoteelik and Akjar. There was hope that from these three new families would come many children so that the Ihalmiut could turn their faces away from the narrowing angle of their declining years and look forward into the widening perspective of a new futurity.

Indeed it was a time of hope. The men awaited the return of the deer that spring with a new enthusiasm and with an excitement that fired the blood as it had not been fired for a full decade. They believed that the days ahead would lead them to the life that they had lost.

* * *

During the last month of winter the deer began to move north from timber to seek the open plains; but where once they had surged out of the forests from Hudson Bay to Great Slave Lake, treading a hundred highways to the north—now they came by only half a dozen roads. The shrunken river of life which still flowed up from the famous wintering grounds near Reindeer Lake was no longer supported, nor channeled north, by the pressure of other rivers on its flanks. It flowed into an empty land and it had hardly cleared the edge of timber when it faltered and began to bend toward the west as if frightened by its own loneliness and bent on seeking union with the great tides of the past which had been wont to inundate the entire Barrens in one contiguous sea of life. Farther and farther to the westward the meager river swung, and still it was alone. It became seized with an inexplicable and feverish compulsion, nor did it cease to flow until it had reached the Dismal Lakes, hard on the arctic coast beyond the Coppermine—and nearly six hundred miles to the northwest of Ennadai.

It was an almost incredible and inexplicable migration, and to this day the biologists can offer no concrete explanation of why it happened. But it did happen, and the result was that the Keewatin plains from Ennadai to the Back River saw almost no deer that spring.

It was an occurrence which should have underlined the findings and the prophecies of the caribou survey biologists with such dramatic emphasis that no one, not even a government official, should have been able to avoid the conclusion that the deer were done for. But that was a truth which the authorities, and which the old arctic hands too, were unable, or unwilling, to assimilate. Although the scientists had presented their findings, and were in no doubt about the accuracy of them, they were ignored.

They had proven to the satisfaction of any thinking man that the deer were doomed by a combination of the destruction brought about by rifles and unlimited ammunition, and by the wanton and gigantic wastage of the forests to the south by fire, and the consequent destruction of the lichens and mosses which alone enabled the great herds to survive upon the winter range. The biologists had shown that it takes seventy-five to a hundred years for the spruce-lichen forests to renew themselves after a fire; and they had shown that as much as fifty per cent of the winter grazing grounds of the deer had *already* been destroyed by fires set, for the most part, by prospectors, anxious to expose the naked rocks, or by settlers anxious to clear land, or simply as a result of the kind of casual carelessness with which white men treat their heritage—and the heritage of others.

The biologists had demonstrated that it was starvation which was now primarily responsible for the decimation of the deer; even as it was starvation, either outright or by degrees, which was destroying the peoples of the deer—the inland Eskimos and the northern Taiga Indians. But those who had the power and the authority to use this knowledge for the salvation of men and beasts alike chose rather to deny the evidence, and thereby to ensure that men and deer should perish.

The year 1955 failed to bring the deer back to the Ihalmiut, but it did bring a remarkable influx of white men, all of whom were more or less concerned with their welfare. In a sense, this year marked the real discovery of the Ihalmiut, and their recognition as a segment of humanity.

The invasion began with the first visit of the N.S.O. who was responsible for the Keewatin Eskimos. This man, an ex-R.C.M.P. constable, had been given the charge of about two thousand Eskimos spread over an area of more than 150,000 square miles. He had no means of transportation at his own disposal, and was almost wholly dependent upon the R.C.M.P. to carry him about in police aircraft. He was stationed at Churchill, where his primary task was the establishment of an Eskimo community composed of exiles from Ungava Bay, who were to be taught to work for the Army establishments at Churchill. In his spare time he was expected to look after the needs of all the inland peoples, as well as those of the Eskimos along the whole west coast of Hudson Bay.

He made his first trip to Ennadai in January, accompanying an R.C.M.P. patrol, and he was shocked by the condition of the people, though they were then doing very well as compared to previous years. He was, however, helpless to do any more for them than was already being done by the police and the Department of Transport staff. He therefore confirmed the existing arrangements and returned to Churchill. His report on the Ihalmiut eventually reached Ottawa, where it seems to have caused considerable surprise, and even more incredulity.

An unofficial visitor who followed the N.S.O. to Ennadai was a member of the Northern Evangelical Mission to the Eskimos, a businesslike young American who flew to the camps of Owliktuk's group in July and was able to remove three of the children from the camp and carry them off to attend a three-week revival meeting.

The next visitors had a legitimate reason for coming to Ennadai, for they were members of the first medical inspection team ever to visit the inland peoples. Until 1955 all medical inspections of the Eskimos had been carried out by parties aboard either the Hudson's Bay Company vessels, or the new Canadian government arctic supply ship, *C.D. Howe.* Until 1955 no more than 40 per cent of the total *known* Eskimo population of Canada had ever been medically examined in any given year; but in 1955 the addition of airborne teams was expected to extend the coverage to about 80 per cent.

The team which visited Ennadai found that tuberculosis was present, but not widespread (during the preceding four years sixteen of the Ihalmiut had been evacuated at one time or another as a result of tuberculosis), and that apart from the usual disabilities and diseases associated with malnutrition, the people were fairly healthy.

The medical team had barely departed when another official visitor arrived. This one was a rare bird indeed. He was a young Dutchman who had, for some inscrutable reason, perhaps associated with his strong partisanship for the Oblate missions, been employed by one of the branches of the Department of Northern Affairs to investigate the legal structure of the Ihalmiut society. Though his investigations were somewhat hampered by the fact that he did not speak Eskimo and had no interpreter, he was nevertheless able to prepare a long and learned account of law concepts amongst the Ihalmiut, together with some concrete suggestions as to their future.

The Dutchman was still present when, on August 13, the Ihalmiut were at last properly discovered—by a party from *Life* which had flown to Ennadai to do a picture-story on Stone Age Man.

If the activities of the Dutchman puzzled the Ihalmiut, the activities of this new group baffled them completely. Nevertheless they were, as always, hospitable in the extreme; and they courteously obliged the strangers, even when the cameraman insisted on moving tents about, and in generally upsetting the tenor of the camps.

These minor inconveniences resulted in Anoteelik and Akjar, together with their baby son Igyaka, eventually appearing in full color on the cover of *Life* above an illuminating title which read: "Stone Age Survivors." It was a distinction (the appearance, not the comment) which many white men would have envied—but it was of little concrete value to the People.

By August 29, the autumnal deer had not yet appeared and a serious food shortage was already developing. In early September, when a few stragglers from the vanished herds began to pass through the land, the Ihalmiut were unable to hunt, for they had no ammunition. It was not until September 15 that the R.C.M.P. flew in the season's supply of shells, but by then there were almost no deer remaining in the Ennadai area.

On September 23, when the young Dutchman departed, he noted that the people had not been able to get enough meat to last them for more than a few weeks. Clearly the Ihalmiut were again in difficulties; but the expert on Eskimo law had a solution to their continuing problem, a solution which he included in his official report.

"No experiments," he wrote, "should be made with the few hundred Eskimos of the inland. Only a close teaching of the gospel, after my opinion, will save their small communities and offer some perspective for the future. It needs no elucidation that the conditions for their personal happiness can be assured by this."

It was a sincere, if somewhat incredible, statement, but it was dictated directly by the Oblate policy which was frankly one of holding the Eskimos in their present and primitive conditions despite all odds, and in resisting the first hesitant efforts of the few thoughtful men in Ottawa who foresaw that eventual survival for the Eskimos could only be ensured by bridging the gap between their culture and ours, and by admitting them to full equality in our society. The Oblate resistance to this as yet nebulous trend was being effectively demonstrated at Garry Lake where the majority of the Hanningaiormiut were now firmly under the control of Father Bulliard, who was using every method at his disposal to prevent them from establishing relations with the outer world, and to ensure that they remained "unspoiled."

Before coming to Ennadai the young Dutchman had arranged to be joined there by Father Ducharme, an Oblate priest from Eskimo Point who could have introduced the "conditions for the personal happiness" of the Ihalmiut, as these were presently being enjoyed by the Hanningaiormiut at Garry Lake. Fortunately the R.C.M.P., who had volunteered to fly the priest to Ennadai, were unable to do so due to an accident to their aircraft, and so these plans went unrealized.

"The caribou hunt at Ennadai in the fall of 1955 was just short of a total failure," to quote the words of the N.S.O. In fact the people obtained only enough meat to last them until November, and when it was eaten they were back where they had been two years earlier—on the dole once more.

The N.S.O. was not able to visit them until January when he again accompanied the R.C.M.P. patrol. His time at Ennadai was too short to allow a visit to the rest of the camps at the Little Lakes, but the N.S.O. authorized the Department of Transport staff to issue some frozen buffalo meat which had been in storage at the station since the starvation summer of 1954, and which was now perishing. With one notable exception this was to be the only meat the Ihalmiut would see until the spring.

The police and the N.S.O. paid a second visit in February, bringing supplies of flour, lard and oatmeal, and the N.S.O. subsequently reported to Ottawa that he had found almost no fur waiting to be taken out, and that the people appeared to be completely shiftless. He recommended that a competent person be employed to supervise and direct their activities on the spot. Unfortunately no such person was available.

So things continued as before. Most of the people clustered as close to the station as the Transport men would allow, and huddled in their snow-banked tents, there to outwait the winter in the kind of physical misery which had become second nature to them. But this year they were totally without hope, and abjectly resigned to an acceptance of their lot. Their very will to live seemed to have been stifled by this renewed descent into despair after the previous winter's brief journey into hope. There seemed to be no room in their minds now for anything except an all-embracing apathy.

12

The Promised Land

By early March of 1956 the Ihalmiut were as close to physical and spiritual extinction as people can come, and still survive. The relief supplies had been exhausted and the Department of Transport staff had been forced to issue flour from their own stocks, supplemented by three hundred pounds of ham that had gone bad and been condemned. Some of this foul meat was fed to the handful of surviving dogs, and when they did not die of it the rest was issued to the Eskimos who "ate it with relish."

Such was their condition when, on March 19, they received an epochal visit. On that day the Eastern Arctic Patrol, consisting of a party of officials of the Department of Northern Affairs and the Department of Health and Welfare, flew to Ennadai to make a firsthand assessment of the problem of the Ihalmiut.

Within the Department of Northern Affairs the persistent struggles of the handful of dedicated men were now beginning to have some small effect, and this visit was the first concrete evidence that their efforts might eventually amount to something. In March of 1956 a senior official looked for the first time upon the remnants of the Ihalmiut, and he was deeply disturbed by what he saw.

Later, he described the conditions under which the people were existing as intolerable. He visited some of their tent shelters and discovered that they lacked everything a human being needed to survive in that hard land, including bedding. He noted that the people were suffering so severely from hunger that they were quite unable to fend for themselves; and that their morale was so low that they were incapable of making any sustained effort on their own behalf. He reported that of the seventy-five dogs which the people had possessed at the beginning of the winter, only five skeletal survivors remained.

The visit of the Eastern Arctic Patrol was brief, but it had an immediate effect. During the next two weeks the N.S.O. and the R.C.M.P. flew in several plane loads of supplies to Ennadai, and outright starvation was temporarily halted. The visit also established, beyond any further possibility of evasion, that, unless the pattern of life amongst the Ihalmiut was radically altered to prevent a continuing repetition of the events of the past years, the last of the Ihalmiut would soon vanish from the land, and from humanity.

But even before the visit of the official party to Ennadai, other agencies had been at work preparing a plan for the salvation of the Ihalmiut, a plan which was certainly radical, not to say drastic. This plan seems to have originated with two men, the Hudson's Bay Company manager at Padlei and the R.C.M.P. corporal in charge of the Eskimo Point detachment.

The corporal was a man of parts. During his stay at Eskimo Point he had shown that he possessed vigorous ideas as to how the "natives" should be handled, and most of the other whites in the tiny settlement—it consisted of the trading post, an Oblate mission and the police detachment—seem to have agreed that his methods were at least efficacious. The Eskimos of the area, however, were not inclined to agree with their betters. They were, in fact, terrified of the policeman, for the corporal was a very forceful man.

In December of 1955 he suggested in a memorandum that the only hope for the Ihalmiut lay in their transportation to his area, where they would come under his control and would be subject to his "no-nonsense" policy of native administration. The N.S.O. was not in favor of this plan at first, for he still hoped that a competent supervisor might be found who could go and live with the Ihalmiut in their own country and gradually lead them out of the morass in which they were immersed. However, he was persuaded to change his mind by the combined arguments of the corporal and of the Padlei Post manager.

The trader at Padlei, who was himself of Eskimo extraction, had always been a good friend to the Padliermiut. He had lived with them for fifteen years and knew no other home; but since 1951 he had witnessed an abrupt decline in the numbers of his hunters—a decline due primarily to death by starvation and disease, which was rapidly depopulating the Padlei area and thereby threatening the continued existence of the post itself.

Awareness of this danger may have contributed to the post manager's anxiety to see the Ihalmiut brought to Padlei; yet he believed, in all sincerity, that such a move would be to their advantage. He believed that proximity to a trading post would act as a stimulus to help them regain something of their independence. He was personally convinced that the caribou were not really threatened with extinction, or even with a serious decline in numbers. It was his belief that, under his guidance, the Ihalmiut would soon shake off the apathy engendered by years of dole, and would be able to live adequately, if not well, on the meat and fish the Padlei district could provide.

Essentially his hopes were reasonable; but they were founded on a false premise—that the deer could still remain the mainstay of the inland people's lives.

The recommendations of the R.C.M.P. corporal, backed by those of the trader, made the decision inevitable; for the old orders still spoke in loud and imperative tones. The report of the Eastern Arctic Patrol clinched matters. Something obviously had to be done, and done at once. The decision was made to move the Ihalmiut eastward to the Padlei district.

Although this decision became final in June, it was not until August that the N.S.O., accompanied by the corporal from Eskimo Point and by the Padlei Post manager, could fly to the interior in search of a suitable location for the people. Their choice finally fell on Offedal Lake, which is an inlet on the western shores of North Henik Lake. It was unoccupied territory, being south and west of the area which the Padliermiut themselves still held.

The surrounding country consisted of high ridges and bald rock hills, in whose sheltered valleys stood stunted stands of black spurce trees. It was good white fox country and, while the value of fur had remained high, it had been a favorite trapping ground for numerous white trappers. It was not, however, and had not been in living memory, a good place for caribou.

The last Eskimos who had attempted to live on the land near the two Henik Lakes had been the Taherwealmiut, a people of the Ihalmiut stock who had moved eastward from the Kazan before the turn of the century. They had found that the Henik area was not good caribou country and so they gradually moved down the Th'Anne River toward the coast, where a small remnant of them still exists.

During the late 1920's and the early 1930's a few Padliermiut tried to live at Henik, but by the late '30's the entire western regions near this lake had been abandoned to the white trappers who were not so dependent on the land for food.

These were indubitable facts, and they must have been known to those who proposed that the Ihalmiut be settled at Henik Lake. But if they were known, their implications were totally ignored. Indeed the N.S.O. gave, as one of his main reasons for the choice, that the "Ennadai Eskimos" were intimate with the new area, and considered it to be a good place for deer. The Ihalmiut, when they were officially interrogated about this in March of 1958, denied that they had ever said these things, and they were vehement in their statements that Henik had always been a notoriously bad place for caribou. As for their familiarity with Henik Lake, the only contact they had ever had with the area was when they traveled through it en route to Padlei, together with the two despairing journeys they had made to the vicinity of Otter Lake in 1947 and in 1951.

It is also known that when the projected move was first broached to them they were unenthusiastic. Not only were they aware that Henik was poor caribou country, but they had other cogent reasons for disliking it as a place to live. For countless generations they had avoided broken hill country of the type which characterizes the western shores of Henik, knowing such areas to be the domains of particularly unpleasant spirits. The sincerity of their belief in these hill trolls is amply documented by Knud Rasmussen in his *Intellectual Culture of the Caribou Eskimos* and, as far as the Ihalmiut were concerned, this was an extremely potent reason for giving Henik as wide a berth as possible.

Nor were they favorably impressed by the argument put forward by the N.S.O. that Henik was a good fish lake and that, in the unlikely event that deer might happen to be temporarily scarce, the people could live handsomely on fish.

The idea that Eskimos could survive on fish as their primary article of diet had by now become one of the most widespread, and fatal, misconceptions in the arctic. Almost certainly the idea originated amongst those who wished to keep the Eskimos on the land at all costs, even though the meat mammals were to vanish utterly, and it had been so strongly advocated by these people that men who should have known better had come to believe it too. The Eskimos never believed it. They were fully aware that fish, and particularly fresh-water fish, can provide no more than a starvation diet for those who must cope with the inimical physical environment of the arctic. They knew that fish might suffice to keep a man alive if there was nothing else to eat, but only at a fearful cost in the slow wastage of his body. The inland Eskimos, who had been masters of the land for centuries, had learned *not* to rely on fish. Indeed they thought so little of it as a source of sustenance that they had never devised any fishing techniques beyond the use of the spear. A whole body of tabus and restrictions had grown up about the use of fish and, as any student of primitive society knows, most native food tabus have a solid basis in reality. Amongst the inland peoples these restrictions had no doubt been intended to ensure that men did not come to rely on fish (which were often more easily obtainable than meat) and so court self-destruction.

The presence of these tabus amongst the Ihalmiut was well known, and had been described with exasperation by the N.S.O. and the R.C.M.P. who had often railed at the people for their stubborn refusal to accept the advice of their mentors and turn to fish.

Whether the many arguments against moving the Ihalmiut to Henik Lake were even considered must remain an academic question. For whatever unexplained reasons, the decision had been taken and nothing was to be allowed to alter it.

While the plans were maturing, things had not been going well at Ennadai. The deer again failed to appear in any numbers during the spring migration. Two animals, killed on

May 12, appear to have represented the grand total for that month, and they were eaten in a single day. A report from that period has this to say:

"The natives continue to spend their time hanging about the D.O.T. station begging food, and they seem to be almost utterly dependent on what is being supplied to them. It is believed they could catch fish, but they do not seem to want to. However, good nets have been purchased for them on Family Allowance credits and they will not have any excuse for not keeping themselves well supplied . . ."

In Ottawa the plans for the move were being passed from department to department, and at the headquarters of the R.C.M.P. they elicited some sensible advice from one of the senior officers. This man insisted that the move should not be made at all unless the Ihalmiut could be accompanied by a trained and competent white man who spoke the language and who would remain with the people at the new location until they had become permanently established there. He was emphatic in his opinion that there was a definite risk of failure if the Eskimos were left to their own resources within a month or two of their arrival at Henik Lake.

In August, after the reconnaissance of Offedal Lake was completed, the N.S.O. and the R.C.M.P. corporal, again accompanied by the Padlei Post manager, flew on to Ennadai to inform the Ihalmiut of what was in store for them. Through the medium of the trader the people were told that they would be given transportation to Henik Lake as a gesture of good will on the part of the government, but that if they attempted to leave that place in order to return to Ennadai, they would get no further assistance. They were then asked if they wished to move and, since they clearly had no alternative (or at least thought that they had none), they agreed to do as the white men wished.

It had been intended to move them by R.C.M.P. Otter aircraft, sometime in August; but at the last minute the police plane was called away on other duties, and arrangements had to be hurriedly concluded with the R.C.A.F. for the use of a Canso amphibian. The usual snarl of red tape delayed matters so that it was not until September 16 that this aircraft could reach Ennadai where the people had been patiently waiting since August 2, prepared to leave on a moment's notice. Now it was decided that the season was too far advanced, and that the move could not be made in 1956.

The Ihalmiut did not display any marked unhappiness at the postponement. During early September they had killed a few caribou, and Owliktuk's group had recovered enough incentive to trek back to the Little Lakes in the hope of being able to survive the winter there. Owliktuk was having second thoughts about the move in any case. He remembered all too vividly the events which had followed upon the previous transportation of his people.

The supply of autumn deer lasted Owliktuk's band until the end of January, when they were once again forced to return to the station and to the flour and baking powder diet. Yet the Ihalmiut were luckier than most of the inland Eskimos that winter. To the north, at Baker and Garry Lakes, influenza again swept through the camps of people who were attempting to survive on fish, and twenty-one individuals, most of them children, are known to have died from the disease. At Padlei the annual epidemic was measles; but it killed only four people. It was a normal year amongst the inland Eskimos.

In early April the Ihalmiut received an unpremeditated visit from Canon Sperry of the Church of England, who was forced down at Ennadai while en route from Churchill to Yellowknife. His account of what he saw is worth recording:

> There was a group of about fifty Eskimos nearby and the sound of the plane brought them to the landing strip to see what was going on. They presented a picture of such abject misery and such indescribable filth that I found it hard to believe they were Eskimos at all. They stood huddled together in old skins; were gaunt and dirty and had faces hollowed out with malnutrition. Between the fifty of them they had one dog, if it could be described as such.
>
> I visited their hovels, circular walls of snow with old skins forming a roof. An old fuel can in the centre formed a stove for twigs and willows. That morning, they said, they had breakfasted on pieces of caribou skin—boiled. This meagre starvation diet was supplemented by the leavings of the radio men at the nearby station. Indeed they formed a pitiable spectacle. . . .

The good canon was so appalled, and so distressed, that he was unable to resist some disparaging comparisons between these miserable and apathetic starvelings and other Eskimos he had known in happier times and better places.

Probably he would have found it hard to believe that not much more than a decade earlier these had been a proud, vigorous, and happy people. He was glad enough when his aircraft was able to pursue its journey on the following day.

In late April some caribou miraculously appeared, but the hunters were unable to make more than a token kill due to the fact that the D.O.T. staff had been instructed by the police to issue only ten rounds of ammunition at a time. This necessitated a long and laborious trek back to the station after each sally to the hunting places. Considering the scarcity and dispersion of the deer, and the consequent tendency of the hunters to begin shooting from excessive ranges, a man was lucky if he got one animal with his ten shots. The result of this rationing of shells was effectively to prevent a successful hunt—which may have been the intention, since the restriction of ammunition was apparently imposed by the R.C.M.P. on the recommendation of the Wildlife Branch of the Department of Northern Affairs in order "to prevent the natives from slaughtering the already depleted caribou herds."

In the event, the failure of the hunt was unimportant for on May 6 a radio message reached Ennadai with instructions that all the Eskimos were to be gathered at the station prepared to fly to their new home at Henik Lake.

On the morning of May 10, 1957, the distant mumbling of an approaching aircraft engine reached the people who had gathered about the radio station at Ennadai. Men, women and children came from their tents to stand uncertainly, staring into the northeast. They did not talk amongst themselves. All of them knew what the sound portended, and there was nothing to talk about. Once more the time had come when the People of the Little Hills must leave their land and, submitting to the will of others, must go to a new destiny.

The big R.C.M.P. Otter aircraft circled once and came in heavily upon the ice. Two policemen and the N.S.O. climbed down and walked toward the land where the D.O.T. men waited impatiently—waited with relief writ large upon their faces; for the plane's arrival meant the end of a long and weary period during which the Eskimos had represented an increasing burden.

It was a fine morning. The sun stood high, and was already hot with the distant promise of spring. There was a sharp aseptic glare from the snow on the nearby ridges, and in the distance to the northeast the Little Hills loomed dimly like the backs of primordial and gigantic beasts emerging from a glacial sleep. It was the time of the year when men were used to climb those hills so that they might stare southward in anticipation of the moment when the horizon would begin to shift and shimmer with the oncoming tide of *tuktu.* But there were no living men on the Little Hills that day. There were only the stone *inukok,* the "semblances of men"; and they had no eyes with which to watch the last of the people of that land being herded out upon the ice, to disappear into the bowels of the aircraft.

The Ihalmiut made their farewells to their land in silence. They obeyed the instructions of the whites, and did so quietly. One by one they carried their bundles to the plane.

It took five flights to move the fifty-seven people and the five dogs which the N.S.O. had purchased for them at Churchill. They were allowed no baggage, except what they could carry in their hands and on their backs. Their traps remained upon the land. Their sleds and kayaks, and two canoes, their tents and most of the rest of the heavier gear which was vital to existence on the plains, were left behind. During the preceding few days Owliktuk and Ohoto had even been refused permission to visit the Little Lakes in order to pick up caches which included Ohoto's rifle. Perhaps someone may have feared that they would not return to Ennadai to join the exodus.

On their arrival at Offedal the people were issued with canvas tents and they were given some extra canvas with which to patch their tattered clothes. According to the official reports they were also given a month's supply of flour and other food, paid for out of their Family Allowance credits.

It was felt by the N.S.O., the trader and the policeman that these supplies would be quite adequate to tide the people over a transition period, "for the caribou were expected in a week or two, and in any case it was believed that there were ptarmigan in the hills and fish in Offedal Lake."

Originally it had been intended that the advice of the senior R.C.M.P. officer in Ottawa should have been followed; and an excellent man named Louis Voisie was to have been left with the Ihalmiut until they settled in. In the event Voisie's services were dispensed with. It was the opinion of the three men who conducted the move that he would not be needed.

The transportation of the Ihalmiut was completed on May 11. The people were told that they were now on their own resources—that they were again hunters and men—and should behave accordingly. With a final injunction to remember that they were not to return to Ennadai, the three white men climbed aboard the Otter and it soon vanished eastward over the ice of Henik Lake.

Without enough dogs to make sled travel possible while the ice remained, and with no canoes to provide transportation during the season of open water, the Ihalmiut were virtually cut off from Padlei, though it lay only forty-eight air miles away. Their isolation was intentional. They were to be subjected to a cure for their lethargy, their indolence, and their passive acceptance of the dole. It was, to be sure, a somewhat drastic cure; but those who devised it must have had confidence that it would work.

When I talked to Owliktuk about those early days at Offedal he told me a remarkable story. To preserve the flavor of it I repeat it here in the first person, translated into free English from the original tape recording.

We were surprised when the white men told us this was a good place for caribou, for we knew it was a hungry country. All the same it was the right time for the deer to come north and we needed meat. The food that had been left for us only lasted a few days. Our people were hungry and they ate a lot.

The white men had made us pitch the tents under a big hill. We knew this to be an evil place but we let the tents stay there for a while and took our rifles and went looking for deer trails and crossing places. We found no trails. We knew there had not been any deer in this place for a long time because there were no old trails. After a while we came back to the tents and we decided to move because we were afraid of the hill spirits.

We knew we could not go back to our own country, but we thought if we went a little way to the west we might find level ground where the deer might pass. Some of the people would not move, because they said it was no use. So they stayed at the camp the white men had chosen for us. They were Pommela, Alekahaw and Onekwaw. All the rest of us walked for a day to the southwest until we had crossed the big hills and reached some little lakes where we could see flat country to the west. Here we set up our camps. There was lots of wood here, and we had fires, but we had no food. There

170

were some ptarmigan but not enough to be much use. We tried to fish in the lakes, but the ice was very thick [it would then have been from six to eight feet in thickness], and when we had cut through it we did not catch any fish by jigging. I do not think there were any fish in those lakes.

It was on the second day after we had come to Henik that we moved to the new place. While we were making the new camp we heard some airplanes flying to the southwest and Anoteelik thought they were landing. So he and Mounik and another walked that way. They found some white men with a big camp, and with a tractor, and one of the white men gave them some food.

The next day all of the men walked to that camp and they gave us food again, but they did not have very much to give us.

One day Alekahaw arrived at our camp and said that Pommela had died and that he had starved to death. He said there was nothing to eat at the first camp and so he had come to see if there was food where we were. We did not have any food, for no deer had come at all and we could not get any fish.

Some thought we ought to walk back to our own country but it was too far when the children were hungry, and anyway the white men had told us we had to stay where we were.

One day a white man from the camp came to visit us with Anoteelik. He slept with us and went back the next day. He said he would send a message that we were hungry and that some food would be brought in. Nothing happened for a long time. We were all hungry, but the white men at the camp could not give us much food. Mostly we stayed in the tents and some people wished they had run away and hidden when the plane came to Ennadai to take us away.

It was by an unlikely coincidence that, on the day before the Ihalmiut were moved from Ennadai, an advance party for a large mining corporation should have established a base for their summer prospecting operations at Bray Lake, only fifteen miles southwest of Offedal. This camp was established with considerable secrecy, and it appears that the police

171

corporal at Eskimo Point was not aware of its existence. If he had known about it, there is a strong possibility that the Ihalmiut would have been settled elsewhere—and that would have been unlucky for the people. Had it not been for the accidental propinquity of the mining camp it is probable that most of the remaining Ihalmiut would have died that spring.

The Bray Lake operation was a large one. While the four white men in the advance party erected buildings and hauled supplies to the site with a caterpillar tractor, a big Canso aircraft from Churchill brought in load after load of supplies, landing with them on the lake ice. It was this Canso which Anoteelik heard, and on May 12 he walked south to try and find its landing place. What follows is from the personal record of Mr. P. Lynn, who was one of the party at Bray Lake:

> One day shortly after a Canso had landed and taken off I was sitting in my tent when the flap was thrust open and a figure stepped in. He was a grotesque looking fellow and I was momentarily startled. He introduced himself as Anoteelik. I offered him tea and food which he readily accepted. He asked if I had seen any caribou and I said I had not. I asked where his village was and he said it was some hours off to the northeast and that there were many of his people there. I kept offering him food and he ate in such a famished way that I thought he had not eaten in some time. Later I discovered that this was the case, not only for him, but for his whole tribe. Later more Eskimos came and I offered them food, but they were eating so much that I became apprehensive about our fresh meat supply which was limited.
>
> In the evening I explained to the foreman that these Eskimos wanted to work for us and would accept food in lieu of wages. He said that this was not possible, and the Eskimos went away.
>
> The following day the Eskimos returned and brought some of their fellow hunters. They seemed to be in desperate need of food and accepted every opportunity to take it. [There are photographs extant of this visit which show Anoteelik and Yaha grubbing through the camp garbage pile.] Unfortunately we were not fully aware of their dire

circumstances and had to save our meat for ourselves, so we did not offer them too much.

In the afternoon Anoteelik brought another Eskimo named Uhoto [Ohoto]. I learned from Uhoto, who could speak a few words of English, that the little group was in need of food for they were starving and already one of their elder tribesman had died of starvation.

The next day a Trans Air Norseman arrived and the pilot listened to Uhoto tell of the conditions of his people. He said he would mention this to the authorities when he returned to Churchill. Uhoto then asked if he had seen any caribou. The pilot told him that he had seen thin trails to the south and that they should be here in a few days. Uhoto seemed to feel better about this. Later the pilot told me that the caribou were few and were slanting off to the north and west and the chances were they would pass a number of miles to the west of us.

A few days later an old Eskimo woman with two children came to the tent. [This appears, from the photographs, to have been Nanuk, Ohoto's wife, who was then forty-one years old.] I gave them a sack of flour, thirty pounds, which they eagerly accepted. I noticed that the old woman's eyes were in poor shape; red-rimmed and almost completely swollen shut. I gave her a pair of sun-glasses for I thought she was going snow-blind.

After the Eskimos had been dropping in for about a week I made up my mind to visit their village. I asked Anoteelik if he would take me and he agreed. We started on May 17th. The journey took about six hours. At four in the afternoon we arrived at the shores of a small lake and I could see eight or nine tents in a huddle near a grove of stunted spruce trees some of which had been cut down. As we approached, the whole village turned out to greet us. I noticed that bark had been stripped away from some of the trees. I questioned Anoteelik about this. He said some of the people had taken this bark and boiled it for a long time and then drank the liquid and ate the bark. I resolved to try it. Anoteelik's wife seemed surprised and asked if I was starving too. I gulped some of the liquid. Immediately I retched up this bitter and most distasteful substance.

In my inspection of the camp I saw no food whatsoever except the sack of flour I had given to the old woman some days earlier. Most of the women were making a kind of biscuit out of this. They gave it to the children and to the men who were able to go out hunting. The men seemed to be very demoralized and confused and they looked to me as if expecting that I could do something for them.

In the morning I gave what food I had with me to Anoteelik's wife and returned to my own camp.

That afternoon we had a visitor. A well-dressed and healthy looking Eskimo arrived with a fine set of huskies and a sturdy *komatik* [sled]. [This man was Karyook, the post manager's servant from Padlei.] I was very much interested in this man for he was in direct contrast to the other Eskimos who were in poor shape. At length the stranger asked for a piece of paper and a pencil. Without hesitation he quickly wrote a note which he gave to me. [It was written in syllabic script.] Uhoto told me the stranger wished me to give this note to the R.C.M.P.—it was an explanation of the circumstances in which Uhoto's people found themselves. Some days later when the plane returned I gave this note to the pilot and he said he would give it to the R.C.M.P.

Near the end of June our job was finished and we prepared to leave. All the perishable food-stuffs we had left—it wasn't much—we gave to the Eskimos. All canned and boxed food-stuffs were piled in one of the aluminum-clad huts. This food was to be used by the exploration crews who would come in after break-up.

Uhoto, seeing we were about to leave, tried again to impress on us the seriousness of the situation that he and his fellows found themselves in. He said to me: "What shall we do? We starve, and in there (pointing to the building containing the food) there is food. If we starve we will have to take the food in the hut."

Even before this I felt that the Eskimos might be forced to do this as a last resort. I mentioned it

174

to the foreman, but while he sympathized with the Eskimos, he could not accept the responsibility of giving the Company food to the Eskimos. I thought that once we got to Churchill everything would be all right, for the R.C.M.P. would immediately handle the situation once they were aware of it. I told Anoteelik and Uhoto that I would inform the R.C.M.P.

On June 1, we arrived at Churchill and the following day I went to the R.C.M.P. headquarters. I explained everything about the circumstances of the Henik Lake Eskimos. I mentioned that one of the elders [Pommela] had starved to death and the strong possibility that the Eskimos would break into our food cache unless help got to them soon. I even showed the place where the Eskimos were encamped, on the map in the office. The Constable seemed bored with the details, and curtly informed me that the R.C.M.P. were quite aware of the location and the circumstances of these people, for they sent in an aircraft periodically to check on these people. There was nothing to worry about and these people were being looked after.

Despite the lack of concern displayed by the R.C.M.P. constable at Churchill, a report that the Ihalmiut had not been able to kill any caribou did reach the N.S.O. He radioed Padlei to ask about the deer, and he was told that the caribou *were* returning to the district. Nevertheless he seems to have been uneasy, and on June 5, after flying to Eskimo Point with a number of Eskimos who had been released from tuberculosis sanatoria, he continued inland to Offedal Lake.

Only four tents still stood at the original site. The people who were living in them told the N.S.O. that the majority of the Ihalmiut were somewhere to the southwest. From another source, presumably the R.C.M.P. in Churchill, the N.S.O. had already heard that these people were in touch with the prospectors' camp and "had been trading fish for tea and tobacco." When the Offedal families told him that the rest of the people were also very hungry, the N.S.O. was therefore not inclined to believe them. He suspected that Owliktuk's group was not really hungry, but had deliverately spread a famine story in order to keep the prospectors' bounty for themselves, and to discourage the Offedal families from joining them.

Convinced that there was nothing to be gained by visiting the outlying camp, the N.S.O. unloaded some relief supplies and departed. He assumed that Owliktuk's group would hear his plane (the airline distance between the two camps was about eight miles, and there was a high intervening range of hills), and come to Offedal to share in the supplies if they had need of them. Athough he recognized that the deer were alarmingly late, he felt that the Ihalmiut now had sufficient relief supplies, together with what ptarmigan and fish they could obtain, to see them through. In point of fact the relief supplies were insufficient even for the people at Offedal, and they were completely consumed within a few days.

There is no doubt but that the N.S.O. was a conscientious man—if a harried one—and it can be assumed that the reason he failed to comprehend and investigate the situation fully was because the R.C.M.P. either failed to place much reliance upon the report submitted by Lynn, or did not see fit to relay it in its entirety to the N.S.O. In any event it is known that the corporal at Eskimo Point, within whose jurisdiction the Ihalmiut now lived, had assured the N.S.O. that conditions at Henik Lake gave no cause for concern.

Meanwhile, the nine families at Owliktuk's camp were striving desperately to stay alive. Owliktuk built a kayak which he covered with part of his tent, in order to ensure the killing of some deer when the migration came. The migration never came.

With the advance of spring, the only food available was the occasional hare or ground squirrel, a few ptarmigan, a very few fish and the bark of the spruce trees. By mid-June the situation had become desperate.

The people starved, though all the time they knew that ample food existed within easy reach. The mystery is not why the mining company's cache was eventually broken into, but why it was not raided earlier. Yet this is not so great a mystery in reality, for though the beliefs which had governed the lives of the Ihalmiut for centuries were now in decay, they still retained some power over men's minds; and foremost among those old beliefs was the conviction that to steal food was to commit a crime almost as heinous as murder.

It was Ohoto who eventually brought the matter into the open when he suggested to several of the men that they would have to enter the cache. Owliktuk stood firm against the idea, and in doing so he found himself in direct conflict with his son Mounik. Mounik was young, he had a baby son to worry about, and he had grown up during the dissolution of the Ihalmiut society so that he had known much bitterness against the whites. Not only did he side with Ohoto, but he now took the lead in demanding that food be taken from the cache. In thus going counter to his father's will, Mounik created an intolerable situation, for it is one of the great tenets of Eskimo belief that a son must defer to his father in all things. Not knowing how to deal with Mounik's rebellion, Owliktuk withdrew into silence, but in that famine camp the tension between father and son mounted steadily toward an open rift.

At this juncture the camp received a visitor. He was a Padliermio called Iootna, who was a distant relative of Miki's. Iootna had come hunting far afield, for the caribou migration had largely bypassed Padlei too. He had also heard of the arrival of the Ihalmiut in the land and he decided to visit their camps to see if they had managed to kill any deer.

Iootna was immediately drawn into the struggle of wills regarding the cache. Although he was a professing Christian, he had also had a fairly wide experience of the flexibility of white men's moral and ethical codes. Consequently he did not hesitate to throw his weight on Ohoto's and Mounik's side. One day the three of them visited the storage cabin, broke down the door, and stole what food they needed.

After the deed was done the rest of the people shared in the results; but they were uneasy and upset by what had happened. Iootna hurried home with his part of the loot, and word of the affair soon spread through the Padliermiut camps.

In early July, when the inland lakes were free of ice, the mining company's field parties flew in to Bray Lake, to find that their food stocks had been rifled. This was a serious matter, since it involved dispatching their aircraft to Churchill for more supplies, and thus losing several valuable days which could have been devoted to exploratory surveys. They were discussing the problem when a figure appeared over a nearby ridge and came slowly down to join them.

It was Ohoto, come in all good faith to explain what he had done, and why it had been necessary.

His reception was hardly what he had expected. His friend Lynn was not present, and the prospectors were so enraged at the damage done to their supplies—and to their plans—that they were not of a mind to listen to someone else's tale of woe. They dealt with Ohoto as if he had been a sneak thief and a wanton vandal. Their words struck him with the effect of physical blows, and after a little while he turned from them and walked back toward the hills—toward the empty hills.

The plane returned to Churchill where a representative of the mining company visited the N.S.O. and reported what had happened. The N.S.O. recommended that the information be passed on to the R.C.M.P., and toward the end of the month a complaint was laid before the corporal at Eskimo Point.

If the police had been slow to react to the reports of starvation from Bray Lake, they made up for it by the celerity they displayed now that there was a question of lawbreaking involved. The corporal at Eskimo Point seems to have been properly outraged that Eskimos under his jurisdiction should have dared to steal—and particularly from white men. On August 2, therefore, he and the N.S.O. flew into the interior determined to arrest the perpetrators of the crime and bring them out for trial.

At Padlei, Iootna's part in the affair was easily uncovered, and he was arrested and loaded aboard the plane which then flew on to Offedal. The main Ihalmiut camp was eventually located, but it proved impossible to arrest Mounik and Ohoto, since the aircraft could not approach the shore because of rocks; while the two Eskimos could not get out to the plane unless they swam—a skill which they did not possess. It was a statemate, and the aircraft had to return to Eskimo Point with a fuming corporal, to try again some other time.

Five days later these policemen of the modern era managed to establish dry-land contact with their quarry, and the two Eskimos were arrested and flown to the coast. Their wives and children remained behind, unattended and without assistance, and dependent for existence on what little help the remaining people in the camp could offer.

The N.S.O., perhaps reverting to his own years as a policeman, concurred with the corporal that "the ring-leaders of the gang should be fully prosecuted as an example to the other Eskimos."

The punishment of the three men began soon after they arrived at Eskimo Point, and almost two months before their trial. There is, in the Northwest Territories and Yukon Prison Regulations, a useful statute which permits prisoners to be given employment while awaiting trial, *if they so desire*. In the light of what follows, it must be assumed that Mounik,

Ohoto and Iootna "desired" to be employed—with sledge-hammers, breaking stones on a rock pile. At any rate this was what they were soon doing.

The idea of pre-trial punishment was not, however, unfamiliar to the corporal. On one occasion in 1951 he had kept a Padliermio named Okalik in chains while under custody awaiting trial. When questioned about this event a few years later, the constable stated that, in his opinion, "seeing Okalik in chains did more to prevent crime [amongst the other Eskimos] than the entire subsequent sentence."

Whether Ohoto and his companions did in fact ask to be allowed to break stones probably cannot be established now. Ohoto himself denies that he ever made such a request. His story is that he was *put* to work upon the direct orders of the policemen. The corporal, on the other hand—backed by the Commissioner of the R.C.M.P. himself—insists that he was only obliging Ohoto.

Whatever the truth of that may be, the fact remains that while Ohoto was breaking stones, a chip flew up and ruptured his right eye. He was eventually evacuated to Churchill after, as Commissioner Nicholson has said, "aggravating the injury by rubbing it." The doctors at Churchill hospital found that the damage was too severe for them to deal with, and Ohoto was sent on to a hospital near Winnipeg.

Ohoto missed the trial, which was held at Eskimo Point on September 20. The defense of Mounik and Iootna, that they had broken into the cache only because they were starving, could not offset the evidence of the chief witness for the prosecution, the R.C.M.P. corporal, who testified that relief rations had been delivered to their camp and that, with great care, they would have had enough food without stealing from the cache. Mounik and Iootna were found guilty and sentenced to three months imprisonment.

Ohoto missed that trial—but the law has a long arm. In August of 1958, between two bouts in hospital, he too was brought before the judge, was tried, and was found guilty. He was sentenced to the time that he had already spent in custody.

With the approach of autumn, the problem of what to do with, or about, the Ihalmiut again began to grow acute. The police corporal strongly recommended that they be brought to the coast in the spring and placed under his direct control so that he could be in a position to curb their lawless propensities more easily. The N.S.O. thought that the people

179

should be taken entirely away from their old land, and their old ways, and placed in the newly established rehabilitation settlement at Churchill, where they could come to an adjustment with our way of life, where their children could attend schools, and where they would have no need to fear starvation; but his was too daring a suggestion. The old orders looked askance at it, for both the police and the missions were now making a public outcry against the increasingly determined efforts of the new men in Northern Affairs to lead the Eskimos out of their despair and into a world where there was hope for their survival. This battle was being fought on the highest levels, where policy is made, and where politicians balance precariously between contending forces. But as yet the old orders held the edge of power, and in the end it was their will which prevailed.

It was agreed, therefore, that in the spring the Ihalmiut should be transported once again; this time to a desolate spit of rock called Term Point which juts out into Hudson Bay between Rankin Inlet and Eskimo Point. There they would learn to become seal hunters while, in the words of the police, "They would be removed from the temptation to commit theft . . . [for they] are not suited to live without supervision, and as yet are not ready for adaptation to life in or near a settlement."

Meanwhile the winter months had still to run their course before this new plan could be implemented.

On August 28, young Louis Voisie was at last permitted to go to the Ihalmiut. He was instructed to remain amongst them for as long as they had need of him, and to assist them to make a sufficient kill of caribou to last until the spring.

When he arrived at Offedal Lake, Louis found the People widely dispersed. The events of the spring and summer had shattered even the tenuous bonds of unity which Owliktuk had managed to maintain for so many years, in spite of Pommela and all his works. Fear of the police; a state of chronic unease arising from the theft and its aftereffects; and finally the crumbling of the last remaining tower of strength amongst them—Owliktuk—had turned the gradual dissolution of the People into a climactic and almost total disintegration. Strangers in a strange land, haunted by fears of many kinds, they no longer had even the comfort of propinquity. The individual families had drifted away from one another like the isolated bits of human flotsam which they had now become.

Now that Pommela was dead, the way might have been

clear for unopposed leadership; but Owliktuk, the only possible leader, had suffered a blow more severe than any the old shaman had ever dealt him. He had never recovered from the turmoil of the spring days when Mounik had rebelled against him. He had been unable to resolve the difference between himself and this well-loved son before the police took Mounik away. Owliktuk seems to have believed he would never see the boy again, and this, together with the draining of his last reserves of hope and purpose, had left him a beaten, silent, and empty man.

Alekahaw, who had quietly made the best of evil during the days of Pommela's power, one day struck his tent and vanished. He did not go back toward Ennadai but made his way to Padlei where he had many relatives. He had never been a true member of the Ennadai Ihalmiut in any case, and now he abandoned the doomed remnant of that people in order to save himself and his own family.

The wives and children of Pommela, Ohoto and Mounik were without men to help them through the winter which lay ahead, and they drifted from tent to tent, looking for the strength which had now vanished from the People. Two years earlier Kaiyai, the eldest of Pommela's adopted sons, had married Alekashaw, who was the adopted daughter of Onekwaw; now he did what he could for his stepmother Ootnuyuk and her two remaining children—but he could do little enough, for he had two babies of his own to keep alive. The boy Angataiuk, who had been orphaned for a second time by Pommela's death, attached himself to Onekwaw, that poor dull-witted fellow who had only managed to survive down through the years because he had been useful to Pommela.

Miki and Yaha still clung uncertainly to Owliktuk; but they got no comfort from his presence, for Owliktuk gave them no leadership and no direction.

Almost alone of all the men, Halo seemed to have retained something of his old indomitable assurance. He and Ootek remained inseparable, and in their camp there was still some semblance of vitality, though it was but a pallid shadow of what once had been.

Louis Voisie's presence provided a nucleus for this broken people and they gathered to him. He spoke their language as one of them, for he *was* one of them in part at least. Owliktuk said of him:

"He knew our minds. While he was with us we were happy. We did not worry. We hoped that he would stay for a long time. But after a little while he went away."

Louis was permitted to remain with the Ihalmiut only until September 20. During this time (which should have seen the mass migration of the deer pass through the land), he and the other hunters killed only eighteen caribou. An attempt to establish a fall fishery came to nothing, for few fish ran up the streams from Henik Lake that fall. By mid-September both Voisie and the Eskimos could recognize the sure shape of the future which awaited the Ihalmiut.

Voisie walked overland to the prospectors' camp and sent a radio message to Churchill to the effect that the People were *already* hungry and that he and they had failed to obtain a winter supply of meat or fish.

On the 20th of the month an aircraft arrived at the camps bearing 1400 pounds of relief supplies—consisting, as usual, mainly of flour. The plane also brought instructions for Voisie to return at once to Churchill.

He left unwillingly. On his arrival at Churchill he reported that the People would not be able to survive the winter without considerable help, and he offered to return to Henik Lake; but Ottawa had other plans for Louis Voisie. His services were more urgently needed to serve the deer than to serve the People of the Deer. He was instructed to spend the winter killing wolves.

Ottawa was notified of Voisie's opinion as to the prospects for the Ihalmiut, and the Department of Northern Affairs at least made an effort to do something about it. The R.C.M.P. were asked to take whatever action was required; and the police replied that the matter was well in hand. The corporal from Eskimo Point said that he intended to make an air patrol to the Ihalmiut early in December, to be followed by a full-scale dog patrol a little later, at which time he would spend a week or two at the Henik camps.

Ottawa accepted this, and let the matter rest.

There is some confusion as to what actually did happen to these projected patrols. The Commissioner of the R.C.M.P. has since claimed that, to use his own words, "There was a police patrol at an Eskimo camp on Henik Lake on December 8, 1957." On the other hand, the surviving Ihalmiut claim that they saw no white man at their camps after Voisie departed on September 20. If a flight was indeed made on December 8, to an Eskimo camp, it would appear that it must either have been to a Padliermiut camp or to the camp of one of the Ihalmiut families which did not survive. In any event, it is admitted by the police that the dog patrol was never made at all.

The Ihalmiut began that winter with 1400 pounds of food for forty-eight people—a little less than thirty pounds for each man, woman and child. They had no meat after the middle of October, and almost no fish. Some of the men were able to make a trip to Padlei for relief supplies in November; but they had no dogs after that month ended, and they could not carry back enough food on their backs to make further trips worthwhile. In the first weeks of December the Ihalmiut were starving; and if they *were* visited by a police plane at that time, its passengers must have been blind men.

As the snows grew deeper the dispersed camps (for the People had again separated into their component elements after Voisie left) seemed to diminish and to be absorbed into the winter plains. The People themselves seemed to be physically diminished, as they fought their way through the snow wraiths to sit for hours jigging through the ice for fish which seldom took the hook. They lost form and substance, until they began to be as unreal, as disembodied, as the very spirits of their ancient land.

The days grew shorter, and the nights colder. The fish grew scarcer—and no one came to Henik Lake. January dragged its weight slowly across the buried lakes and hills, while the winter darkness became a winding cloth.

13

The Ordeals of Kikik

On the morning of April 14, 1958, the Territorial Court of the Northwest Territories convened in the beer-parlor-cum recreation hall of the North Rankin Nickel Mine which squats upon the western shore of Hudson Bay a hundred and fifty miles north of Eskimo Point. Ceremoniously the judge took his place behind a deal table while on his right six jurors shifted their bottoms uncomfortably upon a wooden bench. In front of the judge (and awkwardly aware of the needs of propriety), an audience consisting mainly of off-shift miners' wives tried not to drown out the proceedings in the clatter of folding chairs. Outside the doubly insulated building a husky nuzzled at a garbage can as the sun beat down upon the white immobility of a frozen world.

The prisoner sat at the right hand of the judge. She smiled steadily at the assembled court, but in her eyes there was the blankness of total bewilderment, of such an absence of comprehension that she might have been no more than a wax mannequin. Yet perhaps, since there was the flush of life under the brown shadows of her skin, she more nearly resembled a denizen of some other world who had become inexplicably trapped in ours. It is not too far-fetched a simile, for this woman had indeed been plucked out of another time and space in order that she might be brought to this alien place to answer to the charges laid against her.

Those to whom she would have to answer had also come great distances in space. The judge and the crown attorney had flown eastward from Yellowknife, some 700 miles away. Another plane had brought a learned doctor, together with the young attorney for the defense, from Winnipeg which lay 900 miles to the southward. From Ottawa, more than 1400 miles distant, representatives of the Department of Northern Affairs had come to serve as friends to the accused. Through many days, aircraft had been converging from across half a continent upon the transient cluster of drab buildings which huddled under the gaunt head-frame of this arctic mine. Between them they had spanned vast distances; yet none had come a fraction of the distance that this woman had traversed in order that she might stand before this court and listen while a white man spoke incomprehensible words to her.

"You, Kikik, of Henik Lake, stand charged before his Lordship in that you, Kikik No. E 1–472, did murder Ootek . . . How say you to this charge?"

During the long night of February 7, the great wind from off the congealed white desert of the arctic sea came seeking south across five hundred miles of tundra plains, to strip the unresisting snows from the black cliffs at Henik Lake and to send the snow-devils dancing like dervishes across the ice. The driven snow scoured the darkness like a blast of sand until no living thing could face it. Nothing ran, nor crawled, nor flew over the broken ridges, the frozen muskegs and the faceless, hidden lakes.

Yet there was life unseen beneath the wind. On the shores of a narrow bay in North Henik Lake two snow houses crouched against the implacable violence of the gale and, within their dark confines, people listened to to the wind's voice. Its muted roar changed pitch as the night hours advanced, until before the dawn it had become a high-throated wail that sank into the mind like needles into naked flesh.

In the smaller of the two houses—it was in reality no more than a snow-block barricade roofed with a piece of canvas—there were four people. One of these, the year-old boy Igyaka, lay rigidly inert, and did not hear the wind. His small body was shrunken into a macabre travesty of human form by the long hunger which, two days earlier, had given him over to the frost to kill.

Beside him on the sleeping ledge of hard-packed snow his two sisters lay. There was Kalak who had been born deaf and dumb out of a starvation winter ten years earlier, and there was little Kooyak who was seven years of age. They lay in each other's arms under the single remaining deerskin robe—and they were naked except for cotton shifts grown black and ragged through the months. There were no more robes to lay across their bloated bellies and their pipestem limbs, and none to hide the frozen horror of the boy who lay beside them—for the other robes which the family had possessed when winter came had long ago been eaten, as had the children's clothes; for all of these had of necessity been sacrificed to hunger.

Oddly contorted from the paralysis which had stricken her in 1949, the mother of the children crouched over a handful of white ashes by the sleeping ledge. These ashes had been cold through the three days of the blizzard, for the willow twigs which were the only fuel available had long since passed in evanescent flame. Howmik crouched motionless; and in that meager shelter the darkness was so absolute that she could not see her husband, Ootek, who lay against the farther wall and stared with wide open eyes that saw through darkness, and which could see death as vividly before him as other men might see the sun.

In the second of the two shelters, a hundred yards away, were Kikik, her husband Halo, and their five children. Hunger had laid its mark upon all of these, but death had as yet been unable to take any of them; its long assault upon this family had not yet overmastered the indomitable resistance of a man who could not comprehend defeat. Through all his years Halo had never known defeat, nor had he even recognized its shadow, for always he had looked no farther than the hour in which he lived. He had not looked back into the dark days of the past, nor yet had he stared forward into the obscurity of the future which awaited him and all his race. He had been free to live within the confines of the moment—to live with a kind of frenzied vigor which made each day give life to him and his. And he owed this special freedom to his song-cousin and lifelong companion Ootek, who had been the visionary and the unraveler of timeless questions for the two of them.

They complemented each other so completely, these two, that they were almost a single man. Slightly built, and with no great reserves of physical stamina, Ootek had never been more than a mediocre hunter, relying often enough on Halo's help to keep his family fed. Yet Halo had always relied upon Ootek to shoulder and resolve those nebulous problems of the mind and spirit which have confronted man since he *was* man. In a true sense they were the two archetypes of Man: the one, who sought to limit and assuage the hostility of fate with his mind's weapons—the other, with the weapons of his hands.

These two families were the people whom the wind had found, and they were almost alone in the wind's world on that February day; alone in a particular hell that had not been of their own contriving, but which we had contrived for them. They were almost alone, because eight of the nine other Ihalmiut families had seen their doom approaching and had made desperate efforts to escape it by attempting to trek, on foot, to Padlei Post.

Owliktuk, he who had tried to stand against acceptance of the soul-destroying dependence on the whites for so many years, had been amongst the first to flee the Henik country and to beg for food at Padlei. With his defection, there was no strength left in the People, and the rest began to follow after. Not all of them survived that savage journey to the sanctuary which they sought.

Onekwaw and his wife Tabluk, with the orphaned boy Angataiuk, made their attempt to escape inevitable death during the last week in January. As with the rest of the Ihalmiut, they had almost no caribou skin clothes, and were dressed largely in castoff cloth garments given them by the white men. They might almost as well have gone naked into the white winds. The boy survived five foodless, fireless days and nights; but on the last day of the passage of the ice of Henik Lake, he died.

Onekwaw only lived a few days longer. He died a mile or two beyond the lake, and many measureless miles from Padlei Post. Thus, of that little group of doomed and driven people, only Tabluk survived; and she did so only because she was discovered by a Padliermio hunter with a dog team, who brought her safely to the post.

Ootnuyuk and her two children had left Henik early in December, for she knew the land, and knew what winter portended there. When she reached Padlei she reported that the young man Kaiyai lay helpless in his snow house. He had frozen his leg, she said, and it had thawed and then been frozen a second time, and thawed again so that now it had swelled like a great dead fish in summertime, and stank like one.

The post manager radioed Eskimo Point and asked that the police plane fly a rescue mission to Henik Lake at once to bring Kaiyai to hospital—for he had recognized the description of gangrene. But the short days and the long nights passed, and the plane did not come, and Kaiyai could wait no longer. His wife Alekashaw placed him on a small hand-sled, and with her two baby sons upon her back, she set out to haul her husband to the post. She had fifty miles to go. She hauled that sled for eight days—and then there was no need to haul it any farther, for Kaiyai was dead. Alekashaw with her two children eventually reached Padlei—but her feet were frozen marble white and hard, and she spent many months in hospital.

This was the pattern of that winter flight. By the time the belated dawn was staining the storm with the opaqueness of a blind man's eye on February 8, the flight was almost over. Yaha's family was still en route, and only Halo and Ootek and their families remained in the promised land to which they had been led by the white men.

For these families, too, the time had come when they must flee, or meet a certain death within their wind-swept camps.

Ootek was aware of this, but he was also aware of a harder truth—it was too late for him to go. He and his family had stayed too long. Having now eaten most of the skin clothing and robes with which they had begun the winter, they could no longer escape from the snow-shelter which had become Igyaka's coffin. Ootek knew this beyond any doubt, and yet in the morning he spoke to Howmik saying:

"I shall go to the trading place; and in a little time I will return with food for all."*

Howmik looked slowly up into her husband's face but she made no reply. She knew that he could not reach the post alive. But Kooyak, who knew only that she was bitter cold and that her bowels were twisted in agony by the glut of

---

*The events and conversations in this chapter are taken from the detailed police interrogations, the transcripts of the trial and from independent interrogations of survivors.

caribou hair and crushed bones which filled them, moaned—
and cried aloud.

That cry must have been an intolerable reproach, and
Ootek, who had never before raised his hand against any
man, least of all against a child, stumbled toward the sleeping
ledge, his smooth and gentle face contorted into a sudden
savagery. He raised his hand so that it hung trembling over
the girl. "I *shall* bring food!" he cried—and struck his
daughter on her shrunken lips . . .

Indeed it was too late for Ootek, but it was not yet too
late for Halo and his family to flee, for they still had the
means. As Halo took his ice-chisel and fought his way against
the gale toward the lake, there to chip laboriously through
two feet of new-made ice which covered his fishing hole, he
knew that the time had come when he must try to reach
Padlei. He thought about the implications of his decision as
he squatted, back to the whining wind, keeping his jigging
line in motion. Two hours later he caught a small fish. He
took it back to the snow house and the family shared it—and
when they had finished they were starving still.

Meanwhile, Ootek had crept out of his own place and
had turned to face the north. His eyes were blind as he took
half a dozen faltering steps toward the goal that he would
never reach. The gale scourged him until he staggered and
fell to his knees—and he sobbed deep within his emaciated
chest, and turned away defeated and went stumbling across
that lesser distance to the house of his companion and his
friend. He came into Halo's house and crouched exhausted
and blank-eyed against the inner wall.

So they sat, these two who had been closer than brothers. Halo offered Ootek the tail of the fish, and Ootek wolfed
it. When it was gone he asked for the few remaining bones of
the fish to take home to his family, and these were given to
him; but still he sat against the wall and waited. Perhaps he
sensed what Halo would say even before the words were
framed. Yet it was a long time before Halo could bring
himself to speak.

"There is nothing left in this place," Halo said at last.
"And so, when the storm weakens, I must take my family and
go somewhere. There are few fish in this lake. If we stay we
will all be as Igyaka is."

Thus it was done. With those few words Halo dissolved
the bonds which had held these two men through the many
years. He cut them ruthlessly, for he had no other choice. But

he did not look again at Ootek as he picked up his line and went out once again to take up his vigil at the fishing hole.

Ootek made no protest even though sentence of death had been passed on him and on his family. He knew that he no longer had the strength to travel, nor to endure at the fishing hole, nor even to scrabble under the snows for willow twigs. He knew all this, yet he did not protest. He sat silently for a long time watching Kikik, who was his half-sister for, though these two had been born of different fathers, their common mother had been Epeetna who had starved to death in the spring of 1947.

At last Ootek rose, smiled strangely at his sister, and said quietly, "Now I will go to Padlei. Only first I will shoot some ptarmigan with Halo's rifle so my children can eat when I am gone." So saying he picked up Halo's .30.30 and left the igloo.

He had not far to go—and he had sufficient strength to carry him on that final journey. Perhaps he no longer even felt the cold, or knew the agony within him. He went before the storm, directly driven toward the one thing in all the world which could sustain him.

Unseen, unheard, shrouded by the snow and wind, he did not pause until he stood a single pace behind the crouching figure of his other self. Perhaps he stood there for an eternity, knowing what he would do, yet hesitating until the wind, blowing through the torn cloth parka, warned him that he must finish quickly. For indeed this *was* the finish—not only of the broken life that Ootek had led through the long years but, so he believed, the finish of the interminable struggles of the people who called themselves Ihalmiut.

When such an ending comes, it is not good to go alone. Ootek intended that the few survivors by the shores of Henik Lake should be together at the end—and so he raised the rifle and, without passion, blew in the back of Halo's head.

The wind swallowed the thunder of the shot as the sea swallows a stone. Soundless still, Ootek climbed the slope to Halo's house. He leaned the rifle in the snow outside the tunnel and crawled inside.

He came as nemesis—but he was a weak and tragic emissary of the fates for he was so chilled that he could not even raise his arms until Kikik used some of her few remaining twigs to brew him a cup of tepid water. The warmth revived a little of the purpose in his sad design and he attempted to persuade the children to leave the igloo on some

190

absurd pretext. When they would not go, and when he began to be aware that his sister was disturbed by his strange behavior, he could think of nothing else to do but turn and leave the place himself. He was so easily defeated; as he had been defeated all his life by the necessity of doing. He was the dreamer, and the doer no longer lived; and Ootek was no longer whole.

Standing irresolute, and hopelessly confused, in the arms of the storm again, he picked up the rifle and aimlessly began to brush the snow away from the metal parts. He was still there a quarter of an hour later when Kikik emerged from the igloo tunnel.

Kikik had become seriously uneasy. Not only was she surprised that Ootek had borrowed Halo's rifle and had not brought it back, but she was perturbed by his odd actions. Yet when she scrambled to her feet and looked into Ootek's eyes, she lost all other emotions in a surge of fear.

"Give me the rifle," she said quickly.

Ootek made no answer, and his hand continued to stray over the steel, brushing away the snow. Kikik stepped forward sharply and grasped the gun, but Ootek would not release it and so brother and sister began to struggle with one another in the whirling center of the storm. Kikik slipped and stumbled and when she recovered herself it was to see Ootek slowly bringing the rifle to his shoulder. But his movements were painfully slow and she had time to step in and push the muzzle to one side so that the bullet rushed harmlessly away into the wind.

Now the woman, better fed and stronger, and driven by a fierce anxiety for her five children, easily overpowered the man. He fell, exhausted, and she fell on him and her slight weight was sufficient to pin him, helpless, in the snow. Ootek struggled faintly as Kikik shouted to her eldest daughter Ailouak, telling the child to fetch Halo from the jigging hole.

Ailouak came from the igloo, glanced in terror at the struggling pair, and then went racing toward the lake. She was not gone long. Sobbing wildly she emerged from the enveloping ground drift. "My father cannot come, for he is dead!" she cried.

What followed has the quality of nightmare. Sprawling astride the feebly resisting body of her husband's killer, who was her own half-brother, Kikik began to question him with the quiet and detached voice of someone speaking in an empty room. There was no rancor and no passion in her voice, nor in the steadfast, half-whispered replies of the man. There was only a terrible remoteness as these two emaciated travesties of human beings, whose hold on life was almost equally tenuous, engaged each other in dead words while the wind roared darkly over them and the quick snow drifted up against their bodies.

They talked so—but even as they talked Kikik was coming to the realization of what she must do next. In Ootek's mind the certainty of their common fate might be inevitable; but Kikik would not accept this truth. She was well fitted to be Halo's wife for she too was of adamantine stuff. Therefore she did not think, she *knew,* her children would survive—and of the many obstacles which lay between her and their survival, the first was Ootek.

She called Ailouak again who, horrified and frightened, had retreated to the igloo.

"Daughter! Bring me a knife!" Kikik demanded.

Ailouak crawled out, closely followed by her younger brother Karlak—and both children had knives clutched in their hands . . .

"I took the larger knife from Ailouak and I stabbed once near Ootek's right breast but the knife was dull and would not go in. Then Ootek grasped the knife and took it from me, but as we struggled for it it struck his forehead and the blood began to flow. Karlak was standing near and so I took the small knife which he handed me and stabbed in the same place near the right breast. This time the knife went in and I held it there until Ootek was dead. . . ."

The killing might have been easier for Kikik had there been passion in it—but there was none. She acted out of intellect, not out of emotion, and she knew exactly what she did. She knew too what lay ahead of her. She had no illusions. She was fully aware of the almost insupportable burden which Halo's death had laid upon her. There would be no more food of any kind. There would be no man's strength to haul the sled if she moved camp. The inevitable doom which Ootek had envisaged was in reality only a step away. Yet stubbornly, and with a singleness of purpose which will be her epitaph when she is gone, Kikik engaged her fate in battle. As Ootek died she ceased to be a woman and became instead an unfaltering machine. The humane passions left her. Love, pity, sorrow and regret were past. With terrible efficiency she stripped away these things so that nothing might weaken her indomitable resolve.

After Ootek was dead she placed the two knives upright

in the snow beside his head and went at once into her snow house. She found the children hunched together under the skins upon the sleeping ledge, staring at her out of black, depthless eyes. Brusquely she ordered Ailouak to follow after, and together they went out into the unabated storm, dragging Halo's heavy sled down to the jigging hole. Together they raised the already frozen body of the husband and the father, laid him on the sled, and brought him home to lie beneath the snow beside the door. The effort exhausted both of them and they crawled back into the igloo to lie panting on the ledge.

"We will sleep now," Kikik told her children, and there was a quality in her voice that belonged to the north wind itself. "And in the morning we will go to Padlei where we will find food."

That night, in Ootek's snow house, his children and the crippled woman huddled close to one another so that no part of their ephemeral body warmth would be wasted. Kooyak still whimpered in her agony, and Howmik gave her water, for there was no food. Even water was only obtainable at a fearful cost, for there was no fire, and Howmik was forced to melt handfuls of snow in a skin bag warmed by her slim reserves of body heat.

Howmik herself slept little that night, for with Ootek's failure to return to the igloo she could only assume he had meant what he had said, in which case death would have soon overtaken him amongst the drifts along the route to Padlei. She believed that she was now alone except for Halo and his family, and she knew that they could give her no assistance.

Before dawn on February 9, the wind fell light; the sky broke clear and the temperature plummeted to forty-five degrees below zero. Kikik, who had also slept little enough that night, roused her children, gave them each a cup of warm water in which some scraps of deerskin had been softened, and bade them prepare to travel. They went about their tasks readily, for there was no gainsaying the inexorable resolution in their mother's face. Within an hour the few possessions which were essential for the journey had been placed aboard the long sled; then Kikik tore down the canvas ceiling of the igloo and cut it into halves. One piece she placed over her husband's grave. With the other she made a bed for her younger daughters, Nesha and Annacatha, upon the sled. These children were too young to stagger through the snow and, in any case, they had no skin clothing left.

Their clothes had long ago been sacrificed as food for Halo and the elder children so that they could hunt, and gather fuel.

It was at this juncture that Howmik emerged from her snow-shelter and came hobbling across toward the others. She stopped beside the sled, shivering uncontrollably, for her own clothing had been reduced to tattered remnants. She did not need to ask what was afoot, for she could see and understand the implications of the loaded sled. She knew too, as Ootek had known, that there was no point in protesting; and so she contented herself with asking Kikik if she knew where Ootek had gone.

Kikik was evasive. She denied any knowledge of her brother, except to intimate that he had probably gone towards Padlei in which direction, so she said, Halo had already gone to break a trail for Kikik and the children. This was a very thin explanation for Halo's absence from the scene, but Howmik did not question it. Her mind was filled with thoughts of Ootek, and with the certainty of his fate.

"If he has gone for Padlei, he is dead by now," she said, half to herself.

Kikik made no comment. Imperturbably she continued with her preparations. She had been Howmik's best friend, and had helped the other woman with domestic tasks for fifteen years; but as of this moment that was past and dead. She could do nothing more for Howmik, nor for Howmik's children and, since this was so, she dared not even allow herself the luxury of pity.

And this was the second of the bitter things that Kikik was forced to steel herself to do—to deny her friend, and to leave her by the shores of Henik Lake to die.

Howmik understood. As unemotionally as if she had just concluded a casual morning visit, she said, "Well, I am pretty chilly now. Perhaps I will go home till Ootek comes."

And Kikik, straightening from her task, watched as the cripple limped away across the snows.

So Kikik left the camp by Henik Lake. With the hauling straps biting into her shoulders she dragged the awkward sled upon which Nesha and Annacatha crouched beneath two deerskin robes. Her youngest child, the eighteen-month-old boy Noahak, rode upon her back in the capacious pocket of her parka. Karlak and Ailouak trudged stolidly along behind.

For a time the going was good. The gale had packed the

snow, and the route lay over the level surface of the lake. Seldom pausing to rest, Kikik forced the pace to the limit of the children's endurance. When the pace began to tell upon Karlak, she ordered him to climb upon the sled, and she toiled on. By late afternoon she had gone ten miles; and then something occurred which must have made Kikik believe she had outdistanced the hounds of fate.

A mile ahead, near the tip of a great rock point, she saw a centipede of human movement on the ice. She came erect, stared for a long moment, and then her voice rang out through the crystal air—and the distant movement slowed and ceased.

In a little while Kikik was talking to four of her own people.

The four were Yaha (who was Howmik's brother), his wife Ateshu and their six-year-old son Atkla, together with the last survivor of Pommela's adopted children, the young man Alektaiuwa. They too were making for Padlei, but Ateshu's lung sickness (it was tuberculosis), and the fact that both of Alektaiuwa's feet were frozen, had slowed their progress to a fatal crawl. They were in desperate straits, and they could offer no island of hope and strength to which Kikik could drag herself and her own children.

Kikik's sick disappointment when she discovered that Yaha's family had barely enough resources to enable them to survive for a day or two longer, let alone a surplus to share with others, must have been a crushing blow. Yet she could bear that too. She told her tale and Yaha heard that his own sister and her children lay abandoned only ten miles distant— and he knew he could do absolutely nothing for them. He was carrying on his back the last food that his family owned—two or three pounds of caribou entrails dug from underneath the snows where it had been discarded in the fall. Yaha had no sled, and his pace was therefore that of the sick woman and the injured boy. He was by no means hopeful that his family would ever get to Padlei alive, and he knew that to turn back for Howmik would only mean certain death for all. He made his inevitable decision, as he listened to Kikik's story, and when she was done he said no word, but turned again toward the northeast. Into the darkness of that frigid evening the little group clawed slowly forward. When they could no longer see their way, they made camp in a tiny travel igloo which Yaha built, and here exhaustion held them till the dawn.

That night *Kaila*, the unpredictable and heartless goddess of the weather, struck again. Before dawn the wind was back in all its frenetic fury; but the ten people who fled could not hide from it. They dared not stay in their minute igloo and hide. So they went on.

The agonies of that day, facing a growing blizzard, freezing, and pitifully weakened by the long starvation, were such that the younger children who took part in it have lost its memory—to them it is now no more than a blank white space in time. But the older ones, and the adults remember. . . .

As the long hours passed and the straggling column slowed even more (for Kikik, with her load, could not keep up), Yaha knew that they would find no sanctuary except beneath the snows. When dusk came he and his family, with Karlak and Ailouak, had left Kikik a mile behind. Such was the exhaustion of these people that Kikik could not close the gap to the travel igloo Yaha built, nor did any of those at the igloo have the strength to go back for her. Kikik crouched in the snow all that roaring night with her three youngest children huddled underneath her body.

In the morning Kikik threw off the snows that all but covered her and faced north. She saw the little igloo and struggled to it. Yaha's wife gave her warm water and a fragment of caribou gut, and when she had drunk and eaten, Yaha spoke to her. His speech was gentle, for he was a gentle and a childlike man.

"You must stay in the snowhouse," he told Kikik. "If I take your sled to pull my wife, we may go fast enough to reach Padlei before we starve. Then we will send help. Perhaps the airplane will come. If it does not, then the trader will send his dog team. But you and your children must remain here and wait."

Kikik, recognizing the truth of this, made no demur. Yaha and his family left soon afterwards and she remained with her five children inside the frail snow shelter, and strained her hearing to catch the rustle of receding footsteps against the whine of the wind.

Kikik and her children remained in that travel igloo through five full days.

During that timeless interval they ate nothing—for there was nothing to eat; but Kikik gathered some dead spruce branches and she made a tiny fire so that they at least had water. More than that, she was even able to squeeze a few drops of bluish liquid from her shrunken breasts for the child Noahak.

For five interminable days the children and their mother huddled together under their two robes and the fragment of canvas, and simply waited—with no certainty. They did not talk much, for even words require strength to utter them. They waited while the storm waxed and waned, and waxed again; and while the keening of the wind heralded the sure approach of the malevolent pursuit.

But Yaha's promise had not been made in vain. On February 13, three days after leaving Kikik, he and his family reached the shelter of Padlei Post, where the trader fed them first, then listened to their tale. With Yaha's arrival all but two of the Ihalmiut families had been accounted for, and now the trader knew what had happened to the rest.

He was appalled. He had earlier radioed his concern about the people to the police at Eskimo Point and now he sent a message which brooked of no delay. In the outer world the slow and almost toothless gears of bureaucracy meshed suddenly. The R.C.M.P. patrol plane which had been so fatally delayed in Kaiyai's case came thundering out from Churchill and on February 14 it reached Padlei. With the trader aboard as a guide, it took off again for Henik Lake, landing on the wind-swept ice of that place shortly before noon.

The policemen went ashore toward the two almost buried igloos and at Howmik's house they found the crippled woman and two children miraculously still alive. They, and the body of Igyaka, were carried to the plane—light burdens all, for the living too had been reduced to skeletal caricatures of human beings. Then the police found Halo's grave, and after a little time they stumbled on the snow-covered body of Ootek. These two were also taken to the plane, and so Halo and Ootek, those enduring friends, came together for the last time, lying stiffly contorted at the feet of Howmik and of her two surviving children.

What followed must constitute the most inexplicable aspect of this whole dark tale. The police aircraft left Henik Lake for Padlei and though it flew directly over the area where Kikik and her children were known to be waiting in the travel igloo, no real attempt was made to find them. Nor can the entire weight and majesty of the police prevail against this truth. The events which followed provide corroboration which cannot be assailed.

The patrol aircraft returned to Padlei. But despite the suggestion of the trader that it remain overnight in order to have the advantage of the precious extra hours of daylight to search for Kikik the next day, the police decided to fly on to Eskimo Point, bearing three dead bodies out of the land, and leaving six who might be alive to wait a little longer. In making this decision the police sacrificed the advantages of having two more hours of daylight for a search on February 14—assuming that they had indeed intended to make such a search.

In the event, however, the patrol aircraft did not return to the interior at all the following day.

It was not prevented from doing so by bad weather, or by any other physical cause. It was not sent back simply because it was considered to be more important to send the aircraft north to Rankin Inlet in order to fly the coroner down to Eskimo Point to conduct an inquest into the cause of death of the three bodies which were already on hand.

Had the trader at Padlei known that the police had no intention of returning, he would undoubtedly have sent his post servant Karyook by dog team to search for Kikik; and Karyook would easily have been able to reach her on that day. But in the belief that the police plane would arrive at any time, the trader did not send Karyook out.

Thus for two additional days and nights, Kikik and her children remained abandoned.

Sitting in Yaha's travel igloo Kikik heard the double passage of the plane on February 14, and when that day drew to a close and no help had come, she was convinced that none would ever come.

This should have been her moment of ultimate despair—but no fiber of her being would acknowledge it. There was no more hope—but what of that? On the morning of February 15, while the police plane was winging its way north to Rankin Inlet on official business, Kikik wrapped Annacatha and Nesha in the skin robes and used the piece of canvas to make a crude toboggan on which to haul them. Then these six, who had eaten no food for seven days, and little enough in the preceding months, set out for Padlei.

It was a blind, almost insensate, effort. Staggering like demented things, they moved a yard or two, then paused as Karlak or Ailouak collapsed on the hard snow. Blackened by frost, and as gaunt as any starving dog, Kikik would rest beside them for a moment and then remorselessly would goad them to their feet—and they went on another yard or two.

Kiki drove the children with a savage, almost lunatic obsession. She drove herself, hauling what had become a gargantuan weight behind her, and bowed beneath the incubus of the child Noahak upon her back. She had become a vessel filled with a kind of stark brutality—filled with it to the point where there was room for nothing else.

In six hours they moved two miles closer to their goal—which still lay twenty-seven miles ahead.

It was dark by then, but Kikik had no strength to build a shelter. The best that she could manage was to scoop a shallow hole in the snow using a frying pan as a shovel. Into this depression the six of them huddled for the night—the long and bitter night, while the ice on nearby Ameto Lake cracked and boomed in the destroying frost.

That shallow hollow should have become a common grave for all of them. They had no right to live to see the slow dawn's coming. Yet when the gray light broke in the east, Kikik lifted her head and looked toward the unseen Padlei Post. Still she would not give her hand to death.

And now she came to the most frightful moment of her years; for Kikik knew that they could not all go on. She could no longer think to save them all; and so in the dark half-light of morning she came to the most terrible of all decisions.

Quietly she roused Karlak and Ailouak from their mindless sleep, and firmly forced them to their feet. Then she drew a caribou hide softly across the faces of the two little girls who still slept on. While the elder children watched, wordless and mercifully uncomprehending, she laid sticks across the hole and piled snow blocks on top.

Early on the morning of February 16, three figures moved like drunken automata on the white face of a dead land . . . and behind them, two children slept.

In the morning of February 16, the R.C.M.P. plane came back. It did not reach Padlei until the day was well advanced and then it landed to pick up the trader once again. It was noon before the search began.

On his arrival at Padlei, Yaha had given the trader explicit instructions as to how to find the travel igloo, and this time the aircraft went directly to it, experiencing no difficulty in locating it—as there would have been no difficulty two days earlier. But by now the igloo was empty.

Airborne again the plane lumbered uneasily through the frigid edge of dusk while the men aboard strained their vision for a sight of motion on the snows below. They saw nothing. Dusk was rushing into the land as they turned back for Padlei—but then, on a last suggestion from the trader, the plane deviated slightly to pass over an abandoned trapper's cabin. There, by the door, the searchers saw a human figure, its arms upraised in the immemorial and universal gesture of a supplicant.

As for Kikik—as she watched the plane circle for a landing—that indomitable structure which she had created so ruthlessly out of her own flesh and spirit began to crumble into senseless ruin. She could sustain it no longer, for there was no longer need of it. As the plane came to a halt and policemen began to run toward her, she faced them with nothing left in her but dust, and the apathy of nothingness.

They asked many, and urgent, questions, for it was almost dark, and they were very anxious to get away. Where were her children? Three of them were in the shack. Where were the other two? What had she done with them? Coherence left her and she could explain nothing, for out of the emptiness an old emotion had quickened into life within her. She who had known no fear through the eons of her travels now remembered fear. She answered out of fear of those who were her rescuers. She lied. Believing that Nesha and Annacatha must now be dead, she told the police that they had died and she had buried them.

The police were not so anxious this time to recover bodies, and so they flew Kikik and her remaining children out of the land to Eskimo Point, after leaving a constable behind at Padlei with orders to collect the dead children by dog team the next day.

The constable followed his instructions and late on February 17 he reached the unobtrusive hummock in the snow where Nesha and Annacatha lay. The Eskimo guide who had accompanied him stopped in terror as they approached the grave, for he had heard a voice—a muffled, childlike voice. The constable tore away the snow blocks and the twigs, and there he found the children. Insulated from the killing cold by the snow crypt, Annacatha was alive—but Nesha had not lived.

So the ordeal of the winter ended for all of the Ihalmiut—except for Kikik, and her ordeal had only just begun.

The flight to Eskimo Point bridged the final chasm between her time and ours in one gigantic and immutable step. Within the day she ceased to be the woman she had been, for now she sat under arrest in a small igloo beside the police barracks, a woman of *our* times destined to live or die according to our laws. The transcendent fortitude she had displayed; the agony that she had voluntarily embraced when she left Nesha and Annacatha to their long sleep; the magnificence of her denial of death itself—all came to this: Kikik had killed a man—Kikik had willfully abandoned two children in the snow—Kikik must answer for her crimes.

Through interminable weeks she remained at Eskimo Point, her children taken from her and she herself subjected to endless interrogations. She was not even told that Annacatha had survived until it suited the needs of the police to confront her with this information in a successful attempt to force her into the admission that she had lied. She endured two preliminary hearings before a justice of the peace at Eskimo Point and she was searchingly examined by a very competent crown attorney who was flown from Yellowknife for the occasion. There was no defense attorney present at either hearing. The verdict of the justice was that she must stand trial on both charges.

She knew nothing of the shape of what awaited her; she only knew that her life remained in jeopardy. She endured. She who had already endured so much could still endure.

In the middle of April they flew her to Rankin Inlet and there the whole mighty paraphernalia of our justice closed about her, and she was tried.

But here, if anywhere in this chronicle, there emerges some denial of the apparent fact that man's inhumanity to man is second nature to him. Kikik was tried before a judge who understood something of the nature of the abyss which separated Kikik from us, and who was aware that justice can sometimes be savagely unjust. In his charges to the jury, Judge Sissons virtually instructed them to bring in a verdict of acquittal. And be it to the everlasting credit of the handful of miners who held the woman's life in their hard hands, they did acquit her, not only of the murder of Ootek, but also of the crime of "unlawfully, by criminal negligence, causing the death of her daughter Nesha."

Thus, on the sixteenth day of April in the year of our civilization 1958, Kikik's ordeal ended. At 9 P.M. under the glaring lights of the improvised courtroom the judge looked at the woman who sat, still smiling blankly, still uncomprehending, and he spoke gently:

"You are not guilty, Kikik. Do you understand?"

But Kikik did not understand, as she had understood so little through the days since she had come to Eskimo Point, except that a threat she could not comprehend, and one more fearful, therefore, than any she had met and mastered in the months and years behind, lay over her.

201

At length a white man who is almost an Eskimo in his feeling for the people came forward and led her, unresisting, from the room. He took her into the adjoining camp kitchen, sat her down, and gave her a mug of tea. Then, standing over her and looking down into her eyes, he spoke in her own tongue.

"Kikik," he said softly. "Listen. It is all finished now—it is all done."

And then at last that fixed smile faltered—and the black eyes looked away from him toward the darkened window, and past it, and into the void beyond.

14

For Us to Say

During the morning of August 19, 1958, the Beaver aircraft in which I was a passenger swung northward up the coast of Hudson Bay. To the west the Barrenlands rolled inward from the sea: a muddied palette sponged into weird designs, flecked with innumerable lakes, and shattered by the quicksilver cracks of many rivers.

The sky was the Barrens sky—pale with unlimned distances and hard as winter ice. The plane drifted through it and after a time the minute white excrescences which were the buildings at Eskimo Point slipped into view over the horizon. There was a trail of smoke hanging pendent above the anchorage to mark the *Rupertsland*, the Hudson's Bay Company supply ship for the Eastern arctic, which was making its annual visit to the settlement. The Beaver took the water close beside the ship, and taxied toward shore.

Forty or fifty coastal Eskimos in their best clothes crowded the landing place, while still others piloted their big seagoing canoes across the anchorage, drawing frivolous patterns in the calm waters around the ship. Watching them from the vessel's rail were the government agents, a medical party, R.C.M.P. constables resplendent in their crimson jackets, and even a few tourists with glittering cameras slung aggressively about their craning necks.

They were engrossed in the spectacle provided by the boisterous and jovial welcome being given to the ship by the Eskimos; they were enjoying the atmosphere of this gala day which comes to most arctic outposts only once in every year.

Ship-time is the best of times to see the Eskimo, for then he wears his happiest and most carefree guise. Then he is indeed the living embodiment of the myth we have so painstakingly created in his image.

After a while some of the *Rupertsland*'s passengers came ashore, and one of them stopped to talk to me. He waved his hand toward the gay throng on the beach and said:

"God! What I wouldn't give to stay right here and be an Eskimo. No problems. Lots of meat, and hunting, and nothing to worry about. Do you guess they *know* how lucky they are?"

A smart young Mountie who was also a passenger on the ship overheard the remark and added:

"It's a pretty good life they lead. The way they are, they're about the most contented people in the world."

As for me, I turned away from the most contented people in the world and walked toward another people whom the young policeman, and the tourists, did not know existed.

Beyond the trim red-and-white buildings of the trading store, beyond the neat rectangle of the R.C.M.P. barracks, I walked over the frost-shattered rocks toward six tents that clustered grayly in the distance. I went to meet again, after an absence of ten years, the men, women and children who call themselves Ihalmiut.

I had a companion on my walk, an Eskimo special constable of the R.C.M.P. He was a little dubious about my visit to the distant tents, and he tried to prepare me for what I would find there. He told me—and it was not pride of race, but pride of his association with the white police which put the edge on his voice—that the people in the six tents were a shiftless and hopeless crowd with whom nothing could be done. He was still echoing the opinions of his superiors when we came to a halt outside the first of the dirty canvas shelters. The constable called out a peremptory command. There was a stir within and a man crawled out and rose slowly to his feet, blinking against the brilliant sun. I recognized him, though that was not an easy thing to do, across the years which he had lived since last I saw him. His name was Yaha.

I spoke to him and after a time he replied—but he did not look at me. Neither did he look toward the beach where the happy Eskimos were gathered, nor toward the harbor where the great ship—such a one as he had never seen nor yet imagined—lay to her anchors. Yaha looked inland; away from the sea, into the yellowing distance of the tundra plains. He spoke when he was spoken to; but for the rest he stood as immobile as an *inukok*—those men of stone who stand upon the far ridges in the land towards which Yaha's hazed eyes stared.

We left him standing there and went on to Ohoto's tent. When Ohoto failed to obey the constable's summons, I stepped inside, past the hanging flap which shut the world away.

Ohoto sat in the center of the floor space, his legs extended straight before him and his eyes cast down. He wore an ancient woolen sweater-coat, caked with dirt and unraveled at the sleeves and hem. He gave no sign that he was aware of my presence, even when I squatted by his side and spoke his name.

The constable, who had thrust his head and shoulders into the noisome space, said loudly:

"He is a little crazy. He got hurt once. You got to yell at him."

I did not yell—instead I touched his arm; and as I did so his fingers twitched so that my gaze was drawn to them and I saw that he was clutching the weathered tine of a caribou antler, gripping it so hard that the knuckles shone almost as white as the deer bone. I looked away, and my eyes met those of his wife Nanuk, who sat, grim and corroded, staring back at me with dead black eyes.

Suddenly Ohoto raised his head. For a long moment his one living eye searched my face, and then he smiled, and in a voice unchanged from that which I had known, he spoke in English.

"Ello, Skibby."

It was the name the People had called me by a decade

205

earlier, and his use of it helped dissipate the horror which had come upon me. I burst into talk and Ohoto listened with his head bent to one side and a half-smile on his broad lips, while I strove to recall and to restore the times that now were gone.

But he only seemed to listen; for his gaze dropped slowly until he was again staring blankly at the piece of bone in his right hand.

The constable was sympathetic with me in my distress.

"You see," he explained. "His mind gone bad. Nothing to do. We go look some other tent."

Nanuk had not spoken, nor had she relaxed a muscle of her harsh rigidity.

We went to all six tents. In some there were living people—the very young—but for the rest there was only a pallid animation that had no reality. Howmik crouched speechless with her crippled arm about her daughter's waist. Old Hekwaw mumbled amiably and pointed to a great herd of nonexistent caribou. Miki came reluctantly from his tent and looked at me for a moment—not with recognition, but with a blind, insensate hatred—and turned his back on us.

Of them all, only Owliktuk still seemed to be aware. He asked me to enter his tent, but I could not face that. It was not dirt or stench which held me back—it was the knowledge that, once inside, I would be shut off from the world of neat white buildings, ships and airplanes, and laughing people.

So we sat outside, on the gray rocks, and Owliktuk talked. His voice was low and listless, but he could still remember things. He talked of the events of the preceding winter and of the death of men and women I had known. He ignored the presence of the special constable and it may be that he also ignored the reality of my presence, for he spoke with a steady and monotonous insistence that was proof against the interjections of the constable or against my own hesitant questions. His face was in repose, but it was the repose of total apathy.

I did not remain long during that first visit, for the plane was waiting. And it was with a sense of relief, of which I am ashamed, that I said good-by to Owliktuk. I stopped once, on the ridge beside the barracks, and I looked back at the six tents. There was not a living being to be seen. The People had vanished into the shadows of their canvas caves. Having no part in the bright world around them, they had returned into darkness to wait, as they had been waiting through the months since they had been brought to this place.

On the 27th day of February in the spring of 1958, the surviving Ihalmiut were loaded into a police aircraft at Padlei and flown to Eskimo Point, where they came under the direct aegis of the R.C.M.P. They were ordered to build igloos behind the barracks, out of direct contact with the local Eskimos. After the thaw, they were given tents; but they were still in effective isolation. They were no asset to the settlement. The ordeal which they had just passed through had left them in a condition bordering on coma.

They were fed an average of fourteen pounds of flour per family each week. Under the eye of the police they were made to work for this ration, first by shoveling snow for an airstrip on the ice, and later by carrying rocks from one part of the settlement to another—and then back again.

Late in March they were visited by two officers of the Department of Northern Affairs. The visitors found them, quite literally, starving. They were told that this was the Ihalmiuts' own fault because they were too lazy and shiftless to catch fish. Unhappily, as the visitors soon discovered, there *were* no fish available locally, but this did not alter the general judgment of the whites that the hunger of the Ihalmiut was their own fault, for they were too lazy to even try to fish.

Unimpressed, the senior official took it on himself to order a planeload of meat from the south, together with a full issue of warm clothing—for the people had nothing but rags to cover their starving bodies. This action drew much adverse criticism from the local whites, some of whom were still complaining in August that such generosity was wasted on "those arctic Irishmen" and had tended to "spoil the good natives" of the area.

The visitors further alienated the good will of the whites by insisting on investigating the Ihalmiut story firsthand, and by recording in detail the account given by each individual Eskimo. Their obvious sympathy for the Eskimo point of view irritated many of the local whites, for as one of the most important of these said:

"These inland Eskimos are unfeeling and without emotion, and they live like dogs."

This was by no means an entirely inaccurate assessment. Certainly the Ihalmiut had but few remaining outlets for emotions, and those which they still possessed were not encouraged. When some of them made a pathetic attempt to draw together in the unity evoked by a drum-dance, the tent was invaded by the police, the drum—presumed symbol of abhorrent paganism—was smashed; and they were denied even this meager anodyne in future.

The official visitors departed—but the Ihalmiut remained at Eskimo Point. The local priest, the Rev. Lionel Ducharme of the Oblate order, was sure that no one needed to feel disturbed about their fate, for he was convinced that the Ihalmiut were contented with their lot, and, as he expressed it later in a letter to a newspaper, they were both grateful and full of respect toward the R.C.M.P.

Some members of the Department of Northern Affairs did not share his convictions and they were anxious to implement their own plans to "save" the remaining Ihalmiut. However, a combination of limited personnel and funds, together with the reluctance of government to reach a policy decision about what might be done for the Eskimos, delayed any action until the impact of another and even grimmer arctic tragedy was felt.

The Ihalmiut had not been alone in their ordeal that spring. At Garry Lake the attempt to establish a church-state among the last of the true inland Eskimos had collapsed in an atmosphere of unadulterated horror, when nineteen of the fifty-eight remaining Hanningaiormiut starved to death during February and March.

The magnitude of the disasters which had overwhelmed the Keewatin Eskimos that spring was such that it could not be adequately concealed, nor glossed over, as innumerable similar tragedies of the past had been concealed or ignored. Finally, and one suspects reluctantly, the government of Canada felt compelled to attempt some positive action to prevent the utter dissolution of the inland people. For the first time since Canada assumed the wardship of the Innuit, *laissez faire* was abandoned and a policy for Eskimo affairs was devised. It was decided that the Eskimos could only survive if they became fully assimilated into our culture, totally abandoning their own.

The rationale was succinctly expressed by a senior official when he said, "It is amply demonstrated that Eskimos cannot go on living in a state of nature. Death and disease is all they can expect under such circumstances. It is therefore imperative, and it is the desire of this government, that they be brought fully into the twentieth century as soon as possible."

At the time there appeared to be no immediate alternative to the solution proposed by the government, so it drew considerable support from concerned southerners, myself included. I supported the new policy because I was convinced that, without it, many of Canada's Eskimo peoples would simply vanish. In 1958, when the new policy was promulgated, infant mortality among the Innuit was more than 30 per cent in the first year; tuberculosis was so widespread that nearly 80 per cent of the Eskimos contracted it at some point during their all-too-short lives; the average life span of an Eskimo was under fifty years; and chronic malnutrition was the handmaiden of almost every individual from birth until the grave.

In early September of 1958 I returned to Eskimo Point just in time to see the first unfolding of the brave new policy. A rehabilitation center was to be established by the Department of Northern Affairs at Term Point on the coast of Hudson Bay not far from Rankin Inlet. It was to contain not only the Ihalmiut survivors but all the broken remnants of Eskimo groups from the whole of the Keewatin area. Here, these shattered fragments of humanity were to begin their transformation from "stone-age men" into machine-age men.

Term Point was an omen, for it was an unmitigated disaster. Autumnal gales burst over Hudson Bay while the materials and equipment for the enterprise were being offloaded from a freighter standing-to on a dangerous lee shore. Much of the material was lost or ruined; much of what was saved was unsuitable to the land and the climate. The whole affair was a defeat for technology. As for the Eskimos, the defeat meant that they spent the winter in a make-shift camp, in a state of complete disorganization, and without the vaguest idea of what the future might portend for them.

This was something they would have to learn to live with.

In 1959 Term Point was abandoned. Some of its inmates were shipped back to Eskimo Point where they again came under the aegis of the Mission, the R.C.M.P., and the trader. The rest were moved to Rankin Inlet where another great experiment in rescuing the Eskimos was already in progress.

Under the management of a remarkable man named Andrew Easton, a small nickel mine had been opened at

Rankin. Easton was an Eskimophile and a man of good intentions who prided himself on being a practical sort of fellow. He was convinced that the answer to the problem of Eskimo survival was to make use of the Innuit in the new and burgeoning exploitation of the north. To this end he prevailed upon the federal government to let him train Eskimos for mine jobs. He was given carte blanche and at first his approach seemed phenomenally successful. By midsummer of 1959 more than three-quarters of the mine employees were Eskimos, and some of them were earning wages that ran as high as $800 a month. It appeared that the Innuit were capable of making a rapid adjustment to our way of life, for they were now living in wooden houses, buying and using electrical appliances, shopping at the new Hudson's Bay Company supermarket, and even learning how to obtain credit from a newly established bank.

This apparent adaptation was so impressive that most observers, again including myself, were deluded into believing that this must indeed be the way to salvation for the Eskimos. In an article which I wrote at that time for a national magazine, I said:

"It is true, of course, that most of these things represent material benefits, and there has been a cry raised by the exponents of the old orders that the Rankin Inlet Eskimos are being changed into mere carbon copies of ourselves and are losing their age-old cultural heritage. There is but one answer to these criticisms. The Eskimo of today has only one choice open to him. He can eschew some elements of his ancient culture, become an equal citizen in our common land, and so survive; or he can remain an anachronism whose own aboriginal culture has now disintegrated to near the vanishing point—and die. Rankin Inlet has proved beyond any possibility of doubt which course the Eskimo himself prefers to follow. . . ."

Men believe what they wish to believe. I believed those words when they were written. I believed the visions that I saw . . . and was blind to the fact that they were little more than the creations of wishful thinking.

For I was wrong . . . dead wrong!

Early in the 1960's the Rankin Inlet mine closed down. The ore reserves had been small, but high grade, and the company had made a satisfactory profit. The nearly one hundred Eskimos who had been employed by the mine, and who were no longer capable of reverting to their earlier mode of life, had no choice but to go on the dole with their families. A very few of them were later shipped to distant mining towns such as Yellowknife, but they did not stay long. Yellowknife was a white man's community, and the Eskimos soon learned what the local Indians already knew so well—that their acceptance was conditional on their being content with second- or third-rate human status.

Meanwhile other Eskimos, particularly from the western arctic, had been sent south for special training courses in mining, heavy machinery handling and other technical trades. Suddenly, large sums of government money had become available to aid the Eskimos in making the transition; whereas in the past almost no funds had ever been available to help them survive in their own way of life. There were cynics, even in 1959, who equated the government's sudden and generous interest in the Eskimos with a spate of grandiose plans for the exploitation on a massive scale of the oil and mineral resources of the arctic regions, and the anticipated need for a large and highly trained local labor force.

In the event the Eskimos demonstrated that they could easily master the machine skills of our technology yet, with rare exceptions, they did not make their white employers happy. They were labeled as unreliable because they would not accept the vital necessity of being slaves to a time schedule. When an Eskimo, who had become a first-rate mechanic, decided it was time to take a week off and go seal hunting, he went seal hunting—and his employer fumed, and finally fired him. The Eskimo was required to make great accommodations to our culture, and he did so—but we were not prepared to make any meaningful accommodations either to his culture or to his nature. The results were inevitable.

By the late 1960's the great experiment in total assimilation had collapsed into chaos although then, as now, this fact was not officially admitted. Because it has never been admitted there has never been any official explanation for the failure. Yet the explanation is a simple one. In 1966 it was explained to me by one of the Hudson Bay Eskimos who had been sent to work in a gold mine at Yellowknife:

"What's the matter? I'll tell you . . . the government fellows, they came to us like white men always came to us, and they said, 'This is what you have to do.' Sometimes they said it like, 'This is what you ought to do—what is *good* for you to do.'

"Eskimo people was used to doing what white men told them. They just thought, 'Well, that's what they *say* we got to do, that's what we *got* to do.' What was wrong was nobody ever asked our people what *we* wanted to do. And if some of us tried to say, white people never listened. Just turn away, and get mad at us.

"I tell you something else. Not so many of our people believed you wanted us to work in the mine, drive the bulldozer and stuff like that to make *us* happy . . . make us rich. We know what you want anyway . . . just some Innuit to work for you up in the north so people down south get rich from our land.

"And having all that stuff—the TVs and all that stuff—it don't make our people so happy. Maybe it makes you happy, but you don't act so happy.

"Our young people now, they're different from us. They don't want to listen to white men tell them what to do anymore . . . they see how much we lose from listening to white people.

"Now they going to say, 'Why don't you listen to *us*, white man? You better start listen to us for a change!' "

In 1966 I flew the length and breadth of the Canadian arctic, stopping at almost every inhabited Eskimo settlement. They were all nearly identical in appearance: rows of shoddy prefabricated shanties laid out like company towns . . . or like high-grade concentration camps. The new white administrators, the teachers, nurses and police lived in elite enclaves a safe distance from the people they were supposed to be serving. Very few of the Eskimos were employed, or even occupied. Most of them sat in their bleak shanties simply waiting. Almost all of them survived on welfare. They were already a dispossessed people—*dispossessed in their own land.*

On this journey I learned to listen. I listened to and recorded the feelings and opinions of more than a hundred Eskimos and northern Indians. One of them was Ohoto.

By then he had gone stone-blind. He was living in squalor in a plywood shack supplied by the government, at Eskimo Point. Nanuk was dead, and he was alone, totally dependent on the dole.

". . . Twenty years ago when we first met, Skibby, I told you I wanted to be *kablunak*—a white man. In my head I thought it was the best way to go on staying alive. I wanted to be like you so I could go on living . . . I tried to be like you, and now I am not living. That was foolish, eh? All of us who tried that, all dead now. Maybe you are dead too? I can touch you, but maybe you are dead too? . . . Goodby, Skibby."

Ohoto never understood ... had never understood. ...
But in the spring of 1973 I listened to an Eskimo at Frobisher
Bay, that pretentious administrative capital and showpiece of
the eastern arctic where a high-rise apartment, complete with
indoor swimming pool, symbolizes all that we are, and all that
we have done for, and to, the people of the north. This man
was young, and tough, and he knew us. He had gone to one
of our universities, and had lived in our world in order to be
sure that he knew us.

"I read that book you wrote—*The Desperate People*.
When you stuck to the story of what happened you wrote
close to the truth about us. But when you got talking about
what we needed and wanted you talked bullshit! You and
pretty near every other white men I ever heard. I'll tell you
what we want!

"We want you whites to leave us make our own decisions. *We'll* decide how much of your phony world we have
to have to stay alive. I heard so much crap about freedom
when I was down south I could stuff an elephant with it!
What the hell do *you* know about freedom? You *take* freedom away from people! You used us as long as you could get
any good out of it; the traders, the missionaries, the government empire-builders, the hot-shot exploiters. Now we don't
go for that shit anymore.

"There's no big difference between you people and any
other colonial sons-of-bitches. You don't give a frigging hell
that it's *our* country—always *was* our country ... You and
your democracy! You can sure take your democracy and
shove it ... all the way!

"Just give us back the chance to live in our own country
the way *we* figure out we want to live. A place to live
in ... that's what we want! Our *own* place to live in."

This is the true, the authentic, voice of the Desperate
People of the Canadian north. But will we listen? And will we
attempt to make amends?

It is for us to say.

Epilogue

Across the northern reaches of this continent there lies a mighty wedge of treeless plain, scarred by the primordial ice, inundated beneath a myriad of lakes, cross-checked by innumerable rivers, and riven by the rock bones of an elder earth.

It is a land uncircumscribed, for it has no limits that the eye can find. It seems to reach beyond the finite boundaries of this planet. Brooding, immutable, given over to its own essential mood of desolation, it showed so bleak a face to the white men who came upon its verges that they named it, in awe and fear, the Barrengrounds.

Yet of all the things that it may be, it is not barren.

In the brief summer it is a place where curlews circle above the calling wildfowl on the ice-clear lakes. It is a place where gaudy ground squirrels whistle from the sandy casts of vanished glacial rivers; where the dun summer foxes den, and lemmings dawdle fatly in the thin sedges of the bogs. It is a place where minute flowers blaze in a microcosmic revelry, and where the thrumming of insect wings assails the greater beasts, and sends them fleeing to the bald ridge tops in search of a wind to drive the unseen enemy away. And, not long since, it was a place where the caribou in their unnumbered hordes could inundate the land in one hot flow of life that rose below one far horizon, and reached unbroken past the opposite one.

In all its harsh hostility it is not barren; nor has it been since the first crawling lichens spread like a multicolored stain over the ice-scoured rocks. And in the cold millennia since the lichens came, life in ten thousand forms has prospered on the plains, where the caribou became a living pulse fleshed by the other beasts, and waiting for the day when man brought sentience into a new world.

That world is sentient no more.

The living pulse which was the caribou flutters with the almost imperceptible beat that speaks of dissolution.

And the great plains roll to the white horizons under the unseeing eyes of the stone *inukok*—the semblance of men— who have inherited an empty land.

Appendix - The Ihalmiut from 1946 to 1958

This list includes all the Ihalmiut who were alive in the spring of 1946 and who were born thereafter until September 1958, divided into family groups.

As explained in the foreword, all names are the actual names of individuals, replacing the occasional pseudonyms used in *People of the Deer*. Children who later married appear twice, but the number beside their names refers back to the original family group from which they came.

Certain children are listed as "nameless." Ihalmiut children are not named until about ten days after birth; thus a child who dies in the first ten days dies without a name. Only a portion of the nameless children born in the twelve-year period are here included, for a nameless child is soon put out of memory by its parents.

The dates of birth for people born before 1946 are only approximate, since the Ihalmiut themselves keep no accurate record of the years.

One or two complete families which emigrated from the Ihalmiut area to Padlei in 1946 are not shown in this list. Individuals who remained behind when their family groups emigrated are, however, listed.

The spelling used in the list is arbitrary. Since no fixed system of writing Eskimo names exists, and since as many as ten or fifteen variants of a single name have been recorded by an equal number of whites, it is impossible to produce a standard version.

Repetition of the same name, within the same family, and applying to people of both sexes, is common practice amongst all Eskimos.

Surviving individuals, as of May 1959, are indicated by the use of italic type.

1. *Alekahaw* (b. (1932) — Living at Rankin Inlet.
   2. *Kaluk* (wife, b. 1928) — Living at Rankin Inlet.
   3. *Keluharut* (son, b. 1938) — Living at Rankin Inlet (an adopted son).
   4. *Kowtuk* (son, b. 1942) — Living at Rankin Inlet.
   5. *Ookala* (daughter, b. 1948) — Living at Rankin Inlet.
   6. Nameless child (b. 1950) — Died at birth, or soon after.
   7. *Oolipa* (son, b. 1954) — Living at Rankin Inlet.

8. Anarow (b. 1910) — Died of diphtheria, 1946.
   9. Jatu (wife, b. ?) — Died of diphtheria, 1946.
   10. Emyekuna (child, b. 1925) — Emigrated to Padlei, fate unknown.

11. Angak (b. ?) — Died, 1946, cause unknown.
   12. Kahutna (daughter, b. ?) — Died of diphtheria, 1946.

13. Angleyalak (b. 1900) — Died of starvation, 1947. (2 children starved in 1944).
   14. Itkuk (wife, b. ?) — Died of starvation, 1947.
   15. Tiktuk (daughter, b. ?) — Married a Padliermio, fate unknown.
   16. Pama (daughter, b. 1932) — Died of starvation, 1947.
   17. *Anoteelik* (son, b. 1934) — Living at Rankin Inlet (see below).
   18. *Kunee* (Rita) (daughter, b. 1942) — Taken to Churchill by trader, now married to Arlow, at Rankin Inlet.

19. Angolia (b. 1916) — Died of diphtheria, 1946.
   20. *Tabluk* (wife, b. 1918) — Remarried Onekwaw, 1946, remarried at Eskimo Point, 1958 (see below).
   21. *Alekashaw* (daughter, b. 1938) — Married Kaiyai (see below), living at Rankin Inlet.
   17. *Anoteelik* (b. 1934) — Living at Rankin Inlet (see above).
   22. *Aiyai* (Akjar) (wife, b. 1938)
   23. *Owliktuk* (son, b. 1953) — Living at Rankin Inlet.
   24. *Igyaka* (son, b. 1955) — Living at Rankin Inlet.

25. Atunga (b. 1915) — Died of diphtheria, 1946 (3 children died prior to 1946).
   26. Kekwaw (mother, b. ?) — Died of diphtheria, 1946.

27. *Nanuk* (wife, b. 1916)	Married Ohoto (see below), widowed at Rankin Inlet.
28. Aljut (son, b. 1944)	Died of starvation, 1947.
29. Elaitutna (son, b. 1946)	Died of starvation, 1947.
30. Aveaduk (b. 1890)	Died of diphtheria, 1946 (wife and 3 children died prior to 1946).
31. Onikok (daughter, b. 1912)	Married Pommela, died of cancer, 1951 (see below).
32. Elaitutna (b. 1900)	Died of starvation, 1947 (2 children died prior to 1946).
33. *Epeetna* (wife, b. ?)	Died of starvation, 1947.
34. *Ohoto* (son, b. 1920)	Living at Rankin Inlet (see below).
35. *Kikik* (daughter, b. 1918)	Married Halo, remarried at Padlei (see below).
36. Ootek (son, b. 1923)	Killed at Henik Lake, 1958 (son of Epeetna, but adopted son of Elaitutna) (see below).
37. Halo (b. 1914)	Killed at Henik Lake, 1958 (see below) (1 child died prior to 1946).
35. *Kikik* (wife, b. 1918)	Remarried at Padliermio, living at Padlei.
38. Noahak (son, b. 1943)	Died of exposure and starvation, 1951.
39. *Belikari* (Ailouak) (daughter, b. 1946)	Living with mother at Padlei.
40. *Karlak* (son, b. 1948)	Hospitalized with tuberculosis.
41. *Annacatha* (daughter, b. 1952)	Living with mother at Padlei.
42. Nesha (daughter, b. 1954)	Died of exposure and starvation, 1958.
43. Aklaya (daughter, b. 1955)	Died of unknown cause, 1955.
44. *Noahak* (daughter, b. 1956)	Living with mother at Padlei.
45. *Hekwaw* (b. 1897)	Living at Rankin Inlet (6 children died prior to 1946).
46. Kala (wife, b. 1898)	Died of "old age" and/or pneumonia, 1950.
47. Eepuk (wife, b. ?)	Died of starvation, 1947.
48. Ohotuk (son, b. 1926)	Died of poliomyelitis, 1949.
49. *Belikari* (son, b. 1928)	Living at Rankin Inlet.

20. *Tabluk* (daughter, b. 1918)	Living at Eskimo Point (see above).
50. Pama (daughter, b. 1933	Died of diphtheria, 1946 (adopted).
51. Homogulik (b. 1908)	Died of diphtheria, 1946 (wife and 2 children died of starvation, 1944).
52. Petow (son, b. 1924)	Died of diptheria, 1946.
53. Kaiyi (b. 1939)	Died of gangrene and exposure, 1958.
21. *Alekashaw* (wife, b. 1938)	Widowed at Rankin Inlet.
54. *Pommela* (son, b. 1956)	Living with mother at Rankin Inlet.
55. *Boonlak* (son, b. ?)	Living with mother at Rankin Inlet.
56. Kakut (b. 1885)	Died of diphtheria, 1946 (3 or more wives and 7 children died prior to 1946).
57. Okinuk (wife, b. ?)	Remarried Katelo, died of starvation, 1947.
58. *Nanuk* (daughter, b. 1916)	Married Ohoto, living at Rankin Inlet (see below).
59. *Alektaiuwa* (son, b. 1939)	Living at Rankin Inlet with Yaha.
60. Katelo (b. 1899)	Died of starvation and/or disease, 1950 (2 wives and 7 children died prior to 1946).
61. Oquinuk (wife, b. ?)	Died of starvation, 1947.
62. Onekwaw (son, b. 1918)	Died of starvation and exhaustion, 1958 (see below).
63. Kowtuk (daughter, b. 1926)	Married a Padliermio, fate unknown.
64. Iktoluka (son, b. 1935)	Drowned in 1951.
65. Kokea (widow of Kudjuk, b. ?)	Died of diphtheria, 1946.
66. *Miki* (b. 1918)	Living at Rankin Inlet (1 child died of starvation, 1944).
67. *Kahutsuak* (wife, b. 1920)	Living at Rankin Inlet.
68. *Kokeeuk* (Kugiak) (daughter, b. 1940)	Living at Rankin Inlet.
69. *Ilyungyaiuk* (son, b. 1945)	Living at Rankin Inlet.

70. Nameless child (b. 1949)	Died, probably of poliomyelitis, 1949.
71. *Hekwaw* (daughter, b. 1952	Living at Rankin Inlet.
72. *Mounik* (b. 1934)	Living at Rankin Inlet.
73. *Ookanak* (wife, b. 1940)	Living at Rankin Inlet.
74. *Tabluk* (daughter, b. 1956)	Living at Rankin Inlet.
34. *Ohoto* (b. 1920)	Living at Rankin Inlet, blind in one eye (2 children died prior to 1946).
75. Kekwaw (wife, b. ?)	Died of diphtheria, 1946.
58. *Nanuk* (wife, b. 1916)	Living at Rankin Inlet.
76. *Ilupalee* (daughter, b. 1946)	Living with parents at Rankin Inlet.
77. Nameless child (b. 1953)	Died at birth or soon after.
78. *Kirkut* (daughter, b. 1957/58)	Living with parents at Rankin Inlet.
62. Onekwaw (b. 1918)	Died of starvation and exhaustion, 1958.
20. *Tabluk* (wife, b. 1918)	Remarried and living at Eskimo Point.
21. *Alekashaw* (daughter, b. 1938)	Daughter of Angolia-Tabluk, married Kaiyai (see above), living at Rankin Inlet.
79. *Oolie* (b. 1917)	Believed alive at Padlei (wife and 2 children died prior to 1946, later married Ootnuyuk).
36. *Ootek* (b. 1923)	Killed at Henik Lake, 1958 (3 children died prior to 1946).
80. *Howmik* (wife, b. 1920)	Widowed, at Rankin Inlet.
81. *Kalak* (daughter, b. 1947	Born deaf and dumb, now in institute in Winnipeg.
82. *Kooyak* (daughter, b. 1950)	Living with mother at Rankin Inlet.
83. Nameless child (b. 1952/53)	Died at birth or soon after.
84. Igyaka (son, b. 1956)	Died of starvation, 1958.
85. *Owliktuk* (b. 1912)	Living at Rankin Inlet.
86. *Nutaralik* (wife, b. 1914)	Living at Rankin Inlet.

72. *Mounik* (son, b. 1934)	Living at Rankin Inlet (see above).
22. *Aiyai* (Akjar) daughter, b. 1938)	Living at Rankin Inlet (see above).
87. *Arlow* (son, b. 1942)	Living at Rankin Inlet, married Kunee, 1959.
88. *Katelo* (son, b. 1945)	Living at Rankin Inlet.
89. Uktilohik (son, b. 1946)	Died of starvation, 1947.
90. *Tanugeak* (son, b. 1948)	Living at Rankin Inlet.
91. *Neebalnik* (son, b. 1952)	Living at Rankin Inlet.
52. Petow (b. 1924)	Died of diphtheria, 1946.
92. Kena (wife, b. ?)	Remarried to a Padliermio, fate unknown.
93. Ota (child, b. ?)	Accompanied mother, fate unknown.
94. Takwa (child, b. ?)	Died, probably of disease, 1946.
95. Homoguluk (son, b. 1937)	Died of starvation, 1947.
96. Pommela (b. 1885)	Died, probably of starvation and old age, 1958 (note: all his children fathered by other other men).
31. Onikok (wife, b. 1912)	Died of cancer, 1951.
97. Ikok (Itkuk) (wife, b. 1915)	Died of poliomyelitis, 1949.
98. Inoyuk (wife, b. ?)	Died about 1946, cause unknown.
99. *Ootnuyuk* (wife, b. 1922)	Widowed at Rankin Inlet.
53. Kaiyai (son of Inoyuk, b. 1939)	Died of gangrene and exposure, 1958 (see above).
100. Angataiuk (son of Ikok, b. 1943)	Died of starvation and exposure, 1958.
101. Ahto (daughter of Ikok, b. 1941)	Killed at Nueltin Lake, 1950.
102. Pameo (daughter of Ikok, b. 1946)	Died of starvation, 1950.
59. *Alektaiuwa* (son of Kakut, b. 1939)	Living at Rankin Inlet with Yaha.
103. *Rosie Akagalik* (daughter, b. 1945)	Ootnuyuk's daughter, leg amputated, now in foster care in Winnipeg.
104. *Rosie Enitnak* (daughter, b. ?)	Ootnuyuk's daughter, at Rankin Inlet.

105. *Aksak* (child, b. ?)	Ootnuyuk's child, in foster care at Churchill.
106. *Yaha* (b. 1907)	Living at Rankin Inlet.
107. Kooyuk (mother, b. ?)	Died of starvation, 1950.
108. *Ateshu* (wife, b. 1919)	Living at Rankin Inlet.
73. *Ookanak* (daughter, b. 1940)	Married at Rankin Inlet (see above).
109. Itkilik (son, b. 1942)	Drowned in 1954.
110. Nameless child (b. 1949)	Died at birth or soon after.
111. *Atkla* (son, b. 1951)	Living at Rankin Inlet.

ABOUT THE AUTHOR

Farley Mowat, author of such distinguished books as *People of the Deer, Never Cry Wolf, A Whale for the Killing, The Snow Walker,* and *Sea of Slaughter,* has long been eloquent in his indictment of man's exploitation of human and non-human life on this planet. He was born in Belleville, Ontario, in 1921 and began writing for a living in 1949 after spending two years in the Arctic. He has lived in or visited almost every part of Canada and many other lands. More than ten million copies of Farley Mowat's books have been translated and published in hundreds of editions in over forty countries.

SEAL BOOKS

Offers you a list of outstanding fiction, non-fiction, and classics of Canadian literature in paperback by Canadian authors, available at all good bookstores throughout Canada.

The Mark of Canadian Bestsellers